"[*Everybody*] brims with empathy. . . . [Olivia] Laing teases out similarities and contrasts [between her subjects] that deliver sizzling insights. . . . [A] piercing book. . . . [S]he encourages us all to ask new questions to discover how it feels, and what it means, to be free—queries that are as vital as they are resistant to any single answer."          —Aziz Huq, *Washington Post*

"Laing's gift for weaving big ideas together with lyrical prose sets her alongside the likes of Arundhati Roy, John Berger and James Baldwin. In other words, she is among the most significant voices of our time."          —Rachel Spence, *Financial Times*

"Drawing consistently surprising corollaries from history and art, Laing vaults from subject to subject. . . . [H]er paths of inquiry are engrossing and illuminating."          —*The New Yorker*

"Daring and complicated. . . . The method of *Everybody* [is] framed as an extended conversation between the author and her sources, in which De Sade blurs into Reich, who blurs into Sontag, and back again. The key to all this movement is that it also invites us to participate in the conversation."
          —David L. Ulin, *Los Angeles Times*

"A beautiful, strange and sprawling meditation on the relationship between the body and freedom."
          —Sophie McBain, *New Statesman* (UK)

"We are lucky to be living in the time of Olivia Laing. . . . [T]o spend time with Laing as she works through a topic, finding the unlikeliest of connective ideas wherever she looks, is to come away with a view of the world that—if not exactly clearer—is strange and rich and profound."

—Jonny Diamond, *Literary Hub*

"[*Everybody*] travels buoyantly through a rich swathe of cultural history. . . . It's a formidable undertaking, one that Laing executes savvily, her plainly diligent research synthesized in lucid, coolly urgent prose."     —Megan Milks, *4Columns*

"Laing makes an entertaining tour guide, moving like a magpie through art, history and politics, and accumulating an exhilarating set of connections. . . . [*Everybody*] is an ambitious, absorbing achievement that will make your brain hum."

—Jessie Thompson, *Evening Standard*

"Laing is a truly thrilling thinker, with an impressively roving intellectual eye."     —Lucy Scholes, *Telegraph*

"Radically subversive and learned."

—Kate Webb, *Times Literary Supplement*

"Laing's finely crafted blend of incisive memoir and biography [vitalizes] this unique chronicle of the endless struggle 'to be free of oppression based on the kind of body' one inhabits, a work of fresh and dynamic analysis and revelation."

—*Booklist*, starred review

"Laing creates a penetrating examination of the political and cultural meanings ascribed to bodies as well as the relationships of bodies to power and freedom. . . . Intellectually vigorous and emotionally stirring." —*Kirkus Reviews*, starred review

"Impassioned and provocative. . . . This lucid foray into some of life's deepest questions astonishes."

—*Publishers Weekly*, starred review

"This is an astonishing project, written with equal parts stirring passion and capable intellect. Laing puts into words experiences I had never before seen in print, and the world is better for it. I love this book."

—Esmé Weijun Wang, author of *The Collected Schizophrenias*

"*Everybody* is a riveting and fascinating innovative historiography of twentieth-century Euro-American radical thought. Olivia Laing's eagle eye connects previously dispersed impulses to understand and express with her lucid writing, revealing mostly Jewish, Female, and Black desires for radical social transformation through sexuality, liberation, and the body. Brainy, open-hearted, and bold."

—Sarah Schulman, author of *Let the Record Show*

"A free-wheeling and joyful exploration of the works and lives of a range of artists and thinkers who brought libidinal and creative energy together with spectacular results. Laing's particular gift lies in her unique ability to line up unlikely juxtapositions—of artists, ideas, and works—and then draw clear and illuminating insights from such constellations. What her earlier work did for loneliness, this book does for liberation." —Jack Halberstam, author of *Gaga Feminism*

"Reading *Everybody* felt like hanging out with my absolute smartest friend, having, somehow, the precise conversation I need to have in this historical moment. Olivia Laing's mind is a thrill to watch, and the connections she draws between the body, sex, art, and freedom made the world around me buzz with new depth and possibility, connections revealed and illuminated. Rare is the book that makes you feel more alive just in reading it, but *Everybody* does just that."
—Alex Marzano-Lesnevich, author of *The Fact of a Body*

"A provocative inquiry into the body's power and vulnerability, *Everybody* combines deep research, historical gossip, unsung queer lives, and deliciously readable prose. Laing reckons with her own gender and embodiment alongside major and minor theorists, artists, and activists, [casting] fresh light on the unending struggles for freedom and autonomy."
—Jenn Shapland, author of *My Autobiography of Carson McCullers*

"Laing's *Everybody* animates flesh with the incandescent force of histories both individual and collective. Through [her] incisive lens, the body—that knot of mind, matter, culture, and society that we dwell inescapably within—becomes almost impossibly fascinating." —Alexandra Kleeman, author of *You Too Can Have a Body Like Mine*

# EVERYBODY

# OLIVIA LAING

# Everybody

## A Book About Freedom

**W. W. NORTON & COMPANY**
*Independent Publishers Since 1923*

Image credit: *Orgone accumulator* (Topfoto)

For information about permission to reproduce selections from this book, write to
Permissions, W. W. Norton & Company, Inc., 500 Fifth Avenue, New York, NY 10110

For information about special discounts for bulk purchases, please contact
W. W. Norton Special Sales at specialsales@wwnorton.com or 800-233-4830

Manufacturing by LAKESIDE BOOK COMPANY, Harrisonburg

Library of Congress Cataloging-in-Publication Data

Names: Laing, Olivia, author.
Title: Everybody : a book about freedom / Olivia Laing.
Description: First American edition. | New York : W. W. Norton & Company, 2021. |
Includes bibliographical references and index.
Identifiers: LCCN 2021000768 | ISBN 9780393608779 (hardcover) |
ISBN 9780393608786 (epub)
Subjects: LCSH: Human body—Social aspects. | Body image. |
Human rights movements. | Freedom.
Classification: LCC HM636 .L44 2021 | DDC 323—dc23
LC record available at https://lccn.loc.gov/2021000768

ISBN 978-1-324-02202-2 pbk.

W. W. Norton & Company, Inc., 500 Fifth Avenue, New York, N.Y. 10110
www.wwnorton.com

W. W. Norton & Company Ltd., 15 Carlisle Street, London W1D 3BS

1 2 3 4 5 6 7 8 9 0

For Rebecca and PJ,
with love and gratitude

'I don't want a body anymore. Fuck the body.'

Ryan Trecartin, *Sibling Topics*


'In my life politics don't disappear but
take place in my body.'

Kathy Acker, *Blood and Guts in High School*


'May we not say there is probably some sort of
Transmutation of essences continually effected
and effectible in the human frame?'

Edward Carpenter, *Love's Coming of Age*


'My life held precariously in the seeing/
hands of others'

Frank O'Hara, 'Poem'

# Contents

This is a book about bodies in peril and bodies as a force for change. I started it during the refugee crisis of 2015, and finished it just as the first cases of Covid-19 were being reported. The new plague has revealed the frightening extent of our physical vulnerability, but the global Black Lives Matter uprisings of the past year prove that the long struggle for freedom isn't over yet.

# 1

# The Liberation Machine

IN THE FINAL YEAR of the twentieth century, I saw an advert in a herbal pharmacy in Brighton. It was pink, with a hand-drawn border of looping hearts, and it made the bold claim that all symptoms, from headaches and colds to anger and depression, were caused by stuck energy from past traumas, which could be loosened and induced to move again by way of body psychotherapy. I knew this was a controversial statement, to say the least, but the idea of the body as a storage unit for emotional distress excited me. I'd had a strong sense since childhood that I was holding something, that I'd locked myself around a mysterious unhappiness, the precise cause of which I didn't understand. I was so rigid and stiff I flinched when anyone touched me, like a mousetrap going off. Something was stuck and I wanted, nervously, to work it free.

The therapist, Anna, practised in a small, soupy room at the top of her house. There was a professional-looking massage bed in the corner, but the overwhelming impression was of slightly grimy domesticity. Frilly cushions proliferated. My chair faced a bookcase crammed with charity-shop dolls and toys, awaiting their casting into Gestalt pantomimes. Sometimes Anna would take a grinning monkey and clutch it to her chest, talking about herself in the third person, in a high-pitched, lisping voice. I didn't want to play along, to pretend an empty chair contained a family member or to wallop a cushion with a baseball bat. I was too self-conscious, painfully alert to my own ridiculous-, ness, and even though I found Anna's antics mortifying I was aware she was inhabiting a kind of freedom to which I did not have access.

Whenever I could, I'd suggest we ditch talking in favour of a massage. I didn't have to undress completely. Anna would don a stethoscope and lightly work at odd places on my body, not kneading but seeming instead to directly command muscles to unclench. Periodically she'd lean over and listen, the bell of her stethoscope pressed against my stomach. More often than not, I experienced a sense of energy streaming through my body, moving through my abdomen and down my legs, where it tingled like jellyfish tentacles. It was a nice feeling, not sexual exactly, but as if an obstinate blockage had been dislodged. I never talked about it and she never asked, but it was part of why I kept coming back: to experience this newly lively, quivering body.

I was twenty-two when I began seeing Anna, and the body was at the centre of my interests. When bodies are discussed, especially in popular culture, it has often meant a very circumscribed set of themes, largely to do with what the body looks like or how to maintain it at a pinnacle of health. The body as a set of surfaces, of more or less pleasing aspect. The perfect, unattainable body, so smooth and gleaming it is practically alien. What to feed it, how to groom it, the multiple dismaying ways in which it might fail to fit in or measure up. But the element of the body that interested me was the experience of living inside it, inhabiting a vehicle that was so cataclysmically vulnerable, so unreliably subject to pleasure and pain, hatred and desire.

I'd grown up in a gay family in the 1980s, under the malign rule of Section 28, a homophobic law that forbade schools from teaching 'the acceptability of homosexuality as a pretended family relationship'. To know that this was how the state regarded your own family was to receive a powerful education in how bodies are positioned in a hierarchy of value, their freedoms privileged or curtailed according to more or less inescapable attributes, from skin colour to sexuality. Each time I went to therapy I could feel the legacy of that period in my own body, as knots of shame and fear and rage that were difficult to express, let alone dissolve.

But if my childhood taught me about the body as an object whose freedom is limited by the world, it also gave me a sense of the body as a force for freedom in its own right. I went to my first Gay Pride at nine, and the feeling of all those marching bodies on Westminster Bridge lodged inside me too, a somatic sensation unlike anything I'd previously experienced. It seemed obvious to me that bodies on the streets were how you changed the world. As a teenager terrified by the oncoming apocalypse of climate change, I started attending protests, becoming so immersed in the environmental direct action movement that I dropped out of university in favour of a treehouse in a Dorset woodland scheduled to be destroyed for a new road.

I loved living in the woods, but using my own body as a tool of resistance was gruelling as well as intoxicating. The laws kept changing. Policing had become more aggressive and several people I knew were facing long prison sentences for the new crime of aggravated trespass. Freedom came at a cost, and it seemed that the cost was bodily too, the loss of physical liberty an omnipresent threat. Like many activists, I burned out. In the summer of 1998, I sat down in a graveyard in Penzance and filled out an application for a degree in herbal medicine. By the time I started seeing Anna, I was in my second year of training.

Though I didn't know it at the time, the type of therapy she practised had been invented in the 1920s by Wilhelm Reich, one of the strangest and most prescient thinkers of the twentieth century, a man who dedicated his life to understanding the vexed relationship between bodies and freedom. Reich was for a time Freud's most brilliant protégé (*der beste Kopfe*, the best mind, in psychoanalysis). As a young analyst in Vienna in the wake of the First World War, he began to suspect his patients were carrying their past experiences around in their bodies, storing their emotional pain as a kind of tension he compared to armour. Over the next decade, he developed a revolutionary new system of body-based psychotherapy, drawing attention to the characteristic ways each patient held themselves. 'He listened, observed, then touched, prodded and probed,' his son Peter later recalled, 'following an uncanny instinct for where on one's body the memories, the hatred, the fear, were frozen.' To Reich's surprise, this emotional release was often accompanied by a pleasurable rippling feeling he called streaming; the same unmistakable sensation I'd experienced on Anna's couch.

Many of the patients Reich saw in Vienna were working class. Listening to their stories, he came to realise that the problems he was seeing, the psychic disarray, weren't just a consequence of childhood experience but of social factors like poverty, poor housing, domestic violence and unemployment. Each individual was plainly subject to larger forces, which could cause just as much trouble as Freud's central site of interest, the crucible of the family. Never one to shirk almighty ventures, Reich spent the interwar years trying to fuse two major systems for diagnosing and treating human unhappiness, wrestling the work of Freud and Marx into productive dialogue, much to the discomfort of the followers of each.

Sex had always been central to his notion of freedom and in 1930 he moved to Berlin, a city on the brink, caught between two disasters, where out of the wreckage of war there arose a great flowering of new ideas about sexuality. Reich believed freeing sex from centuries of repression and shame would change the world, but his activities in Berlin came to an abrupt halt when Hitler seized power in the spring of 1933. In exile in Denmark that autumn, he wrote *The Mass Psychology of Fascism*, a gripping analysis of how Hitler utilised unconscious sexual anxieties, including the fear of infection and contamination, to whip up anti-Semitic feeling.

The first book of Reich's I read was *People in Trouble*, an account of his political experiences in Vienna and Berlin. I found a copy in the old Sunday market that flourished in the 1990s in the car park of Brighton station, picking it up because the title was the same as a novel I loved. Although it was written in the 1950s, it chimed with my memories of becoming involved in activism, the excitements and frustrations of trying to agitate for political change. Reich was not a beautiful writer, like Freud, and nor were his arguments so disciplined or composed. He often sounded boastful, even paranoid, but there was an urgency that tugged me in. It was as if he was writing from the battleground, hunched over his notebook, sketching out high-stakes possibilities for enlarging the freedoms of real people's lives.

His ideas seemed so relevant to my own times that I couldn't understand why I hadn't heard about him, either in protest circles or during my training. It wasn't until much later that I realised the reason he isn't more respected or discussed is that the excesses of the second half of his life have overwhelmed the first. The radical, incisive ideas about sex and politics that he developed in Europe before the war have been almost buried beneath the far more dismaying notions developed in his years of exile, which range from pseudo-scientific theories of disease to a space-gun that controls the weather.

When Reich emigrated to America in 1939, he didn't establish himself as a psychoanalyst or an activist, but as a scientist, albeit one proudly uninterested in the process of peer review, the testing ground of all scientific achievement. Shortly after his arrival, he claimed to have discovered the universal energy that animates all life. He called it orgone, and in the laboratory of his house in New York he developed a machine to harness its healing powers. Given the consequences it would have for its maker, it's ironic that Reich's universal healing device was a wooden cell slightly smaller than a standard phone booth, in which you sat in stately self-confinement.

Reich believed the orgone accumulator could automate the work of liberation, obviating the need for laborious person-to-person therapy. He also hoped it might cure disease, particularly cancer. This latter claim triggered an exposé, which in turn drew him to the attention of the Food and Drug Administration, initiating an investigation into the medical efficacy of the orgone accumulator that lasted almost a decade. On 7 May 1956, Reich was sentenced to two years' imprisonment for refusing to stop selling his invention. The following spring he was sent to Lewisburg Penitentiary in Pennsylvania.

The orgone guy: that was Reich! I hadn't put the two things together. As a teenager I was besotted with William Burroughs, and as a young man Burroughs was obsessed with Reich. His letters from the 1940s and 1950s are riddled with references to Reich and his orgone boxes. The flickering blue glow of orgone energy, the 'vibrating soundless hum of deep forest and orgone accumulators' form the pervasive atmosphere of his books, contributing to their apocalyptic chill, 'the message of orgasm received and transmitted'. Like many countercultural figures, Burroughs built his own orgone accumulators. In fact, the first time I ever saw one was when Kurt Cobain tried out Burroughs's rusty garden accumulator in Kansas in 1993. He was photographed waving through a porthole in the door: a melancholy, earthbound astronaut, frozen in time six months before his suicide. Every time I saw that photograph, it seemed retroactively to condemn Reich as a hopeless fraud.

★

It wasn't until the despairing year of 2016 that I returned to Reich. Over the previous few years, the body had become a battlefield once again. Two issues in particular had come to a head: the refugee crisis and the Black Lives Matter movement. Refugees travelled to Europe in leaking boats from regions that had been graphically destroyed, and other people expressed the belief that they were scroungers and crooks, followed by the hope that they would drown. Those who did make it across the Mediterranean were penned in camps from which they would potentially never escape. The presence of these desperate bodies was utilised by the far-right to gain power in Europe, while in Britain they were deployed in the xenophobic scaremongering of the Brexit campaign.

Meanwhile in America, the Black Lives Matter movement had emerged in 2013 in response to the acquittal of the murderer of Trayvon Martin, an unarmed black teenager killed by a white man. Over the next few years, Black Lives Matter protested the ongoing murder of African-American men, women and children by the police: killed for selling cigarettes, for playing with a toy gun, while reaching for a driving licence, while asleep at home in bed. The demonstrations that took place in Ferguson, Los Angeles, New York, Oakland, Baltimore and across the nation seemed as if they must bring change, but on 8 November 2016 enough people voted for Donald Trump, a barely disguised white supremacist, that he became the 45th President of America.

The old bad news of bodily difference was everywhere again. Words and phrases that would have been unthinkable a decade earlier were articulated by newspapers and politicians in countries that had only recently seemed bastions of liberal democracy. The right to abortion was rolled back or rescinded altogether in several American states, even as it was secured in Ireland. In Chechnya, gay men were put in concentration camps, in what was euphemistically described as a 'prophylactic sweep'. The right to love, to migrate, to gather in protest, to reproduce or to refuse reproduction were becoming almost as viciously contested as they'd been in Reich's own time.

It was beginning to seem as if the great liberation movements of the twentieth century were failing, the victories of feminism, gay liberation and the civil-rights movement overturned one by one, assuming they'd ever been secured at all. I'd grown up embedded in some of those struggles, but it had never occurred to me that their painful, inching progress could be so rapidly reversed. What they all shared was a desire to turn the body from an object of stigma and shame into a source of solidarity and strength, capable of demanding and achieving change.

This had always been Reich's subject and as my own era grew more troubled I was haunted by the sense that there was something vital untapped in his work. His ideas felt like time-capsules, half buried in history and still humming with life. I wanted to unearth them, to trace their legacy in the flickering light of the twenty-first century. What Reich wanted to understand was the body itself: why it's so difficult to inhabit, why you might want to escape or subdue it, why it remains a naked source of power, even now. These were questions that burned away at me too, informing many different phases of my life.

The pseudoscience of his orgone theory appalled me, but I

was beginning to wonder whether there wasn't something to be learned from his downfall, too. Throughout his career he'd struggled for bodily emancipation, and yet he ended up in a prison cell, unmoored by paranoia, an end not uncommon to people involved in freedom movements. I felt as if his troubled life formed a pattern that was in itself illuminating. Why had his work gone so catastrophically astray, and what did it tell us about the larger struggles in which he'd played such a dynamic, ardent role? His failures felt just as important to understand in this new moment of crisis as his more obviously fertile ideas.

It turned out Reich's influence was far more substantial than I'd realised back in the 1990s. It was him who'd coined the terms 'sexual politics' and 'the sexual revolution', though what he'd hoped for was closer to the overthrow of patriarchal capitalism than the Pill-abetted free love of the 1960s. According to Andrea Dworkin, one of the many feminists who drew on his work, he was 'that most optimistic of sexual liberationists, the only male one to abhor rape *really*.' James Baldwin had been reading Reich, as had Susan Sontag. He even had an afterlife in pop culture. Kate Bush's song 'Cloudbusting' immortalises his long legal battle over the orgone accumulator, its insistent, hiccupping refrain – 'I just know that something good is going to happen' – conveying the compelling utopian atmosphere of his ideas.

Though I was fascinated by his life, which is charted in a brilliant, troubling biography, *Adventures in the Orgasmatron* by Christopher Turner, what I found most exciting about Reich was the way he functioned as a connector, drawing together many different aspects of the body, from illness to sex, protest to prisons. It was these resonant regions I wanted to explore, and so I took him as a guide, charting a course right through the twentieth century, in order to understand the forces that still shape and limit bodily freedom now. Along the way I encountered many other thinkers, activists and artists, some of whom drew directly on his work and some who arrived in the same places by very different routes.

Reich led me first to illness, the experience that makes us most forcibly aware of our bodily nature, the ways in which we are both permeable and mortal, a revelation that the Covid-19 outbreak would soon forcibly bring home across the world. One of Reich's more controversial theories is that illness is meaningful. This was Sontag's criticism of him in *Illness as Metaphor*, and yet the more I discovered about her own experience of breast cancer, the more it seemed that the reality of illness in our lives is far more personal and complicated than she might have been willing to admit in print. As she put it in her hospital diary: 'My body is talking louder, more plainly than I ever could.'

I didn't agree with Reich that the orgasm could bring down the patriarchy or stop fascism (as Baldwin tartly put it in an essay on Reich, 'the people I had been raised among had orgasms all the time, and still chopped each other with razors on Saturday nights'), but his work on sex took me to Weimar Berlin, the birthplace of the modern sexual liberation movement, the numerous achievements of which seemed less secure by the day. Though Reich placed enormous faith in the liberatory possibilities of sex, sexual freedom is not such a straightforward matter as we might sometimes like to think, since it shares a border with violence and rape. Thinking about these less comfortable aspects of sex brought me to the Cuban-American artist Ana Mendieta, to the radical feminist Andrea Dworkin and to the Marquis de Sade, who between them have mapped one of the most difficult regions of bodily experience, where pleasure intersects with and is usurped by pain.

While the theories of Reich's later years were often bizarre, his battle with the Food and Drug Administration and subsequent imprisonment were clearly not unrelated to the issues with which he grappled throughout his life. What does freedom mean? Who is it for? What role does the state play in its preservation or curtailment? Can it be achieved by asserting the rights of the body, or, as the painter Agnes Martin believed, by denying the body altogether? Reich's liberation machine might not have cured cancer or the common cold, but it did serve to expose a system of control and punishment that is invisible until you happen to transgress it in some way.

His imprisonment in USP Lewisburg drew me to consider the paradoxical history of the prison reform movement, encountering the radical ideas of Malcolm X and Bayard Rustin. They in turn opened up the realm of political activism and protest, the bodily struggle for a better world. Here I came upon the painter Philip Guston, who documented the cartoonish, grotesque forms of those who try to limit freedom, as well as the singer and activist Nina Simone, who spent her life trying to articulate how it might feel to be free, the ultimate Reichian dream.

Like all of these people, Reich wanted a better world, and furthermore he believed it was possible. He thought that the emotional and the political impacted continually on the actual human body, and he also believed that both could be reorgan- ·ised and improved, that Eden could even at this late juncture be retrieved. The free body: what a beautiful idea. Despite what happened to him, and despite what was happening to the movements in which he'd participated, I could still feel that optimism vibrating through the decades: that our bodies are full of power, and furthermore that their power is not despite but because of their manifest vulnerabilities.

# 2

# Unwell

WHEN I WAS SEVENTEEN or so I had irregular periods, also acne, the former concerning enough that my mother decided I ought to see a specialist. We drove into London on a sweltering afternoon, past the dusty plane trees of the Cromwell Road. At the hospital, I was chastised for not having a full bladder and made to drink several penitential glasses of Ribena. The ultrasound technician plied her wand over my belly and then a consultant informed me I had polycystic ovaries and would need IVF to get pregnant, which as it happened wasn't true and was probably a reckless thing to tell a teenage girl.

The condition was enigmatic and basically untreatable, a hormonal disturbance marked by clusters of fluid-filled follicles in the ovaries. Its symptoms included acne, weight gain, hair loss and hirsutism, all related to elevated levels of testosterone. The only treatment on offer, ironically enough, was the contraceptive pill, which would at least give me the illusion of regular periods and might also help reduce my zits, though the small print warned that the opposite was also possible.

It was the mid-1990s, and I was a punk–hippie hybrid, with

an undercut and a pack of tarot cards wrapped in black silk. I didn't want to take a pill, to eradicate symptoms without understanding their cause. I was an awkward occupant of my body at the best of times. It felt like an animal I couldn't talk to, a dumb, not always loyal horse. It went on without me, and its failure to function on schedule accentuated my sense of mystification. Sometimes at night I lay on my bed and tried to project my astral body onto the ceiling. Sometimes too I woke to find my body was paralysed, immobile as a block of wood, a terrifying experience I discovered years later was called sleep paralysis. I'd lie there, concentrating all my energy on the formidable task of twitching my toe, to break the spell. What if I got stuck there, and nobody knew I was still inside?

At around this time, I came across a copy of *The Holistic Herbal* by David Hoffmann, a hippie bible with a beguiling spiral of hand-drawn flowers on the cover. Under its benign guidance, I began experimenting with herbs, jotting down properties and contra-indications in my diary. I bought dried raspberry leaf and chasteberry from a local wholefood shop, to try and regularise my periods. They sounded like prescriptions from a fairy tale but they did possess actual, verifiable effects, at least as far as my ovaries were concerned.

After a brief dalliance with an English degree and a year on protest camps, I decided to apply to do a degree in herbal medicine. I was exhausted and burned out by protest, and I badly wanted to do something positive with my life, to contribute to a future that didn't despoil the environment. I wanted to formalise my understanding of the body, and I was fascinated too by the idea that it might have its own language, distant from speech but just as eloquent and meaningful, composed of symptoms and sensations rather than words. A Mickey Mouse degree, my dad liked to say, but it was four solid years of Mickey Mousing, plus a foundation year to make up for my lack of science A-levels. Most of the courses were the same as in a standard medicine degree, but there were witchier modules in materia medica and botany too.

Over the next two years, I drew every bone, muscle and organ in the body, memorising their functions and their names, right down to the tiny bones of the hand: lunate and pisiform, named for their resemblance to moons and peas. On sheets of butcher's paper, I mapped the metabolic transformations that went on inside the miniature factory of each cell. At the beginning I had only the crudest notion of how the body worked, but I struggled gamely on, fascinated and a little appalled by how much of my life happened beneath the Plimsoll line of conscious control. Gradually it all came into focus. The body was a device for processing the external world; a conversion machine, hoarding, transforming, discarding, stripping for parts.

We studied the ideal body, the theoretical version, and then what could go wrong, working our way through hundreds of disorders, each with its own idiosyncratic pathology. The process of distinguishing between them was called differential diagnosis. We learned how to recognise the finger clubbing that foretells congestive heart failure, to differentiate the rash of eczema from that of psoriasis, to spot the bulging eyes and racing pulse of hyperthyroidism or the classic 'lemon on sticks' presentation of Cushing's syndrome.

We were initiated into the art of physical examination in a training clinic in pre-gentrification Bermondsey, spending giggly, embarrassed afternoons taking each other's blood pressure and palpating livers and kidneys, which had to be caught between two jabbing hands like a bar of soap. Everything was meaningful. A wince as you poked at the base of a patient's rib might indicate gallbladder disease. Fingernails that curved inward like spoons could mean iron-deficiency anaemia or haemochromatosis. The sheer amount of information was overwhelming but also wonderfully orderly, at least on paper.

I began to see patients in my second year. Because the clinic was in central London and offered subsidised appointments, the diversity of patients was greater than tends to occur in private practice. I soon found that diagnosis was far more tangled and confusing than Davidson's *Principles and Practices of Medicine* had led me to expect. For a start, people rarely had one illness, but came with a concatenation of conditions. An elderly man might have diabetes and heart disease and swollen ankles; a teenage girl Raynaud's syndrome and painful periods and depression. You had to painstakingly assess each symptom, to trace it back to the source, before even beginning to consider a treatment plan.

Herbal medicine is narrative medicine, a tutor once said, and that phrase stuck with me. Because the prescription was dispensed at the very end of the session, the bulk of the hour was spent listening to the patient, drawing out their whole life story by way of their body. It was as close to psychotherapy, the talking cure, as any form of physical treatment could be. From the beginning, I was fascinated by the sense patients made of their own bodies, the way they experienced their physical and emotional lives as interwoven. In their telling, a divorce prompted cystitis, old griefs attached to tumours, the bereaved developed ulcers or lost their voices, like Freud's famous patient Dora.

After qualifying, I set up practice in a large white room in Hove, overlooking a long garden I wasn't allowed to enter. There was a tiny dispensary off the hall, where I'd weigh out tisanes of meadowsweet and lavender on an old brass scale, digging out the five and ten gram counterweights and sneezing at the aromatic clouds of dust, an activity I still find myself carrying out sometimes in dreams. My patients were of all ages, from infants to the very old. I saw anorexic girls and whole families beset by anxiety. I saw people desperate to conceive, women who were so lonely it was a sickness in itself and men with weeks to live. I listened to their stories, and though I knew why buchu and horsetail would help one patient, and sweet violet and yarrow another, it still seemed to me that the abiding assistance I was providing was as a facilitator of narrative, a witness before whom the whole tangled yarn of the body's difficulties could be unfolded and considered. It felt as if this process was in itself a source of healing, and it left me more fascinated than ever by the mysterious nature of illness, which arises and departs on tracks that are not always visible.

There was a pernicious mode of thinking at the time, popular in New Age and alternative circles, which argued that all physical illness is caused by negative psychological states, the body a theatre in which suppressed or unacknowledged emotions wreak total havoc. One of the main sources was an elderly American woman called Louise Hay, a former model with white-blonde hair and a tight, uplifted face, who became a millionaire on the back of her 1984 self-help manual *You Can Heal Your Life*. It sold fifty million copies, making it one of the most read non-fiction books of all time. When her marriage broke up at the end of the 1960s, Hay started attending a spiritualist church, which introduced her to the concept of positive thinking. She claimed to have used it to cure herself of cervical cancer (when an interviewer at the *New York Times* asked her to prove this in 2008, she said she'd long since outlived any doctor who could confirm the diagnosis).

In the Hay universe, the mind was far more powerful than the body. She taught that illnesses as serious as cancer would spontaneously resolve if the underlying psychological woe was addressed, not by medication or therapy but by positive affirmations, the practice of repeating slogans like 'I am a beautiful person' or 'I am radiant with health'. It was as simple as a, b, c, and indeed in 2004 she published an alphabet of physical illnesses and their mental causes: acne caused by dislike of the self, arthritic fingers by a desire to punish, asthma by suppressed crying. Cancer was resentment and hatred, while polio was paralysing jealousy (a condition that apparently became vanishingly rare in England after the 1950s, when the polio vaccination was introduced).

It didn't surprise me that she'd become one of the best-selling authors of all time, a mere rung beneath the titans, Danielle Steele and Agatha Christie. Somehow it is more comforting to believe that sickness is consequential, a response to suppressed emotions or undigested traumas, than to confront the existential horror of randomness, the knowledge that anyone, no matter how good or innocent or emotionally healthy, might be afflicted at any time. To believe that illness is caused by their own mind gives the patient a kind of power over it, though also a terrible culpability. What I most hated about Hay's theory was that it manoeuvred the blame for illness onto the person who was experiencing it. It was anti-science, and it housed a more insidious notion, too: that there is a right way for the body to be, and that illness or disability is the consequence of failure, while physical health is a reward for psychological balance.

My own experience with patients made me certain that the relationship between soma and psyche was far more complicated than either Hay's model or mainstream medicine allowed. Sometimes it was plain that emotional distress was at the root of physical symptoms (there's evidence, for example, that past trauma has a substantial impact on the functioning of the immune system, as the psychiatrist Bessel van der Kolk discusses in his fascinating book *The Body Keeps the Score*). But the relationship wasn't always that simple, or that unidirectional. The patients I saw were ill, and at the same time their illness was grounds for thinking about other arenas of their lives. Illness functioned as a way for them to acknowledge or express otherwise inadmissible pain, the afflictions of the body providing a ready language by which other things could be conveyed.

At the very end of the Patrick Melrose quintet, the novelist Edward St Aubyn put this phenomenon into words so precise that I was jolted when I read it.

His body was a graveyard of buried emotions; its symptoms clustered around the same fundamental terror . . . The nervous bladder, the spastic colon, the lower back pain, the labile blood pressure that leapt from normal to dangerously high in a few seconds, at the creak of a floorboard or the thought of a thought, and the imperious insomnia that ruled over them, all pointed to an anxiety deep enough to disrupt his instincts and take control of the automatic processes of his body. Behaviour could be changed, attitudes modified, mentalities transformed, but it was hard to have a dialogue with the somatic habits of infancy. How could an infant express himself, before he had a self to express, or the words to express what he didn't yet have? Only the dumb language of injury and illness was abundantly available.

It was this dumb language I longed to understand, the body speaking its own stubborn, elusive tongue.

★

Whether they knew it or not, both St Aubyn and Hay were drawing on the work of Wilhelm Reich. The foundation of all Reich's thinking, good and bad, lies in a single idea he developed in Vienna between the wars: that our bodies carry our unacknowledged history, all the things we try to ignore or disavow. This is the seed that gave rise to his subsequent ideas about freedom, but it's also the origin of the troubling, even dangerous theories about health he expounded in America.

When Reich arrived in Vienna in the summer of 1918, he was twenty-one, a penniless Jewish soldier who'd spent the past three years as an infantry officer in the Austro-Hungarian army, trapped in the squalid trenches of the Italian front. The vast empire in which he'd grown up had suffered an overwhelming defeat and there was no home to which he could return. His parents had died when he was still a teenager, and the prosperous family estate in Bukovina had been abandoned during the Russian invasion. When the Austro-Hungarian Empire finally collapsed that November, it became part of Rumania (it's now in Ukraine). Reich couldn't afford the legal case to win it back.

The city he washed up in was also in trouble. Vienna was no longer the capital of a wealthy and cosmopolitan empire, a place so opulent and luxurious it had been nicknamed the City of Dreams. The newly created Republic of German-Austria had lost two-thirds of its pre-war territory, cutting it off from most of its former sources of fuel and food. By the time Reich arrived, part of a mass migration of thousands of homeless and desperate fellow soldiers, hyperinflation had made the krone almost worthless. Wood was in such short supply that there were only paper coffins in which to bury the dead. Many of the corpses were victims of the global Spanish flu epidemic, now raging through the ruined city.

That year, Reich lived off a subsistence diet of oatmeal and dried fruit, along with a slice of jam cake on Sundays and an eighth of a loaf of bread a week. But it wasn't just meat and butter he craved. He was desperate for intellectual stimulation, an outlet for his considerable energy and intelligence, and he also longed for love, companionship and sex. His future sister-in-law, who met him around this time, never forgot how this orphaned boy responded to the warmth of her family. She described him in terms you might use for a stray dog: 'open, lost, hungry for affection as well as food.' Other friends described Willie, as he was invariably known, as brilliant, energetic, far more vital than other people, but also gauche, insecure and arrogant, prone to fits of jealousy and depression. He was so handsome and dashing that you didn't necessarily notice his skin was covered with the itchy red plaques of psoriasis, a condition that had tormented him since childhood.

In October, Reich enrolled at the University of Vienna to study law, and after a dull term switched to medicine, a far more congenial subject, though his living conditions remained gruelling. The single room he shared with his younger brother Robert and another student was so cold he got frostbite despite wearing gloves and a fur coat. Once he collapsed from hunger in a class. Robert, who was working, helped him financially, but even so he was penniless until he started to tutor younger students in his second year, exhausting work that ate up precious hours of the day.

Despite his interest in his classes, the dominant mechanistic model of medicine troubled Reich. He felt instinctively that something was missing: some kind of life essence or vital force that hadn't yet been isolated or pinned down. It was all very well learning anatomy, but what was the thing that made him *him*, the appetite that propelled people through life? Sexual topics weren't covered on the course, and he wasn't the only student to feel it a serious omission. In January, a slip of paper passed from desk to desk during an anatomy lecture, inviting students to join an informal seminar on the secretive, shameful subject of sex. It was in this seminar that Reich first encountered the stunning ideas of Sigmund Freud.

Like Reich, Freud was a non-observant Galician Jew who began his career as a medical student, and like Reich he was insatiably curious, daring and intellectually ambitious. Freud was a scientist who described himself as 'an adventurer', a passionate man who kept his passion confined to two deep pockets: his work and the smoking that he refused to relinquish even when he knew it was killing him. His first research project was to investigate the sexual organs of eels. He moved by degrees into the no less mysterious realm of the human mind, like a diver who plunges into a dark sea.

The discipline of psychoanalysis was only a year older than Reich himself. Freud named it in 1896, a year after publishing his breakthrough work *Studies on Hysteria*, co-authored with Joseph Breuer, in which he argued that hysterical symptoms were not the result of madness, but caused by repressed traumatic memories; a notion made even more shocking by his claim that the trauma was always sexual in origin. Although he later recanted his belief in widespread sexual abuse in favour of an unconscious realm of fantasies and drives, it was his insistence on the primacy of sexuality, even in infants and children, that made Freud such a pariah in academic circles. By the time Reich encountered him, he was sixty-three, recognised across the world and yet a virtual outcast in his own city, regarded as a laughable eccentric, if not a repellent pervert.

Reich was particularly taken by Freud's theory of the libido, which seemed to answer the question of vital force that he'd been fretting over in his own studies. When Freud first began using the word *libido*, it simply meant the energy of sexual desire, which was satisfied by the act of sex. Over time, he deployed it more broadly to refer to a positive life force, an instinctive animal energy that drives each individual from the moment they are born, and which can become damaged or distorted at any stage in their development. Freud saw libido as the force behind all loves, passions and attractions. It made sense to Reich, who by March was writing excitedly in his diary: 'I have become convinced that sexuality is the centre around which revolves the whole of social life as well as the inner life of the individual.'

Ever enterprising, he visited Freud at his apartment at Berggasse 19 to request a reading list for the seminar. I've spent years trying to imagine that encounter. Reich came up the stairs in his army greatcoat, he entered Freud's study, with its subterranean atmosphere, its sense of being filled with an accretion of objects from past eras, as if many civilisations had marched through, abandoning small relics. It was like a museum or a shipwreck, very quiet, and at the centre there was Freud, so alert and lively that Reich described him as a beautiful animal.

In those years Freud was surrounded by disciples, but either they were insufficiently intelligent or they were too obdurate, like Jung, impelled to kill the father whose approval they'd once longed for. Looking back on their first encounter from the vantage point of 1952, Reich thought this heated and unequal environment made Freud intensely lonely, that the reception of his theories had isolated him, and that he longed to have someone with whom he could talk, a need that his youngest daughter Anna was later able to fulfil. He could see that Freud was drawn to him, even excited by him – a new protégé, perhaps at long last capable of both brilliance and loyalty. Freud knelt at the shelves and pulled out essays, assembling a pile of reading material that would introduce this raw young man to the mysterious working of the unconscious, the baffling, telling realm of dreams and slips and jokes.

More than thirty years on, Reich could still vividly remember the graceful way Freud moved his hands, the brightness of his eyes, the appealing glint of irony that ran through everything he said. Unlike the other teachers he'd encountered while gathering material for the course, Freud didn't pretend to be a prophet or a great thinker. 'He looked straight at you. He didn't have any pose.' Looking back, it's apparent that both men brought a weight of need and desire to each other, as we all do when we encounter a stranger to whom we feel drawn, and that the impossibility of those expectations – beloved father, faithful son – would play a heavy role in the relationship ahead.

The 'click' Reich felt was borne out when Freud referred a patient to him, followed quickly by another. In 1920, at the age of twenty-three, Reich was formally inducted into the Vienna Psychoanalytic Society, its youngest member by two decades. He wouldn't finish his medicine degree for another two years. As Christopher Turner explains in *Adventures in the Orgasmatron*, this wasn't totally unprecedented (indeed, it was a trajectory followed by several other members of the sexuality seminar). In the early 1920s, psychoanalysis was 'still at an uncodified, experimental stage, practiced only by a small coterie of faithful apostles.' No training was required, and though it was suggested that new analysts were themselves analysed, it wasn't a formal requirement until 1926. All the same, Reich was special. Capable and burning with intellectual curiosity, he prodded the city's analysts into life. A shark in a carp pool, he once described himself.

The basic technique of psychoanalysis, then as now, was very simple. The analyst sat in a chair, while the patient lay before them on a couch (Freud's was draped in an Iranian rug and littered with velvet cushions). They couldn't see the analyst, and so they simply rested there, speaking of whatever drifted into their mind, a process Freud named free association. There was no need to ask questions or provide solutions. Everything that ailed the patient would emerge, as if by magic, into the charged space between their lips and the analyst's ear. This stream of seemingly random memories, dreams and thoughts could be translated into meaningful material by small, deft acts of interpretation, until the reason for their distress became radiantly clear.

Although Freud had initially touched his patients, by the time Reich arrived the discipline was strictly verbal, conducted entirely in the realm of words. The physical experiences Freud did acknowledge were hysterical, symbolic symptoms that encoded displaced emotional distress. Dora's lost voice, the Wolf Man's constipation, Anna O's inability to swallow: these were the result of a process called conversion, of a psyche frantically signalling that there was trouble elsewhere. They were clues that had to be unravelled, to yield to an expert reader, who could discover in them the existence of unconscious wishes and defences roiling and seething far below the threshold of awareness. Once the occluded memory was recovered by the patient, the symptom would dissolve.

But there was a problem with this method. Helping a patient to become conscious of the reason for their distress, did not, as Freud had once hoped, automatically result in an improvement. Even if you painstakingly discovered the inciting incident, the buried trauma, they didn't necessarily recover. Analyst and patient alike kept getting stuck in the still-unmapped region between interpretation and cure. Did you keep interpreting dreams forever?

The impatient Reich found this process absurdly frustrating, but the lack of signposts did mean he was at total liberty to figure out the next step for himself. As he listened to his patients, his attention kept straying from what they were saying to their bodies, lying guarded and rigid on the couch. Was it possible that they were communicating information they couldn't say in words? Perhaps the emotions they found it so difficult to access were hiding in plain sight. Perhaps the past wasn't just housed in the memory, but stowed in the body too.

What Reich was seeing was not a hysterical symbol to be decoded, but rather a kind of clenching and clamping that pervaded a person's entire being: a permanent tension so solid and impenetrable it reminded him of armour. It was visible in everything they did, from how they shook hands or smiled to how their voices sounded. He thought this character armour, as he called it, was a defence against feeling, especially anxiety, rage and sexual excitement. If feelings were too painful and distressing, if emotional expression was forbidden or sexual desire prohibited, then the only alternative was to tense up and lock it away. This process created a physical shield around the vulnerable self, protecting it from pain at the cost of numbing it to pleasure.

One of the best ways to understand Reich's theory is to consider a soldier, with their military bearing and stiff upper lip, their body disciplined away from feeling. Not everyone undergoes such rigid training, but very few people pass through childhood without learning that some aspect of their emotional experience is unacceptable, some element of their desire a source of shame. 'That's babyish', a parent might say, or 'boys don't cry', and so the child tenses their body in an effort to master and subdue feeling. What Reich realised was that this process inscribes itself permanently, turning the body into a depository for traumatic memories and banished feelings of all kinds.

An uncanny thing happened as I was writing this. An old boyfriend sent me a film he'd made about being sent to boarding school at the age of seven. It was a stop-frame animation, and it told the story as an abduction, the small, grubby, knock-kneed boy shrouded in a blanket and thrust in the boot of a car. 'My body froze,' the voiceover said, and around the sad manacled figure words appeared. *Stiff neck. Headache. Sore throat. Bad back. Painful feet.* 'But perhaps abduction is the wrong word,' the voice continued. 'It was far more English, buttoned up, emotion shut away.' His abductors were the two people in his world he most loved and trusted, and they sent him to a place where feeling was disallowed and abuse was rife. He was nearly sixty, and he hadn't been able to cry since the day he was sent away. This is precisely what Reich was talking about: the way the past is interred in our bodies, every trauma meticulously preserved, walled up alive.

But Reich's revelation did not end there. Over the course of the decade, he began to work with his patients' bodies, first verbally and then, in 1934, by touching them, an act totally prohibited in psychoanalysis. To his amazement, he found that when he worked on these regions of tension – the habitual expressions of fright, the clenched fists or rigid bellies – the feelings lodged there could be brought to the surface and released. Patients remembered long-ago incidents of shaming or unwanted invasion, experiencing the fury or despair they'd been unable to feel at the time. This process was often accompanied by a curious sensation of energy pouring through their bodies, the so-called streaming that I'd experienced during my own therapy in Brighton.

I can still call up the feeling in my body of what that therapy was like. I remember the tension, which lodged in my neck and shoulders and especially in the muscles around my sternum, an area of such extreme discomfort that as a small child I couldn't bear to have it touched or even to point towards it with my own hand for fear of summoning such an overload of abjection and horror that I named it 'the feeling' and clamped down still further to evade it. And I remember too how it felt when those zones of rigidity began to soften and shift, rippling and trickling through my arms and legs precisely as if something too, too solid had been induced to melt, as Hamlet once implored. Was it possible, Reich wondered, that what was being felt was libido itself, Freud's life energy, which had been dammed up and was now flowing freely?

★

The concept of character armour was Reich's single most durable contribution to psychoanalysis. It is the only one of his theories that still forms part of the armature of conventional psychoanalytic thought, and it's also the foundation of what would become the discipline of body psychotherapy, giving rise to the physical approaches that would become so popular in the 1960s, among them gestalt, Rolfing and primal scream therapy.

One of the many people struck by it was a young Susan Sontag, who in 1967 confided to her diary an extraordinary riff about the problem of inhabiting a body. The inner world, she thought, was far more fluid and changeable than the body in which it's housed. She tried to invent a better design: perhaps a body made of gas or cloud, so that it could expand, contract, maybe break apart, fuse, swell, get thicker or thinner according to a person's shifting moods. Instead, bodies were lumps, obstinately solid, practically unchanging. It was 'almost wholly inadequate', she wrote regretfully. 'Since we can't expand + contract (our bodies), we stiffen them a lot – inscribe tension on them. Which becomes a habit – becomes installed, to then re-influence the inner life.' It was Reich's theory of character armour, she added, and then, on a sorrowful line of its own: 'An imperfect design! An imperfect being!'

The Sontag who wrote those lines was thirty-four, and had just published her first work of non-fiction, the widely acclaimed *Against Interpretation*. A photograph taken in her apartment that year reveals her as a demure beauty in ballet pumps and a clinging paisley dress, cigarette caught between two fingers, gazing dotingly at her thirteen-year-old son David, who smirks straight into the camera. The wall behind them is crammed with books and pictures, mostly photographs, shadowed by a jug of peacock feathers. An empty coffee cup cements the image: the intellectual icon, in medias res.

Nearly a decade later, Sontag returned to the idea of character armour in a long, roving interview with *Rolling Stone*. Once again, she praised Reich's idea that people store emotions in their bodies as 'rigidity and antisexuality'. 'Listen,' she said, 'I think there's one idea of Reich's that is a fantastic contribution to psychology and literature and that is his idea of character armour. He's absolutely right about that.' It's not surprising that she was so convinced. Her own childhood resembles an unhappy masterclass in how the past lodges in the body, like a fishbone in the throat.

Her father, Jack Rosenblatt, was a wealthy fur trader who worked predominantly in China (his parents were peasants from a village in Galicia less than a hundred miles from where Reich himself was born). Sontag's mother, Mildred, gave birth to her on 16 January 1933 in New York City and then returned to China, leaving Susan to be raised by her grandparents and a nurse she disliked. When Mildred finally returned to America, she kept telling Susan her father was on his way home. After four months, she summoned her five-year-old daughter to the living room during a lunch break from school. Your father is dead, she said. Now go out and play.

Mildred was an alcoholic, often depressed, cold, tired, furious, frequently and inexplicably away. In a long diary entry also written in 1967, Sontag attempted to disentangle her feelings: how much she admired her mother's beauty, how her mother was dependent on her, how as a child she'd been deputised to keep her happy. She truly believed that without her own project of flattery, her transfusions of energy and interest, her beautiful unhappy mother would die. 'I was my mother's iron lung', she wrote ragingly. 'I was my mother's *mother*.'

Peering back at her past, it was clear that she'd made a contract for her own survival and that it involved her body. 'My earliest childhood decision, "By God, they won't get me!"' She wanted to live, and she'd been born into hostile conditions, among people who did not love her, who moved haphazardly in and out of her life. Very well: she would be extremely well behaved to ward off their criticism, she would put her own needs and feelings to one side, and she would deny the existence of her body, a decision driven by her despair and self-disgust concerning her inadmissible attraction to her own sex. 'The lesson was: stay away from bodies. Maybe find someone to talk to.'

As an adult, she took this lesson of bodily denial to its limits. She avoided washing, refused to brush her hair, chain-smoked, and took speed to suppress her appetite and need for sleep. She was shocked that childbirth caused pain, and had a baby before she had her first orgasm, itself by no means an uncommon experience for women of her generation. Her body remained unreal to her until the autumn of 1975, when she was diagnosed with stage IV breast cancer, a discovery that brought her up hard against another of Reich's theories.

She had no forewarning that anything was amiss, no signs or symptoms. By the time it was discovered, the tumour had already metastasized into seventeen lymph nodes. Privately, her doctor told David, now a student at Princeton, that she was unlikely to survive. In her diary, she wrote about daggers in her dreams, being perhaps irreversibly ill, her 'leaky' panic. She was so frightened that she slept with the lights on, but she was determined to go on living. Survival would be an act of will. Like everything else she did, it would require research and focus, absolute mastery of the available possibilities, followed by swift, definitive action.

She insisted on the most aggressive, extreme treatment available: a radical mastectomy, also known as a Halsted, an operation that is no longer regularly performed. In the Memorial Sloan Kettering Cancer Center on York Avenue that October, her breast and much of the muscle of her chest wall were cut away, the skin and lymph nodes of her armpit excised. She grieved over the ruins of her upper body, carved to the bone, but she was resolute: survival at all costs, no sacrifice too great for the chance of a continued existence.

On the advice of a new doctor, a French oncologist called Dr Israël, she followed surgery with nearly two years of chemotherapy and immunological treatment, a regime so drastic that her son thought it 'bordered on the unbearable'. She had given herself up to doctors, trusting absolutely in the efficacy of science. It was painful, also humiliating, this submergence of her self, her real being, into the passive, damaged body of the patient. 'One pushes and pulls and pokes, admiring his handiwork, my vast scar. The other pumps me full of poison, to kill my disease but not me.'

The martial metaphors came spontaneously, generated from the rough ground of experience. In a later entry, she added: 'I feel like the Vietnam War. My body is invasive, colonizing.

They're using chemical weapons on me. I have to cheer.' After writing these lines in her diary, though, she picked up her pen and scrubbed them out, refusing the image of war. It wasn't just illness she was up against. It was also the way illness was habitually regarded in the culture at large, the toxic and unhelpful metaphors. 'Cancer = death', she wrote, and then set about proving why it wasn't true.

In her hospital bed, she began to assemble the thoughts that would become *Illness as Metaphor*, her spectacular debunking of the myths attendant on disease. In it, she questioned the military language, so pervasive a part of cancer rhetoric that she'd been deploying it herself a few months earlier. She thought all the tough talk of enemies and battles contributed to the stigma of disease; a dangerous process because stigma made people shy away from treatment and disclosure, as they already did with cancer and soon would with Aids. What troubled her even more was the way specific illnesses were conflated with personality traits or types. Tuberculosis doesn't just affect hectic, reckless romantics, she argued, and nor is there a cancer 'type', who bottles up their feelings until they undergo a malignant conversion into tumours. Cancer isn't the result of an emotional blockage, or an inability to express anger. It's not a consequence of inauthenticity or repression.

*Illness as Metaphor* is a strange book, displaying Sontag's genius for aphorism as well as her lamentable propensity for cherry-picking facts. She tears away at stigma like a person stripping ivy from a wall. But throughout the entire performance – the ravishing argument about tuberculosis in nineteenth-century literature; the ardent, necessary refutation of the sick body as anything other than itself — there can be discerned a faint bat squeak of panic: is it my fault, is it my fault? As Denis Donoghue observed in his *New York Times* review, 'it is my impression that *Illness as Metaphor* is a deeply personal book pretending for the sake of decency to be a thesis.'

What she was afraid of was exactly what she was arguing against: that her own cancer was a judgement, a drastic physical reaction to her failings as a person. Later, recalling her diagnosis in the book's 1989 sequel, *AIDS and its Metaphors*, she presented an impregnable self, drily describing her doctors' 'gloomy' prognosis and her own refusal to give way to fears about what her cancer *meant*. Other patients, she notes, 'seemed to be in the grip of fantasies about their illness by which I was quite unseduced.'

Quite unseduced. It wasn't true. She was as scared as anyone. Her body was newly unreachable, 'opaque', while her mind had become something to fear. She couldn't help worrying over the role her own self played in her illness, the vexed and obscure link between biography and disease. Was it something to do with her mother? 'I felt my tumour + the possibility of hysterectomy', she wrote in her diary, 'as her bequest, her legacy, her curse.' Had her repressed feelings somehow caused her sickness? 'I feel my body has let me down. And my mind too. For, somehow, I believe the Reichian version. I'm responsible for my cancer. I lived as a coward, repressing my desire, my rage.'

The 'Reichian version' she mentions here is not character armour. It refers instead to the strange developments that Reich's ideas underwent in the late 1930s. Back when he was

just beginning his medical training, Reich had longed to discover a vital essence that animates all beings. Freud's notion of
libido had seemed to answer this desire, and when his own
patients started to describe streaming in the 1920s he became
increasingly certain that libido was not a metaphorical force,
but a real and tangible energy: a biological substance that he
could isolate and measure in scientific tests. By the time he
arrived in America in 1939, he was convinced of three things:
that there was a life force, which he called orgone; that it could
become blocked because of emotional trauma or repression;
and that these blockages had profound physical consequences.
As he argued in his self-published 1948 book *The Cancer
Biopathy*, they brought about a cellular process of stagnation and
putrefaction that would ultimately lead to illness, especially
cancer.

Despite its pseudoscientific nature, this idea was enormously
influential after Reich's death in 1957. His work was much
circulated in the counterculture of the 1960s, and his theory of
illness chimed with a growing feeling that repression of all kinds
was dangerous and inimical to health. In 1974, the year before
Sontag was diagnosed with cancer, *The Cancer Biopathy* was
brought back into print by her own publishers, Farrar, Straus
and Giroux (they would eventually republish twenty-one of his
books). Reich believed sexual repression was particularly significant in cancer but, as Sontag observes, by the 1970s it was
more often associated with repressed rage.

By way of example, she relays a dismal anecdote about the
novelist, cultural commentator and card-carrying misogynist
Norman Mailer, whose references to Reich in his influential

and frankly barmy 1957 essay 'The White Negro' were at least partially responsible for the resurgence of his ideas. In the autumn of 1960, Mailer hosted a party at his uptown apartment to celebrate the launch of his campaign to be mayor of New York. After getting drunk and picking fights with many of his guests, he stabbed his wife Adele Morales twice with a rusty penknife. It punctured her pericardium and almost killed her. 'Let the bitch die,' he told onlookers.

Mailer claimed that in stabbing his wife he rid himself of 'a murderous nest of feeling', adding that if he hadn't done so, he would have died of cancer himself within a few years, never mind the nest of fear and rage he doubtless bequeathed to his wife. Though Sontag doesn't mention it, this cancer argument was an actual defence prepared by Mailer's lawyers. A woman's body exists as a receptacle for male anger, we all know that. Sontag saves her scorn for Mailer's woolly thinking, his belief that feeling toxifies if unexpressed, taking on its own occult and sinister life, even though her diaries clearly demonstrate that she too was susceptible to the same belief.

*

Do emotions have physical consequences? Sontag's painful question in *Illness as Metaphor* also haunts one of my favourite films. *Safe* was made in 1995 by Todd Haynes, and is about a wealthy white woman assailed by a mysterious disease. Carol White, played by an exquisitely repressed, almost lobotomised Julianne Moore, is a Californian housewife, living with her husband and stepson in the San Fernando valley. She wanders her futuristic house like a baffled child, dressed in pastel clothes, dwarfed by the furniture, asking the housekeeper for glasses of milk, the only food she consumes with relish.

At first Carol seems merely tense, fragile, anxious, absent, with her perfect make-up and sweet, confused smile. Despite her beauty, she doesn't seem wholly at ease in her body. In fact, she's a perfect example of Reich's character armour. She can barely raise her voice above a whisper, she windmills her arms a beat behind the others in her aerobics class. The first sign that something more serious is wrong comes when she almost collapses while driving behind a truck with a filthy exhaust. Later, at the hairdresser, she asks in her tentative, breathy voice for a perm. As she watches the process in the mirror, a thin trickle of blood starts to leak from her nose. These scenes and the ones that follow – a seizure at the dry cleaners, an asthma attack at a baby shower – are as icily constructed and alive with dread as anything by Hitchcock. In fact, they're shot exactly like a horror film: a horror film in which there is no monster, no demonic force beyond the nightmare of a malfunctioning body, the isolation and terror of not understanding why or being believed.

Carol's doctor can't find anything wrong and advises her sceptical husband to take her to a psychiatrist. But Carol is sure her problems aren't inside her head. At the gym she spots a flyer describing a new disease, environmental illness, also known as multiple chemical sensitivities. This must be it, she decides: she's experiencing an extreme immune reaction to the luxurious, toxic world in which she lives. 'I'm allergic to the couch,' she tells a friend; also to make-up, milk, pesticides, her husband's cologne. She responds to this poisonous onslaught by retreating to a New Age community in Montana, a safe zone presided over by a creepy, charismatic leader, Peter Dunning. Peter's message is that each person is responsible for their own illness, which they alone can heal, by confronting their unhappiness and self-hatred, their anger and despair.

At first Carol seems to thrive in the ultra-protective bubble of Wrenwood, but it also encourages her neurasthenic terror of the world. She retreats further and further from other people, other possible sources of contamination. In the final scene, she's insisted on moving to an even more extreme safe house, a pod so devoid of potentially allergenic furnishings that it resembles a prison cell. Her husband and stepson have left and she's dressed in scrubs. Alone, she stares at her own face in the mirror, a strange bruise or blotch on her forehead. 'I . . . love . . . you?' she says, in a tiny voice. 'I . . . love . . . you?' Cut to black. Maybe she'll get better. Maybe she won't.

*Safe* tackles the same weird border between self and world that Sontag patrolled, but it's far more resistant to simple conclusions. Is Carol sick because she's using her body to say things she can't, or is the outside world truly poisoning her? Is this an environmental message about the toxicity of the twentieth century or a feminist parable about the constriction of Carol's life, her limited sphere of influence and control? 'I've been under a lot of stress,' she tells her doctor, though the most taxing thing we see her do is order a new couch. But there's stress and *stress*, the attenuating wear and tear of overwork versus the exhausting psychic fray of living the wrong life. You could view Carol as a kind of Stepford Wife version of Herman Melville's famous character Bartleby the Scrivener: a non-participant, abruptly and inexplicably unable to perform her role, from having sex with her husband to laughing at his boss's misogynistic stories, engaged in a form of passive resistance no less powerful for being entirely unconscious.

'There's nothing wrong with you, Carol,' her doctor keeps saying. I used to see so many people like that in my own practice, armed with a diagnosis of last resort, like chronic fatigue or M.E., unaware that it was often a physician's shorthand for saying *I don't know*, or *go away*, the so-called dustbin diagnoses. They knew something wasn't right, but it wasn't showing up in tests, and they were shamed for not fitting into diagnostic categories. Sometimes it was plain they were depressed or anxious, and that their feelings were being somatised, manifesting on a physical level. But what about the woman who was so allergic to perfume she quit her job, or on the other hand the girl with amenorrhea who turned out after months to be anorexic? There was no clean line between the emotional and the physical, no safe border between self and world.

Part of what's so radical about *Safe* is that it reveals how open that boundary really is. It presents the body as a permeable vessel, not just susceptible to invasion but requiring by its very nature ongoing and risky exchange with the outside world. Carol is terrified of being swamped or invaded, whether by a disease or by people with larger and more forceful personalities than her own. The poisons she encounters damage her, but they also expose the many frightening ways in which her own body is leaky, open, uncontained. Acts like coughing and bleeding involve a body spilling out, exceeding its bounds; shaking, fitting, choking are manifestations of a body no longer under conscious control.

Though it portrays an exceptionally rarefied world, *Safe* is a political film. Haynes made it at the peak of the Aids crisis. It's set in 1987 and was released in 1995, a year before the invention of combination therapy meant that being diagnosed HIV positive was no longer an automatic death sentence. Haynes was in ACT UP, the Aids activist group that fought for treatment and education, and part of his impulse with *Safe* was to explore the horror of being attacked by something invisible, which no one around you understands and against which even wealth is not a prophylactic. Watching it in the autumn of 2019, it was impossible not to recall Aids panic, the confusion and fear attaching to an inexplicable cough or a purple mark on the face. By the spring of 2020, images of Carol in her hazmat suit were circulating on the internet, newly resonant amidst the lockdown of Covid-19, when tens of thousands were dying across the world of a mysterious virus and invisible transmission was once again a source of global terror.

Peter, the leader of the community to which Carol retreats, is loosely based on Louise Hay, the bête noire of my years as a herbalist, who became famous in large part because of her intense and controversial involvement with Aids. As Sontag observes in *AIDS and its Metaphors*, in the early years of the crisis people with Aids were regarded as polluting and perverse, the markers of their disease exposing them as members of a society of deviants and pariahs, widely regarded by politicians, journalists and religious leaders as deserving their appalling fate.

Hay, on the other hand, embraced people with Aids. She hosted massive, charismatic, cathartic weekly meetings in Los Angeles called Hayrides, at which patients, carers and loved ones were encouraged to testify and share their stories. She believed the disease was caused by a lack of self-love and encouraged people to use visualisation and affirmation to strengthen their ability to fight – a strength that would, of course, be enhanced by purchasing her books and tapes. The problem was that when people did inevitably get sicker or die, it became their own fault, their failure to love themselves enough, rather than the ravaging effects of a virus on their immune system, or the political consequences of a government and health-care system disinclined to fund research and treatment.

It was Hay's book on Aids that provided Haynes with the initial impetus for *Safe*. As he put it in an interview in *Bomb* in 1995: 'Her book literally states that if we loved ourselves more we wouldn't get sick with this illness. And that once you get it, if you learn how to love yourself in a proper way, you can overcome it. That's scary. I kept thinking of the people who have no answers to their situation and who turn to this.' In a different interview that same year, he asked precisely the question that had baffled Sontag: 'Ultimately, what was it in people who were ill that made them feel better being told that they were culpable for their own illness than facing the inevitable chaos of a terminal illness?'

★

There's no one I can think of who more clearly articulated an answer to this question than the writer Kathy Acker. Like Sontag, Acker was diagnosed with invasive breast cancer in her forties. Unlike Sontag, she refused chemotherapy, pinning all her hopes on alternative medicine. She had absolute faith in the meaningfulness of disease, right up until it killed her.

The first time she found a lump in her breast was in 1978, when she was thirty-one. A biopsy revealed it was benign, but an overspill of terror ran into *Blood and Guts in High School*, the novel she was working on at the time. Two things especially stood out. Cancer was political, since the doings of the body, particularly a woman's body, were always political. And cancer was inextricably bound up with reproduction, a horrible simulacrum of pregnancy that provoked the question of how you care for and tend the body. ('A demonic pregnancy,' Sontag called it that same year.)

There were more scares in the decades ahead, always benign. And then in April 1996, around the time of her forty-ninth birthday, she found another lump. Although she was by now an acknowledged star of the avant garde, it was a perilous time. Her books weren't selling well and she had taken an adjunct teaching job at San Francisco Art Institute. This time, the biopsied cells were malignant. The tumour was five centimetres in diameter, but the doctor believed it was unlikely to have spread. Acker was offered several choices, including a lumpectomy and radiation. She decided on a double mastectomy, double because she didn't want to have one breast. A few days after the surgery, she was given the results. Six out of eight lymph nodes tested were cancerous. All of us are going to die, the surgeon said flatly.

She refused chemotherapy and radiation, even though she now knew for certain the mastectomy had failed to excise all cancerous cells. She believed the lymph nodes were the body's filter and that the cancer had accumulated there because it was leaving, not proliferating. Like Carol in *Safe*, she seceded from conventional medicine, putting her faith in a retinue of alternative healers, two of whom would later be indicted for medical fraud (her acupuncturist refused to treat her, saying acupuncture could not cure cancer). She severed relationships with friends who disagreed with her decisions. As for the surgeon, she never contacted him again.

Among the therapists she consulted was Georgina Ritchie, a certified Louise Hay healer, who informed her in a session of past-life regression that her mother had tried to abort her. She told Acker that health was based on forgiveness, that she needed to forgive herself. She told her, à la Reich, that disease was trauma, a blockage caused by the scars of past events. 'A healthy person', she said, 'is one who can say, "I no longer have scars from the past that will keep me from doing what I have to do today." ' She made Acker sit on the floor, clutching a stuffed pig, her body rigid, plunged back into the memory of being an unloved infant. It seemed the past lived on inside what she called her emotional body. It was just as Reich had predicted: 'a piece of life history which is preserved in another form and is still active.'

The experience of illness was bringing back old feelings, aspects of her dismal childhood she'd never properly dealt with, despite the fact that they provided the atmosphere and architecture of all her books. A striking feature of Acker's fiction is that it's populated by alter-egos – Janey, Pip, Hester, Eurydice, Electra, O – who remain abject little girls no matter how old they are, abandoned, unloved, precociously sexualised, lost in a psychic landscape that is filthy, dangerous and often deadly. The lineaments of her own family recur in novel after novel, a repeating cast itemised in Chris Kraus's illuminating biography *After Kathy Acker* as 'a girlish mother, a boorish stepfather, a wealthy but disappeared biological father.'

The odd thing about this familial dynamic is that it was also shared by Sontag. Like Acker, Sontag was a poor little rich girl, emotionally impoverished despite erratically plentiful financial resources. Though they took up opposing poles in the cultural landscape, one the epitome of reason and the other a prophetess of chaos, they carried the burden of startlingly similar origin stories. Both women were born in New York City to wealthy Jewish families (Kathy's family on her mother's side, the Weills, had made a fortune as glove makers). Both had unhappy relationships with their mothers, were brilliant students, took refuge in their intelligence, were unpopular, lonely children. Both got married when they were still in their teens, and soon discarded their first husbands. Both were bisexual, and both converted themselves by an act of pure will into icons, instantly recognisable, though not perhaps that easy to get close to.

Acker never met her real father, who left her mother six months before she was born on 18 April 1947. As for Sontag, her father died of what she was always told was pneumonia (snooping in his medical records at the age of ten, she discovered it was actually tuberculosis, the 'passionate' disease that occupied her so intensely in *Illness as Metaphor*, and which also killed Reich's father and brother). She kept her father's ring in a box, asked her mother how you spell 'pneumonia', dreamt that he was coming home, that he was in the act of opening the apartment door. As an adult, she wept at the thought of him.

In Arizona, one of the many stations of a peripatetic childhood, Sontag dug herself a six by six hole in the ground, put a wooden lid on it and spent hours in there, reading and dreaming, grains of dirt falling continually onto her face. She claimed she was digging to China, though even as a child it was apparent that China also stood for death. It was like a scene from Acker's haunted cancer novel *Eurydice in the Underworld*, a descent into a land of the dead populated by girls living in chambers dug into the bare earth.

Like Sontag, Acker also had an absent mother. 'On a very deep level,' she once told a journalist, 'she couldn't stand me.' Claire blamed Kathy for her husband's disappearance, and the other girls at Kathy's school later described how neglected and unkempt she'd been despite the family's wealth. After she left home, Kathy severed contact with her family. She and her mother had only recently begun to rebuild their relationship when Claire took a room at the Hilton and on Christmas Eve 1978 overdosed on barbiturates, apparently because she was running out of money. Acker was thirty. During the sessions of regression at her therapist's office nearly two decades later, she experienced the same revelations of unmet need and cataclysmic loss as Sontag did on her hospital bed. In the libretto *Requiem*, Acker's last published piece of writing, she described these encounters with her small self: unloved, afraid to show anger, so unhappy that she moved wholesale into the other world of the imagination. She wrote about her mother and their life together, calling her THE CUNT.

She wanted to make sense of this past, and she thought cancer was an invitation to do so, that it represented a legacy of pain she'd been trying to ignore for years. In the autumn of 1996, six months after her mastectomy, she wrote an essay for the *Guardian* entitled 'The Gift of Disease'. In it, she says many paranoid, desperate and self-deluding things, including praise for healers who sound closer to charlatans, with their accounts of ancient wisdoms and rusty knives that cut out tumours. But she does make one striking point. She observes that part of the terror of her diagnosis was that it reduced her to a body that was solely material.

I understand this, I think. The terror of the material body is part of why I stopped working as a herbalist, just before my thirtieth birthday. I didn't like practising alone, in what I still think is an unnatural vacuum, without an integrated system of care, particularly for serious conditions like cancer. I thought medicine should be a network, not a charismatic encounter between patient and healer. I wanted to be able to refer, to talk to colleagues, to participate in a shared treatment plan. It disturbed me how many of the patients I saw wanted me to say, Acker-style, that I knew a miracle cure, that they should come off chemo and be healed by coffee enemas or extreme exclusion diets.

The other reason is much harder to articulate. I'd got interested in a French school of herbal medicine, developed by two oncologists. Their focus was not on where illness manifested, but on the originating axis of the hypothalamus and pituitary gland, which together govern and regulate many of the body's systems. Most of the material was in French. I bodged along, intimidated and bewitched. I was beginning to see the body as a network of dazzling complexity, in which any intervention would set off an inexorable cascade of reactions. Nothing worked in isolation. Everything was connected. Get a prescription wrong and you might unbalance a vital defence mechanism, triggering a process that would lead inexorably to disaster. Their vision of the body overwhelmed me: an absolutely implacable machine, in which there existed no self, no meaning, no ambiguity, no other order of existence beyond an endless dance of chemical reactions. I didn't want to meddle any more. I was too scared.

The sense that her own self – her perceptions, thoughts, memories, ideas – was no longer relevant, that she was nothing more than a biological entity, was part of why Acker rejected conventional treatment. 'My search for a way to defeat cancer now became a search for life and death that were meaningful,' she wrote. 'Not for the life presented by conventional medicine, a life in which one's meaning or self was totally dependent upon the words and actions of another person, even of a doctor.' For her, a meaningful body was a far richer source of freedom than health itself.

The *Guardian* essay is different in almost every aspect to *Illness as Metaphor*, from its tone and structure to its intention. In almost all of these ways, Sontag emerges as more reasoned, knowledgeable and controlled. But *The Gift of Disease*, and in particular the statement quoted above, exposes a zone of unreason in Sontag's argument, an odd glitch in her logic. Assuming you are going to be killed by something, doesn't it make sense to allow that experience to illuminate your life, to dwell on what it might mean in terms other than basic biological facts? As Acker's surgeon said, all of us are going to die.

★

A nurse, swabbing Sontag's dry lips with glycerine, had told her the same thing back in 1975. She knew it, of course. It was unarguable, completely obvious, but there was also a sense that she – special Susan, exceptional since childhood – might be the one to give death the slip. Like a matador, she thought, stepping very quickly back and forth in front of a black bull. She wrote about how she would like to run in front of death, have a good look, then let it overtake her, fall back into her proper place behind it.

In a curious interview with the *New York Times* in 1978, not long after she'd received the news that she was cancer-free, she sounded elated, almost drunk on how close she'd come to extinction. 'It's fantastic knowing that you're going to have to die,' she told the interviewer, adding that she would have liked to have kept 'some of that feeling of crisis' – the magnificent focus, perhaps, that mortality brings to bear on one's endeavours and pursuits. She chain-smoked right through the conversation, sweeping her hair off her face, gleeful to be alive.

The sense that she might be uniquely gifted at dodging death grew stronger through the years. In 1998 she was diagnosed with uterine sarcoma. Again she insisted on aggressive treatment, this time a hysterectomy and chemotherapy with the heavy metal cisplatin, which left her in deep pain and unable to walk. She answered the diminishment by learning to play the piano. Again she recovered, though her famous black hair turned grey. Someone had to be the outlier in any statistical analysis. She'd been lucky before, and furthermore believed that her luck was inextricably related to her insistence on the most extreme treatment; therefore with the most extreme treatment she could beat the odds again.

Sontag still despised the responsibility of her body, and her housekeeper, Sookhee Chinkhan, was deputised to take on much of its care. Early in 2004, Sookhee noticed bruises on Sontag's back while running her a bath. Then a routine blood test didn't look quite right. Sontag had more tests and a bone marrow biopsy. On 29 March, at the age of seventy-one, she was diagnosed with myelodysplastic syndrome, also known as smouldering leukaemia, the precursor to what is generally a fatal blood cancer. There were two possible treatments, her doctor explained, though both had very low success rates, particularly for people of Sontag's age, or who'd had cancer before. Defiant, terrified, implacable, she demanded a bone marrow transplant, the only option that could bring full recovery.

The procedure took place at the Fred Hutchinson Cancer Research Center in Seattle. It necessitated the complete destruction of her immune system, a process that turned out to be far more harrowing than she or any of her support network had expected. Isolated in a small room that July, she was exposed to near-fatal doses of radiation. Lying in bed, hooked up to tubes, she kept herself company with *Don Quixote*, the novel about hubris and courage that Acker had so lavishly plagiarised nearly twenty years before. In the aftermath of this procedure, she had endless infections, often couldn't speak or swallow, suffered from gruelling diarrhoea and hallucinations. Her body was grotesquely swollen, her skin covered in bruises and sores.

The transplant itself took place in August. Her recovery was very slow. In November her doctors assembled to tell her that the transplant had failed. A few days later she was medevacked back to Memorial Sloan Kettering in New York, where her doctors began yet another agonising experimental treatment, according to wishes she'd expressed back in the spring. She was no longer capable of communicating whether those wishes had changed. It too was unsuccessful. She died on 28 December 2004, eighteen days before her seventy-second birthday.

All of us are going to die, and yet despite her formidable capacity for reason, Sontag never quite accepted its inevitability. As Katie Roiphe points out in *The Violet Hour*, her beautiful, troubled account of Sontag and five other writers' deaths, there was a precedent of sorts for this heresy. Sontag *knew* her father was dead, but she could never be wholly certain it was true. There'd been no body, after all, and such a succession of lies. Perhaps he was still in China, equivocally absent, biding time until his return. The odds were poor, but poor odds had proved inaccurate before. Maybe you don't have to die.

This – blind spot? refusal? – might account for the glitch in *Illness as Metaphor*, its irrational refusal really to believe in mortality, its sense that people only die if they choose to, its poorly concealed disgust at those who succumb. For all the major aid it offers the stigmatized, *Illness as Metaphor* is engaged in a kind of magical thinking Sontag invented as a child: if you shut down feeling and deny the body, if you exist in a zone of pure thought, you will survive. In the *Rolling Stone* interview, carried out a few months after *Illness as Metaphor* was published in

1978, she explained that it doesn't matter what makes you ill. 'What does make sense is to be as rational as you can in seeking the right treatment and to really want to live. There's no doubt that if you don't want to live you can be in complicity with the illness.' There is no doubt that if you don't want to live you can be complicit with your illness, but the opposite is not true. Millions upon millions of people have died who really wanted to live. Assuming that a desire to live is what makes people survive is a logic that makes the sick as culpable for their own demise as they are in the teachings of Louise Hay.

*

'Each woman responds to the crisis that breast cancer brings to her life out of a whole pattern, which is the design of who she is and how her life has been lived', the poet and activist Audre Lorde says in *The Cancer Journals*, her account of her own struggle with breast cancer. There is much truth in this. Sontag wanted to live so badly she made her final months unbearable. As for Acker, to many people it seemed that she did the opposite, that she put herself through unnecessary suffering because she didn't want to live enough.

She believed her healers when they told her in 1996 that she was cancer-free. She continued her frenetic programme of supplements and yoga classes, moving frequently, to London, Virginia, London again. By the summer of 1997 she was very unwell. She blamed her symptoms on accidentally ingesting bad water, after retrieving and drinking from a bottle of Evian that had fallen into a canal. The weight, she told the *Independent* that September, had been falling off her.

Back in San Francisco the next month, she was finally persuaded to go to hospital, where she was told that the cancer had spread to her bones, kidneys, liver, lungs and pancreas. End stage, the weight of a child, her bones protruding through skin tattooed with a medieval bestiary of fish and flowers, she was still deep in paranoia and denial. She had no intention of dying in a hospital. All her life she'd documented what it was like to live in a culture that was riddled with death, war, violence, cruelty. The hospital was part of it, a staging post in a process that dehumanised people, and she refused to participate.

Somehow she persuaded her friends to get her into American Biologics, an alternative-treatment hospital in Tijuana, Mexico. They drove down on the Day of the Dead, in a rented van, with oxygen tanks and a Buddhist nurse; a far cry from Sontag's high-tech evacuation in a private plane, funded by her partner, the photographer Annie Leibowitz. Acker was assigned Room 101, a mythic location to pass out of a life that she had insisted on making mythic, embellishing and refashioning the shabby, shameful material that she'd been given.

There's a story about Acker's final days that has stuck in my head. She was no longer able to speak, but one of the friends who was staying with her felt she wanted some kind of sexual contact and so lightly touched her vulva and the scars where her breasts had been, while Kathy blew a kiss into the air. She was in bed with her beloved stuffed animals, a little girl of fifty clutching a plush rat, thrust back into a bodily experience of vulnerability that inevitably recalls infancy, with all its terrors and pleasures. Does sex have a place on the deathbed? Maybe for Kathy it did.

How do you make sense of Acker's refusal to have treatment, her seemingly suicidal decision to put her faith in quacks? Why didn't she have chemo, when it could potentially have given her decades more life? She said that she was terrified of the side-effects, of hair loss and muscle wasting. She said conventional medicine would turn her into a puppet. She said that if she uncovered the cause of her illness she might be able to undo it, as if cancer were a bad spell or a just punishment, rather than the random movement of certain cells.

Another reason she gave was money. In 'The Gift of Disease', she did a brisk accounting. Radiation, $20,000. Chemotherapy, $20,000 minimum. Single mastectomy, $4000; double mastectomy, $7000. Breast reconstruction, $20,000 minimum. Her teaching post in San Francisco wasn't tenured and she didn't have benefits. If she wanted any treatment she'd have to pay for it herself. As her friend Avital Ronell observed: 'She remained unsheltered, teaching more or less as an adjunct . . . I will never get over the fact that Acker had to suffer the refusal of medical benefits. Like many Americans, she was uninsured.'

Not everyone bought the maths. Acker's biographer Chris Kraus is particularly sceptical. Kathy, she observes, had $260,000 left in her trust fund; 'her reasoning here wasn't flawless'. But Acker was very short on security: no partner, no family, no permanent job, no permanent home. Her salary didn't even cover her rent in San Francisco. She'd bought many apartments and a great deal of clothes, but now she was getting close to the bottom of the jar. At this point in her career she didn't even have a publisher, a consequence of falling out with everyone she worked with.

Either way, the experience of having a double mastectomy as an uninsured person was brutal. 'The first thing that I did when I came back to consciousness, I remember, was to try to stand up, because I wanted to get out of that hospital as soon as possible. I wasn't staying the night, and couldn't even if I wanted to, because only people with medical insurance were allowed to.' (Audre Lorde told a similar version of this story in 1980, as did the poet Anne Boyer in her radiant cancer memoir, *The Undying*, written nearly forty years later.)

By the time Acker got to American Biologics, the financial situation was desperate. In her last weeks some of her closest friends tried to set up a fund to pay her bills. A group letter sent on 25 November was loaded with more depressing figures. The hospital in Mexico had so far consumed $28,000 of her $40,000 savings (though this doesn't quite tally with the £160,000 Kraus says Acker's London flat had sold for a few months earlier). Staying there cost $7000 a week. In addition, the eight days in the Davies Center in San Francisco had already topped $30,000, though Medicare was expected to cover some of the bill.

Even Sontag, a much more sheltered member of the middle classes, was not immune to the anxiety of getting sick within a health-care system where the ability to pay for treatment is paramount. In a *New Yorker* essay written after her death, her son went through the same dismaying figures, the impossible arithmetic. Medicare wouldn't pay for Sontag to have a bone-marrow transplant until the myelodysplastic syndrome had converted into acute myeloid leukaemia, its more lethal end stage. She didn't believe she could wait that long. Her private insurance did eventually agree to fund the procedure, but insisted it be carried out at a limited group of hospitals, and not at the Fred Hutchinson, which was the most experienced and expert. In the end, she found the money herself. The initial cost was \$256,000, with another \$45,000 to find a compatible donor. Obama changed this story, and Trump changed it again, but it remains true to say that unless there is universal health care, survival is not dependent on a person's will to live, but on their ability to pay.

But it wasn't just the financial cost that caused Acker to shy away from mainstream medicine. Indeed, she must have spent a small fortune on her retinue of healers, one of whom she sometimes consulted at hourly intervals (according to Kraus, he gave out his business card at Acker's funeral). She also refused to have chemotherapy and radiation because she feared them more than cancer itself. There's a depth of paranoia in much of Acker's writing about the body, a grave mistrust of the men in white coats combined with a credulous appetite for pseudo-scientific theories. This isn't to say her paranoia was wholly misplaced. Iatrogenic illness is not a fantasy. The risk factors for the cancer that killed Sontag include previous radiation and chemotherapy. In fact, her lead doctor told her that the particular cytogenetics of her cancer made it a certainty that it was caused by the chemotherapy she had for her uterine sarcoma. Her insistence on aggressive treatment saved her, absolutely, but it killed her too.

This is not a moral judgement. Sontag made the choices that she wished to and so did Acker. The consequences that terrified one meant nothing to the other. Their deaths, like their illnesses, were at once totally random and emblematic, in keeping with the people that they were. The physical self is perpetually affected, as Reich saw, by other things: its past, its state of mind, the culture, society and political climate in which it abides. As the film *Safe* observes, there can be no possibility of a safe zone, no way of keeping yourself isolated from the world. Life demands exchange, a fact that illness by its nature reveals.

Sontag was right to come into the sickroom as a clean broom, to sweep out superstition. I have no doubt that her books alleviated the burden of fear and guilt and shame in a great many lives. And yet, and yet. There is no cure for death. No one has so far invented the 'strange, chemical immortality' that she once hopefully described to her weeping son, when he realised, as children do, that everyone he loved would die. For all that we would prefer to live, and for those who we love to be unharmed, the end of disease is an impossible fantasy. Much as I admire Sontag's work, it seems saner to me to admit that we will never be fully purified of illness, never fully resistant to dying. Maybe some of Acker's choices were wiser than they looked: to know that there is a moment for acceptance, to use the opportunity of being sick to make sense of what has gone before. This isn't to argue against the necessity of getting treatment or of providing care, but rather to remember that these things occur against the fundamental thing that we all share: the fact of a limited lifespan.

# 3

# Sex Acts

BRIGHTON HAD ALWAYS ATTRACTED escapists and refuseniks, people infatuated with freedom, keen to experiment with alternative lives. When I first visited as a child the shabby cream-coloured squares were full of ageing actors, but by the 1990s they'd been supplanted by a transient population of homeopaths, trance DJs and kundalini yoga teachers. Ever since the Prince Regent built his absurd breasted palace, the city had a reputation as a pleasure-dome, primarily queer but good-naturedly accommodating to other tastes, too. On Friday nights the clubs on the beach filled up with Londoners, dressed for business in leather harnesses and fairy wings, their faces streaked with glitter, the whole seedy town throbbing to the pulse of sex.

I moved there in my late teens and stayed a good decade longer than I meant to, finding roosts in tall, rickety houses with high ceilings and bad management companies, redeemed by vertiginous glimpses of the sea. In those end-of-the-line years, sex happened easily, without any strict gender demarcation. It was in the air, part of the particular atmosphere of the city. At the end of parties, the inevitable bodies would be sprawled on someone's bed or by a random friend-of-a-friend's basement pool. I loved it when the mood shifted, platonic affection sharpening into something more focused and greedy. Sometimes the sex was very good, without any of the other necessary components of a relationship, and so a few of these encounters went on for years, on a more or less cheerful basis, fitting into gaps around more serious engagements.

I wasn't alone in this, at least not in the circles in which I moved. It was the cusp of the millennium, and my friends and I were right at the tail end of Generation X, the last gasp, our hedonism shot through with post-Aids caution. We knew the consequences of sex were death as well as birth, we grew up on Don't Die of Ignorance and yet we were still hungry for pleasure – hungry too, and perhaps even more urgently, for experience. The fashionable pose back then was irony, a knowing detachment. We wanted to be older all the time, not grossly innocent and ignorant, like babies. I remember this even from school, bitchy girls in rolled-up skirts and maroon blazers, the endless questioning about how many bases you'd got to the night before. Later, when I read Eve Babitz, I recognized the style I'd grown up with. Better a libertine than a puritan.

Those years contained a lot of sweetness, a lot of late-night honey, but the prevailing ethos made it hard to see that there were striking pleasure disparities. It was apparent, in the heterosexual configurations at least, that the risks weren't shared and neither were the consequences. We fucked and then we went to the GUM clinic on Eastern Road and had painful, frightening tests alone. There were unwanted pregnancies, weeks of steady anxiety over a late period, followed by a visit to the abortion clinic, the requisite tea and plate of sandwiches before you were allowed to dress and leave. It sounds like I'm describing the 1960s, but this was three, then four decades on. We were feminists who'd cut our teeth on riot grrrl fanzines, still somehow incapable of saying *put a condom on*, not just out of embarrassment but because the present-tense surrender was so conclusive it thrust the future out of existence. The poet Denise Riley once titled an essay 'Linguistic Inhibition as a Cause of Pregnancy' and that was us, somehow still buttoned up when naked. We knew only an idiot would have unprotected sex, but that didn't answer the ongoing conundrum, which is that the sex was better, it's just that the life that followed was palpably worse, at least for one member of the experimental unit.

No one could describe this as total freedom and yet everyone knew things could and had been worse. To be sexually active at the turn of the century was to taste the ripe fruit of a long history of struggle, a movement that had grappled with many of the same difficulties and dangers that remained attendant upon sexual exploration in my own lifetime. If I were to trace the roots of the liberties I enjoyed in Brighton, I'd find myself drawn inexorably to Weimar Berlin, a city I first encountered in print the same year that I had sex for the first time.

Johnny was in the year above me at college. I'd seen him around, toting a bass guitar, a beautiful dark-eyed boy with a thin face and hawk nose. For a while we were besotted with each other, electricity passing between us as we moved around the city, thighs brushing, hands interlocked. We were trawling a charity shop when I came across a broken-backed copy of

Christopher Isherwood's autobiographical novel *Goodbye to Berlin*, lured by the black-and-white cover photograph of neon lights cast slickly on wet pavements.

I was seduced and a little unsettled by Isherwood's squalid, sophisticated city, a hot, unsteady bed of erotic activity. On the surface, it sounded a lot like Brighton: girls who looked like boys and boys who looked like girls, high kicks and low dives, cabarets and bars for every kind of taste, decorated for the tourists in thick layers of 'gold and inferno-red'. The difference was that Weimar Berlin was on the brink of economic collapse. Everyone was for sale, and foreign pleasure-seekers like Isherwood could capitalise on a violently skewed exchange rate. It was, as his friend Klaus Mann put it, 'Sodom and Gomorrah at a Prussian tempo . . . Our department store of associated vices.'

Though its glamour is often exaggerated, Weimar Berlin was one of the most sexually tolerant cities in Europe, if not the world. According to the painter Francis Bacon, who spent a dissipated month there as a teenager in 1927, 'you had this feeling that sexually you could get absolutely anything you wanted.' He remembered streets of clubs with people standing at the entrances 'miming the perversions that were going on inside', adding thoughtfully, 'That was *very* interesting.' When the liberal Weimar Constitution was adopted after the First World War, censorship was abolished, and even illicit practices like homosexuality went largely unpunished. The city was far more tolerant of same-sex love than draconian old England, where memories of Oscar Wilde's hard labour still lingered bitterly three decades on, fuelling blackmail and nourishing hatred; a feeling that the 1928 obscenity trial over Radclyffe Hall's lesbian novel *The Well of Loneliness* had hardly helped to dispel.

Isherwood was preceded to the city by his friend Auden, who settled there around the time of the Hall trial, boasting in rapturous letters home about the seemingly infinite potential for encounter, not least because there were a hundred and seventy male brothels, all registered with a tolerant police (this number was at least slightly inflated). His Berlin journal closed with a dreamy list of lovers: *Pieps, Cully, Gerhart, unknown, unknown*. Little wonder he described it as 'the buggers daydream'.

Isherwood arrived on a visit the next spring. He was twenty-four and bristling with appetite and ambition: a small, distinctly boyish figure with a startling white grin and glossy brown hair that kept escaping over his eye, so precociously talented that he'd already published his first novel. Like Auden, he was leaving behind a world of privilege that he found claustrophobic and entrapping. His sexuality set him at odds with English society and he'd come to Berlin to enquire into the possibilities of love, though these pursuits were necessarily occluded in his autobiographical novels of the period. Later, he was more frank. In his 1976 memoir *Christopher and His Kind*, a book that helped ignite the gay liberation movement, he explained: 'To Christopher, Berlin meant Boys.' (To Christopher, I might add, *boys* meant young men in their late teens and twenties, not children.)

He spent his first Saturday night as he would spend a hundred more, in the Cosy Corner, a boy bar in the working-class district of Hallesches Tor. Pushing aside the heavy leather door curtain, he found himself in a shadowy paradise of handsome, tough-looking young men. No one was going to judge him, let alone arrest him if he flirted, danced, kissed, even fucked. His churning stomach and thumping heart reminded him of how he'd felt as a medical student, watching surgery performed for the first time at St Thomas's Hospital. Over the next weeks, and with the help of a handsome blond he called Bubi, he learned how to shed his awkwardness, to feel 'natural' having sex, as a swimmer might come to feel natural in the water, once they'd got past the first difficult, thrashing strokes.

He was embarrassed by his body, disliking in particular a weird patch of hair that sprang from an acne scar on his left shoulder, the source of 'an intimate physical shame'. He was seeing the English therapist John Layard at the time, who persuaded him that it was his animal nature flaunting itself, and that he must embrace it. Layard had trained in Vienna, bringing back his own version of the Freudian speaking body, which communicated buried desires by way of psychosomatic or hysterical ailments. Isherwood kept getting sore throats, which Layard translated as an inability to say what he really wanted. His body was inviting him to be more honest, to live in accordance with his actual longings. (Auden was even more extreme than Louise Hay in his adherence to this theory in the 1920s, telling Isherwood that rheumatism was caused by stubbornness and that tall people were more spiritual than short ones, their height evidence of their striving towards heaven.)

Auden soon left, but the city had cast its spell over Isherwood. Even the language, even the damp streets were redolent of sex.

'This is what freedom is,' he told himself. 'This is how I always ought to have lived.' He returned in November, arriving a few weeks after the Wall Street Crash brought worldwide ruin and staying until Hitler's ascent to power in 1933. After a series of dalliances with hustlers he fell in love with a working-class boy, Otto, with a face like a ripe peach. Otto, he wrote rapturously in *Christopher and His Kind*, 'was the coming of warmth and colour into the drab cold city, bringing the linden trees into leaf, sweating the citizens out of their topcoats, making the bands play outdoors.' This is Freud's libido, truly: an erotic energy that makes everything seem to glow and shiver with life.

But Berlin wasn't just a fleshpot for satisfying one's own personal appetite. Even Isherwood, who arrived believing sex entirely a private matter, recognised that this was a place in which the entire concept of sexual relations was undergoing rapid public change. In the Weimar period, Berlin had become the centre of a thriving liberation movement, a city-sized laboratory for refashioning attitudes to sex in the world at large. By chance as much as design, Isherwood found himself occupying a ring-side seat.

On his first day back, 30 November 1929, Isherwood paid a visit to an English friend, the archaeologist Francis Turville-Petre, also gay, who was living in an enormous house on In Den Zelten, looking out over the bright, leafy expanse of the Tiergarten, a cruising location for at least the last hundred years. The house had once belonged to a famous violinist and was still furnished in such a sumptuous, garlanded eighteenth-century style that you picked your way through 'a Black Forest of furniture'. Though it looked like a domestic residence, albeit an unusually opulent one, it was actually the Institute for Sexual Research, owned and presided over by Magnus Hirschfeld, a chubby, kindly Jewish doctor in his early sixties, with thick glasses, wild grey hair and a walrus moustache. His nickname was Auntie Magnesia and he was the leading sexual reformer in the world. Isherwood's friend Francis had a room above a lecture theatre and surgical unit and below lockable rooms where prisoners on sexual charges were permitted to await trial. 'I suppose you wouldn't care to have lunch here?' he asked a wary Christopher.

Lunch, Isherwood found uncanny. The presence of patients in genteel drag unnerved him, as did the photographs of famous gay couples, among them Edward Carpenter and George Merrill, Oscar Wilde and Lord Alfred Douglas, Walt Whitman and Peter Doyle, which hung alongside images of variant sex organs. Accepting his attraction to tough boys was one thing, but he couldn't yet reconcile himself to what he described in *Christopher and His Kind* as these 'freakish fellow-tribesmen and their distasteful customs'. At home, he'd been aware of his own submerged desires, but hadn't yet seen the possibility of sexuality as the source of a shared, communal identity, something you *are*, as opposed to something you *do*. Even so, he felt a pull. By the time he finished his meal, he was intrigued enough to accept Francis's offer of a room in the house.

The Institute was a very unusual place. It was the first sexual counselling centre in Germany, and one of the first in the world, offering advice on birth control and treatment for venereal disease (Francis was undergoing residential treatment for syphilis, though he also sat on one of the Institute's committees and lectured on sexual ethnology). The world's first sex-reassignment surgery had taken place in its clinic, and the house was also a sympathetic refuge for gay and transgender people (neither term yet in use), an early example of a residential queer community, in which sexually variant people could make an affectionate home together. Even some of the maids were post-op transsexuals. Despite his initial scepticism, Isherwood became so fond of the place that he stayed almost a year.

A beguiling black and white photograph from one of the Institute's famous costume balls shows Hirschfeld in his thick glasses surrounded by a crowd of embracing young people, sprawled across each other's laps. They're dressed for a high old time, in tuxes and top hats, eye masks and elaborate powdered wigs. One figure seems to have come as Marie Antoinette, in a corseted ball gown with frothing satin skirts, three ropes of pearls slung around a pale neck. No one's gender, Hirschfeld aside, is immediately clear. It looks so modern, so familiar I can't quite believe I don't recognise anyone (Season Two of *Transparent* had an arc set at Hirschfeld's Institute, beginning with a scene lifted directly from this photograph). In 1929, Isherwood attended the Christmas ball in make-up and bell-bottoms he'd borrowed from a hustler. The sense of transgression thrilled him, as did an encounter with an aristocratic man who'd inherited a vast wardrobe of ball dresses. Each year, 'he encouraged his friends to rip his gown off his body in handfuls', until he drifted home in luxuriant rags.

As he discovered more about Hirschfeld, Isherwood came to regard him with love and even awe. Despite his cosy appearance, Auntie Magnesia was a seasoned campaigner, a gay man who believed homosexuality could be found in all cultures and countries of the world. In 1921, the year after the League of Nations was founded, he'd established the First International Congress for Sexual Reform (later the World League for Sexual Reform). The timing was significant. Europe was still reeling from violence on an unspeakable scale. Ten million men had died in the Great War, and in its aftermath the horror of the trenches gave way to a burst of utopian dreams: of a world without war, a brotherhood of man, an end to conflict based on arbitrary divisions of gender, class or nationality. Sex was part of that, a fantasy of love without disease or subjugation, free at last from guilt or religious duty, the pervasive association of bodily acts with vice or the demands of procreation.

Since the end of the nineteenth century, Hirschfeld had been driving the campaign against Paragraph 175 of the Prussian (later German) Criminal Code, which punished homosexual acts between men with prison terms of up to ten years. Paragraph 175 had generated a corrosive climate of fear and shame, resulting in blackmail and even suicide. Hirschfeld's own engagement with the subject of sex had been precipitated by the suicide of one of his medical patients in 1896: a young gay officer who was pressured into marriage by his parents and who shot himself on his wedding night. In the suicide note he addressed to Hirschfeld, he explained he couldn't tell his parents about 'that which nearly strangled my heart.'

Many European countries, led by post-revolutionary France, had eliminated anti-sodomy laws a century earlier (Britain, where the death penalty for sodomy had been maintained until

1868, was even more punitive than Germany). Although Hirschfeld's previous campaign against Paragraph 175 had failed, the introduction of the more tolerant Weimar constitution in 1919 convinced him that the time was ripe for repeal and he established the Institute that same year. Cannily, he built a museum of sexuality on the second floor, furnished with dildos, whips and artfully constructed false trousers for flashers, to which Francis took a giggly Isherwood on his first afternoon. The museum drew the crowds, as did a box for anonymous questions on sex. By the early 1930s, fourteen thousand had been submitted, many of them answered by Hirschfeld himself.

This information gathering had a larger aim. One of the great questions of the time was whether homosexual desire was inborn and natural or acquired and aberrant, a consequence of damaging childhood experience or exposure to adult seduction, and either way pathological. Hirschfeld realised that if he could prove it was the former, he could undermine the argument for Paragraph 175 altogether, since criminalisation hinged on the belief that homosexual acts were not only deviant, degenerate and wicked, but – crucially – volitional.

The 'born this way' argument, encapsulated in Lady Gaga's anthem, remains contentious a century on. Many people don't find it liberating to regard their sexuality as innate, and instead fight for the right to choose the consensual acts they wish to engage in, a point of view I share. But in Hirschfeld's era, making a case for an inborn, 'natural' sexuality had real liberatory potential, promising to release individual erotic lives from the burden of oppressive laws.

By no means everyone agreed. In 1928, Freud wrote in a

festschrift for Hirschfeld's sixtieth birthday: 'I have always expressed the view that the life and work of Dr. Magnus Hirschfeld against the cruel and unjustifiable interference of the law in human sexual life deserves general recognition and support.' But though it was Freud who'd formulated the radical idea that the sexuality of infants not only existed but could extend almost infinitely, the so-called polymorphous perversity, even he believed that the purpose of mature adult sex should be procreation. He viewed same-sex desire in terms of immaturity and deviance, portraying 'inversion' as a kind of kink, a disturbance in the functioning current of the libido. He couldn't consider it innate and therefore natural, though it also seemed impossible that it could always be learned or acquired. Indeed, the presence of the *invert* created a snag in Freud's understanding of sex, an inconsistency that made him realise yet again how complicated it was to trace the connection between the pulse of sexual desire and the object to which it attaches.

Unlike Freud and unlike the sexual moralists, Hirschfeld wasn't interested in arbitrating on acceptable practices (assuming always that acts were consensual). He was resistant to the grand Victorian project of cataloguing and classifying in a hierarchical way, determining what is and isn't legitimate. Instead, he wanted to document what people actually desired and did, a venture he carried out decades before Kinsey began to investigate the sexual behaviour of Americans. Over the years, Hirschfeld interviewed tens of thousands of people about their activities and fantasies, taking them through a questionnaire that could take months to complete and run to hundreds of pages (according to Francis Bacon, there were clubs in Berlin that specialised in acting out Hirschfeld's discoveries on stage as titillating tableaux vivants).

These interviews revealed such a diversity of sexualities, not to mention differences in genitalia, that Hirschfeld's belief in the existence of anything so simplistic as two genders was eroded. No, the line between male and female, straight and gay was decidedly blurred. In 1910, he calculated that there were forty-three million possible combinations of gender and sexuality, a near-infinite spectrum of human possibility that goes far beyond our own era's tentative acceptance of gender and sexual fluidity. Imagine telling J. K. Rowling.

'The number of actual and imaginable sexual varieties is almost unending', he wrote that year, sounding very much like Virginia Woolf in her gender-swapping, time-travelling master-piece *Orlando*. 'In each person there is a different mixture of manly and womanly substances, and as we cannot find two leaves alike on a tree, then it is highly unlikely that we will find two humans whose manly and womanly characteristics exactly match in kind and number.' Reading that sentence, I understood why Isherwood was so beguiled by Hirschfeld. I loved him too.

★

Hirschfeld might have been the most visible figure advocating for a new amorous world, but he was certainly not alone in his work. By the time Isherwood arrived in Berlin, there were nearly a hundred different groups involved in sexual liberation in the city, from the radical free love movement to conservative organisations established to protect unwed mothers and their children. There were groups fighting for birth control and sex education, for state maternity benefits, for the prevention of venereal disease and for the decriminalisation of abortion. Many were run by and for women, like Helene Stöcker's Bund für Mutterschutz, which believed '*all* love should be a private matter, free from interference by the state.' Many too were communist, inspired by the Soviet Union's drastic new programme of sexual reforms. Though basically emancipatory, not all their agendas overlapped and there were uneasy alliances as well as open antagonism, especially over the fraught issue of abortion.

Nor was the work confined to Germany alone. Across the world, individuals and small groups had from the late nineteenth century been fighting for a loosening of the stays, a relaxing of laws around sexual behaviour. The British doctor and sexologist Havelock Ellis believed gender was mutable and sex for women should be pleasurable as well as procreative; shocking notions for the Victorians. Along with his sometime-collaborator, the gay socialist and free-love advocate Edward Carpenter, Ellis was one of the first people in Britain to advocate publicly for homosexual rights. His co-authored book on homosexuality, *Sexual Inversion*, was published in 1897, two years after the Oscar Wilde trial, and promptly banned as an obscene publication, while Carpenter's essay 'Homogenic Love and Its Place in a Free Society' had to be published and circulated privately in the aftermath of the trial.

Both Carpenter and Ellis were admirers of Margaret Sanger, the American activist who'd coined the term 'birth control' as part of her campaign to make contraception palatable and legal in the United States (it was banned at the time under the punitive Comstock Laws, which classified it alongside pornography as obscene and immoral). She and Carpenter met in the Egyptian Room at the British Museum in 1914, conducting an impassioned discussion on contraception and sexuality between the tombs of long-dead kings. Sanger was in the country illicitly at the time, after being charged with violating anti-obscenity laws for sending her birth-control pamphlet *The Woman Rebel* through the mail. Rather than face trial in New York, she'd jumped bail and fled to England.

Two years later, she opened the first American birth-control clinic, in Brooklyn. Within four days she was arrested and imprisoned for distributing contraceptives. After her release she founded Planned Parenthood, an organisation that survives to the present day, though it remains imperilled by conservatives still avid to police sexual bodies, protesting under banners that read 'Planned Parenthood LIES to You' and 'Planned Parenthood Sells Baby Parts' (it doesn't). Sanger was a key ally of the German birth-control movement, financially underwriting many of the clinics, thanks to a wealthy husband. She visited Berlin in 1920, describing it as horrifyingly chaotic and impoverished, the streets unlit, the people almost starving (she found herself 'haunting grocery stores like a hungry animal'). Hirschfeld's 'beautiful dwelling' was a respite, and she commented in her autobiography on the striking contentment in the faces of the transvestites whose photographs adorned his walls.

Back in Vienna, Reich too was brooding over sex. In 1919, he wrote a memoir published much later as *Passion of Youth*.

Written in the first flush of his encounter with Freud, this extraordinary document reads as if he's dredging his own past for proof of the sexual nature of the unconscious. He remembers how much he loved puppies, especially their snub noses, and speculates that it was the touch of the mother's breast he longed for. He recalls opening a locked drawer and finding his father's copy of *The Marriage Counsellor*. Leafing furtively through, he became entranced by a diagram of the labia, complete with hair, the acme of forbidden knowledge.

He soon progressed from theory to practice. At the startling age of eleven he lost his virginity to the family cook, a liaison that continued for years. At fifteen, he visited a brothel. '*I had ceased to be – I was all penis!*' (I sincerely hope the girl enjoyed her encounter with this possessed young figure.) As he grew older, his intense sexual desire was sublimated into fantasies about impossibly idealised women. The widespread presence of gonorrhoea in the army made him wary of seeing prostitutes and by the time he arrived in Vienna he was suffering from acute sexual frustration. In 1921, he fell in love with one of his own patients, Annie Pink, and when it was discovered they were sleeping together her father insisted they wed, in what Reich described more than once as a 'forced marriage'. All this is to say that even before he encountered Freud, he already understood sexuality as a wild force, subject to immense control, forced into channels that were tightly circumscribed and hedged about with punishments of many kinds.

When they first met, Freud believed neurosis was caused by disturbances of the libido, and Reich's practice soon bore this out. By the mid-1920s, he realised with a shock that of the hundreds of patients he'd seen, all of the women and around two-thirds of the men were struggling to climax. Though his first orgasm with the cook had been so unexpected that it frightened him, he was starting to harbour a shocking suspicion. If undischarged sexual energy caused neurosis, mightn't it follow that the discharge of sexual energy was in itself a healing force? Was it possible that the orgasm was the body's own innate way of releasing tension, dissolving the rigid armour of trauma and unhappiness in a stream of fluid, libidinous energy? By 1926, the year he wrote *The Function of the Orgasm*, he was convinced that it was a magical biological transaction, the mysterious route by which the psyche restored itself to equilibrium, and as such a source of emotional as well as physical health, for women and men alike.

Reich's version of sexual healing is easy to mock, but it's not as simple-minded as it sounds, and certainly doesn't resemble the genital utopia of sucking and fucking epitomised by something like Nicholson Baker's gleefully lascivious *House of Holes*, in which the pursuit of the orgasm is carried out with a maximum of diligence and ingenuity. Though it's true Reich was obsessed with orgasms (when he presented Freud with the manuscript of *The Function of the Orgasm* as a birthday present, Freud eyed it warily and muttered, 'That thick?'), what he meant was not synonymous with ejaculation. 'It is not just to fuck, you understand,' he explained years later, 'not the embrace in itself, not the intercourse. It is the real emotional experience of the loss of your ego, of your whole spiritual self.' It wasn't the coming that mattered so much as the letting go.

The orgasm as emotional and spiritual awakener was certainly the experience of Susan Sontag. She had her first orgasm in 1959, when she was twenty-six and already the mother of a seven-year-old son. It was with a female lover, the Cuban-American playwright María Irene Fornés (herself the ex-girlfriend of Adele Morales, Norman Mailer's wife, who he would stab a year later). Two months after her momentous experience, Sontag wrote in her diary: 'The repercussions, the shock waves are only now beginning to fan out, to radiate through my whole character and conception of myself. I feel for the first time the living possibility of being a writer. The coming of the orgasm is not the salvation but, more, the birth of my ego.' She described her pre-orgasmic self as 'maimed', 'incomplete' and 'dead'. The orgasm peeled it away, revealing a rapacious new being. Reich would have considered it a good beginning.

His orgasm theory caused an unwitting earthquake in psychoanalysis. While Freud had originally regarded sexual repression as the cause of neurosis, by the time Reich came along his thoughts were in flux. It troubled him that his patients didn't necessarily get better, even after the cause of their symptoms was painstakingly uncovered. It didn't make sense, not if the human organism was driven primarily by Eros, the desire for pleasure. Could there be a counterweight, an equal and opposite drive?

In 1920, the year Reich joined the Vienna Psychoanalytic Society, Freud published *Beyond the Pleasure Principle*, in which he postulated the existence of another drive, a secret current that pulled towards death. He called it *Todestrieb*, the urge towards inertia and non-being, to lying down, drawing up the covers, returning to the dark. In this controversial and even frightening new model of the psyche, he suggested that everyone harboured a secret attraction to death, the cessation of the self. Anxiety was part of it, like bubbles rising from a riptide. It wasn't just a consequence of trauma or damage, but an integral element of what it meant to be a human animal, melancholy and afraid by nature.

In 1926, three years after Freud was diagnosed with cancer of the jaw, he went even further. He declared in *Inhibitions, Symptoms and Anxiety* that instead of sexual repression causing anxiety, it was anxiety that caused sexual repression. If anxiety was innate, this meant that sexual repression too was simply part of what it was to be human; a massive blow to Reich, who believed sexual repression was a malevolent cultural force that warped and inhibited natural human happiness.

In Freud's new construction of maturity, the individual had to come to an accommodation between their own libido, their greedy animating suite of desires, and the social world in which they lived, even if this necessitated *restrictions* or *mutilations* (both words are Freud's) of the erotic life. As he explained in *Civilisation and its Discontents*, written the year Isherwood arrived in Berlin, there was an unavoidable rift between the private, anarchic realm of love and the public, painfully necessary surveillance state of civilisation. It wasn't possible to act on every last libidinous urge. The result would be chaos: rape and violence. The job of the psychoanalyst was to help broker this détente, to encourage the individual to adapt to society. Sex was a dangerous, unruly force, and simply chasing after orgasms was a fool's game, since sexual desire could never be fully satisfied – an argument Freud made so often that I sometimes wonder about his own sex life, six children aside.

'Maimed' and 'mutilated' are strong words, and they underscore why Reich was so adamant that sex was the foundation of emotional health. Unlike Freud, he thought that if people were frustrated and ashamed, if they were hobbled by inhibition or fear of punishment, if they believed their desire was bad and wrong, or if they were not given the opportunity for free and safe expression, then they remained infantile, like permanently unhappy children who channel their frustration into harm. A sexually content human, on the other hand, was by his definition free of anxiety, since sex was the mechanism that discharged it. If society inhibited this healthy expression of sexuality in multiple ways, from puritanical shaming to a lack of availability of contraception or abortion, it seemed obvious to him that it was society that would have to change, to better accommodate the needs of its libidinous citizenry.

Their argument might have been conducted in the realm of ideas, but the breach hurt both men badly. Freud felt betrayed by his stubborn protégé, and Reich was baffled and wounded by his rejection. In an interview recorded for the Sigmund Freud Archives in 1952, he said that Freud turned away from the implications of the libido theory in the early 1920s out of fear and pressure from the outside world, that being a pariah had exhausted him, and that he was forced by his followers to relinquish his more radical ideas. He'd gone out on a limb, and now he was lonely and afraid: an isolated man, who had two, perhaps three friends he trusted, always polite, biting back what he really felt, clamping down on the omnipresent cigar.

In this interview, Reich painted Freud as a strange mixture of a man. On the one hand, he was a free-thinker, an experimental archaeologist of the sexual imaginary who'd weathered years of scorn and disapproval, patiently netting his enormous ideas, which have permanently changed how we understand ourselves. At the same time, he was a tweedy professor, a petit-bourgeois family man stuck in a corset of rigid notions about what constituted civilised behaviour. His marriage, Reich thought, was unhappy and he had resigned himself to loss and lack. 'Freud had to give up, as a person. He had to give up his personal pleasures, his personal delights, in his middle years.'

Reich believed this resignation and despair lay behind Freud's growing conservatism, the tone shift in his work, and he also thought it caused Freud's cancer, which, he observed darkly, had coincided with the conflict between them. Reading this interview (which Reich considered so significant that he published it as a book, *Reich Speaks of Freud*), it is overwhelmingly apparent that the pain of their breach had not diminished with the years. Reich returns to the subject again and again, skating back to it mid-sentence. Decades on, he still felt that he had stayed loyal to his mentor, and that it was Freud who had betrayed himself, terrified of the implications of real sexual freedom.

Poor Reich. It's so easy to mock him, the orgasm man, just as it is easy to mock and minimise sex itself. I thought of him when I watched *Unorthodox*, a TV drama about a nineteen-year-old girl from an ultra-Orthodox community in Williamsburg, New York. When we first see the nineteen-year-old heroine, Esty Shapiro, she is rigid with physical tension.

Her neck is bowed, her body hunched, jerking along the street like a marionette. Expected to have intercourse with her husband on a strictly determined schedule – no foreplay, no kissing, just penetration – and to produce her first child nine months after her wedding, so ignorant about her body that she is shocked when told of the existence of her vagina, and made to undergo rites of purification before her husband can touch her, it's hardly surprising that she suffers from vaginismus, her body literally refusing to be penetrated. After a shattering year of marriage, she escapes to Berlin, of all historically apt places, where for the first time she experiences sexual contact as a consequence of desire rather than duty. Freed of impossible demands, her body gradually unfurls, becoming far more fluid and at ease. This was the liberation Reich was fighting for, the kind of life he wanted people to be able to enjoy, not just ejaculation for its own spumey sake.

★

But Reich's *Steckenpferd*, or hobbyhorse, as Freud called it, might not have had such grave consequences for their relationship if it hadn't coincided with his growing conviction of the need for social change. Since its foundation in 1922, he'd been working at the Ambulatorium, the free psychoanalytic clinic in Vienna. These free clinics (the first had opened in Berlin in 1920) had a very different clientele to the wealthy neurasthenics seen in private practice, and they radicalised the young second-generation psychoanalysts, the so-called *Kinder*, among whom Reich was a prominent figure.

After a long battle for premises, the Ambulatorium was

finally established in the ambulance entrance of the cardiology unit at the General Hospital on Pelikangasse – where, according to the historian Elizabeth Ann Danto, it resembled 'a gatekeeper's house on an opulent estate'. Each afternoon, the four ambulance garages were transformed into consulting rooms, a metal examination table serving as a couch, while the analyst sat on a wooden stool. Despite these unprepossessing surrounds, which illustrate just how highly psychoanalysis was regarded by the Viennese medical establishment at the time, vast numbers of patients streamed through the Ambulatorium's doors. Reich, who had just completed two years' postgraduate training in neuropsychiatry when the clinic opened, was appointed clinical assistant to the director, rising two years later to become deputy medical director.

The patients he saw there were industrial labourers, farmers, housewives and the unemployed, and their stories exposed the tattered inadequacies of the psychoanalytic model. Their problems weren't a result of Oedipal conflict or witnessing the primal scene. They were struggling with poverty, overcrowding, overwork, exhaustion, drunkenness, domestic violence, prostitution, incest, rape, teenage pregnancy, illegal abortions and venereal disease. In short, every individual he saw was being affected by social and economic forces that couldn't possibly be addressed by psychoanalysis.

What Reich longed to do was treat the cause. 'From now onward, the great question was: *Where does that misery come from?* While Freud developed his death instinct theory which said "the misery comes from inside", I went out, out where the people were.' In 1927, he read *Das Kapital* with as much amazed recognition as he had once read Freud. He was gripped by Marx's account of capitalism as a brutal system of exchange that converted people into commodities, objects of arbitrarily fluctuating value. The notion of alienated bodies, estranged from their own needs and desires, chimed with what he'd seen in his own patients, lying stiff and rigid on the couch. He already believed that marriage had deleterious effects on people's sex lives (his own was firmly open), and he was excited to discover that Marx thought social change would require the abolition of the nuclear family. Within a year, he'd joined the Communist Party.

Both psychoanalysis and communism were full of potential for understanding human unhappiness and expanding human freedom, Reich thought, but each had major blind spots. The problem with psychotherapy was that it insisted on treating the individual as if their pain occurred in a vacuum, unmediated by the society they inhabited or the politics that governed their lives. As for Marxism, it failed to recognise the importance of emotional experience, not least the trouble caused by shame and sexual repression, especially to women.

Therapy was not enough. Politics was not enough. Only sex was a sufficiently powerful force to reshape society. Reich kicked off his quixotic campaign in 1928, trawling the suburbs of Vienna in a van he'd kitted out as a mobile 'sex-economy clinic', accompanied by a female doctor who fitted contraceptive devices and arranged illegal abortions for desperate women. He went from door to door dispensing condoms and communist pamphlets, like some lay preacher of the erotic. The following year, and with Freud's uneasy blessing, he established six free clinics in the poorer areas of the city, offering psycho-therapy for the working classes alongside free sex education, contraception and abortion advice. 'What was new about our counselling centres', he explained, 'was that we integrated the problems of the neuroses, sexual disturbances and everyday conflicts. It was also new to attack the neuroses by *prevention* rather than treatment.'

It hadn't escaped Reich that Berlin was the hot zone of sexual liberation, and in 1930 he transferred operations across the German border, joining what he described in *People in Trouble* as 'the great freedom movement'. He moved with Annie and their two daughters to an apartment on Schwäbische Strasse a year after Isherwood first drew back the curtain on the Cosy Corner and a few weeks after Hirschfeld left the city on an epic world tour. While Isherwood was giving English lessons and gallivanting with Otto, Reich was working at the Berlin Poliklinik, the first of the free clinics. He soon established a splinter group of radically-minded young analysts, who met at his apartment to discuss patient case histories, politics, the future. Fascism was on the rise. Surely psychoanalysis had to become politically engaged?

From the moment he'd arrived in Berlin, Reich was aware of the presence of the Nazi Party. Day by day, as Germany tumbled deeper into financial crisis, the Sturmabteilung, SA, became more visible, marching through the streets in their polished knee boots and brown uniforms. Both Reich and Isherwood described seeing anti-Semitic graffiti and smashed windows in Jewish-owned department stores. In 1931, Reich's communist group (which included the writer Arthur Koestler) heard the SA was planning an attack on a Red housing block on Wilmersdorferstrasse. They organised a defence, filling hundreds of glass bottles with water and lining them along the windows, ready to smash on the heads of the troops.

On holiday in Rügen Island that summer, Isherwood observed families decorating their beach encampments with swastikas, a scene he inserted into *Goodbye to Berlin*. As he drifted down the sand, brooding over Otto, he saw that someone had spelled out *HEIL HITLER!* with fir-cones. At the Topography of Terror Museum in Berlin in 2017, I came across a photograph of a similar scene: an embracing couple in bathing suits, hers lavender, his black, their faces close together, their legs entangled. They were curled in the hollow of a dune, and to mark the boundaries of their hedonistic domain they'd planted a line of swastika bunting in the sand, along with three beach-sized swastika flags, snapping gaily.

Even as he'd been preparing to attack and potentially kill a member of the SA, Reich still felt there was a human being inside the uniform. It was plain to him that the young people joining the SA were not that dissimilar to his comrades in the Communist Party. They were all 'individuals living under the same working conditions, in the same material situation, and even sharing the same determination to "do away with the capitalist machine".' Why, then, were some people choosing fascism? Reich suspected the growing popularity of the Nazis was a consequence of the same sexual discontent he saw in his patients, and he was certain that fascism was the malign end product of sexual repression, which made people dangerously susceptible to the authoritarian experience of a dictatorship, from the seductive spitting figure of Hitler to the compensatory pleasure of marches, rallies and uniforms.

Sex was key. Sex was the way to turn the tide, to reach the masses and liberate them from their rigid, infantile fixation with fascism. In the early 1930s, Reich coined the term the 'Sexual Revolution' to describe the universe of happiness and love that would arise once people had shaken off their shackles, divesting the world of its punitive, prurient attitudes. He was undoubtedly naive in this, as the French philosopher-historian Michel Foucault so scathingly observes in the first volume of *The History of Sexuality*, published in 1976. If the orgasm is so powerful, Foucault asks, why is it that the vastly expanded sexual liberties of the intervening years have failed to dissolve capitalism or topple the patriarchy, despite all Reich's ardent predictions to the contrary?

It's an easy criticism to make, but it doesn't mean Reich's utopianism was completely without solid, practical foundations. If people had access to safe sex, and especially to contraception and safe, legal abortion, they were far less likely to produce unwanted children, or to find themselves shackled by poverty or unhappy marriages. As he pointed out in *The Sexual Revolution*, between 1920 and 1932, twenty thousand women a year died in Germany because of illegal abortions, while seventy-five thousand became ill with sepsis. You don't need to believe in the magical power of the orgasm to see why a sexual revolution might be desirable, especially for women.

With Hirschfeld away on his world tour, Reich began to channel the Berlin reform groups into his own explicitly communist organisation, the German Association for Proletarian

Sexual Politics, shortened to the catchier Sex-Pol. Although the limits of his work are contested, he was a prominent, passionate figure in the city, lecturing crowds of thousands. Young people in particular came to him in droves, begging for help with the difficulty of reconciling their own desires with their anxiety and ignorance around pregnancy and disease.

Reich liked to establish demands, and those of Sex-Pol echoed Hirschfeld's World League for Sexual Reform. Even now they sound strikingly progressive: free divorce, birth control and sex education; the elimination of venereal disease; the abolition of punishment for sexual crimes in favour of treatment, combined with robust protection for children against paedophiles. In addition, they demanded free and legal abortion, something the more conservative groups in the World League had refused to countenance.

But there were limits to Reich's radicalism. What he didn't want, and what Sex-Pol refused to address, was the abolition of the homophobic Paragraph 175, which criminalised sex between men. The World League had made a clear case for sexual diversity, demanding a rational attitude towards sexuality, 'and especially towards homosexuals, both male and female'. Reich didn't agree. Like Freud, he was depressingly proscriptive about sex, believing it had to be heterosexual, penetrative and orgasmic. His genital utopia, it turned out, required a passport and visa at the door.

In *People in Trouble*, he writes contemptuously of how sexology in the period after the First World War was 'shrouded in darkness' because the 'great names', Hirschfeld and Ellis among them, 'dealt with (and could only deal with) the biopathic

sexuality of the time, that is to say, the perversions and procreation of the biologically degenerate human animal.'
Homosexuality he regarded as a product of sexual repression, a
kind of warping. Years later, in New York, he refused to treat
Allen Ginsberg because he was gay.

★

When Reich referred to 'the biologically degenerate human
animal', he was drawing on a concept that has had malign consequences on bodily freedoms across the world. Degeneration
is a pseudoscientific theory about bad and undesirable bodies
that emerged in the nineteenth century, played a disturbing role
in the sexual liberation movement, contributed to the rhetoric
that underpinned the Holocaust, and which continues to drive
prejudice, racism and even genocide in our own century. When
Darwin's *On the Origin of Species* was published in 1859, the
limits of inheritance were poorly understood. Was evolution
always progressive, or was there a counter-movement of stagnation, regression and relapse, passed on through the generations?
Perhaps you could inherit insanity, weakness, laziness, even
criminality. This latter belief was popularised by the Italian
criminologist Cesare Lombroso, who argued in his influential
1876 work *Criminal Man* that the criminal was a throwback to
a more primitive, atavistic being.

Throughout the Victorian era, the category of degenerate
people kept expanding. Paupers. Homosexuals. Prostitutes.
Alcoholics. Vagrants. Beggars. The sick, the diseased, the disabled, the suicidal, the insane. The idea gathered immense
racist force, justifying imperial violence as well as missionary

zeal against so-called backward or primitive nations. Its frequent association with parasitism intensified a feeling that the bad, degenerate body should not be supported, perhaps not even tolerated at all.

If degeneration was inborn, it meant the problems it was associated with weren't caused by poverty or social regimes, but were the consequence of the body itself. This brutal worldview, still prevalent on the right today, regards the welfare state, charity and even vaccination as powerless and wasteful in the face of inherited weakness and incapacity. It's visible, for example, in a controversial document written in 2013 by the-then senior advisor to the UK Education Secretary, Dominic Cummings, which questions the value of programmes like Sure Start, arguing that 'most of those that now dominate discussions on issues such as social mobility entirely ignore genetics and therefore their arguments are at best misleading and often worthless'.

By the end of the nineteenth century, the question had arisen as to whether the degenerate should be allowed to reproduce. Though it sounds like pure Third Reich rhetoric, the concept of eugenics was invented in 1883 by Darwin's cousin Francis Galton. He thought that just like sheep and cows, humans could be improved by selective breeding. He proposed two pathways to what he regarded as a utopian future populated by 'the best stock': positive eugenics, which meant encouraging the reproductively desirable to breed, and negative eugenics, which meant preventing the so-called Unfit from reproducing.

Although positive eugenics is regarded as less horrifying than negative eugenics in its effects, both models clearly depend on establishing a sliding scale of human value. It's not enough to simply possess a body. It has to be the right kind. Eugenics always involves identifying which types of bodies are worth preserving and which should be discarded from the communal store of humanity. The question of which court or power would define the Unfit, what police would enforce it, and what punishment there would be for resistance and refusal would soon be amply addressed. But there was abundant evidence of the authoritarian potential of eugenics long before the rise of Hitler. The first sterilisation to eliminate 'inferior' offspring took place illegally in Germany in 1897. The procedure was rapidly popularized, particularly in the United States, where it was used to carry out an outspokenly racist agenda. Race hygiene, as eugenics was also called, wasn't always literally an imperial programme designed to ensure the survival of a pseudo-scientific white or Aryan race, but it was a quest for homogeneity and purity.

What seems truly astonishing now is that a great many people involved in the sexual liberation movement of the 1920s were in favour of some kind of eugenicist programme. In the period before the wars, and despite evidence that it was already being used non-consensually, so-called 'welfare eugenics' (as opposed to 'racial eugenics') was still considered a utopian tool, a rational way of engineering a world without sickness and inherited disease. Just as Fabians like H. G. Wells and Beatrice Webb joined the British Eugenics Society, so Marie Stopes, Margaret Sanger and Helene Stöcker all subscribed to eugenic theories of one kind or another.

By providing a rationale for legalising birth control, eugenics seemed to offer a way of uncoupling sex from pregnancy, thereby allowing women to fully participate in sexual liberty. In Germany, as in many other countries, part of what drove prohibitions against abortion and contraception was a desire to increase population. Sexual hygiene arguments allowed the liberationists to argue for legalising contraception by reframing it as part of a patriotic campaign to increase the quality of the nation's offspring, rather than polluting the communal gene pool. Even the seemingly innocent rebranding of contraception as 'birth control' and later 'family planning', terms now so ubiquitous as to be unquestioned, were actually a way of making non-reproductive sex – sex for sheer pleasure – acceptable by smuggling it beneath a conservative, eugenicist banner. Many sex liberationists used the spectre of degeneracy to bolster their arguments, writing in hostile language of the feckless, asocial poor and reproductively unfit, whose fecundity must be disciplined if not actively prevented.

Reich was disturbed by all this. In *People in Trouble* he described how frustrating it was to hear eugenicist arguments trotted out by people who had evidently never spent time in a working-class clinic, seeing women who slaved at piecework, who were beaten by their husbands and who already had six children they couldn't feed. 'They demanded whether or not tuberculosis, mental retardation, or flat feet in a family constituted indications for abortion,' he recorded wearily. 'Only the extreme radicals advocated the woman's "right to her own body".' His solution, as ever, was fusion, this time between Marx and Malthus: 'social struggle to eliminate the misery of the masses *and* selective birth control.'

One might have hoped that Hirschfeld too would have

refrained from demonising the Unfit. He didn't believe in the concept of racial purity, and regarded nations as communities of hybrids. In *Racism*, he wrote emphatically: 'There is no difference between the races, only individuals. I can appeal to an experience which must be almost, if not quite, unrivalled, so numerous are the men and women from every part of the world who have consulted me on sexual matters.' As the world descended into war, he dreamt of a *Menschenheitsstaat*, a republic for all humanity. Forced to decide whether he was primarily a German or a Jew, he stated that he was a citizen of the world (when the British Prime Minister Theresa May told the 2016 Tory party conference, 'If you believe you are a citizen of the world, you are a citizen of nowhere', I thought of Hirschfeld).

But in the interwar period, even Hirschfeld believed in welfare eugenics. In 1913 he was one of the founders of the Medical Society for Sexology and Eugenics. According to his biographer Ralf Dose, he represented the society at public hearings of the Imperial Council on Health, where he agreed with the compulsory sterilisation for paedophiles as well as people who were 'mentally . . . stupid'; an extreme idea even at the time, and one that he was arguing passionately against by 1934, by which time its implications had become frighteningly clear. He also expressed doubts about whether transvestites should have children, fretting over the possibility of degenerate offspring, before adding uncertainly: 'on the contrary, the children of the transvestites whom I saw gave me the impression of being good and healthy.'

His first biographer, Charlotte Wolff, is somehow even more damning. Wolff was a German doctor, sexologist and lesbian who was herself active in Berlin's sex-reform circles before the war. In a biography otherwise explicitly designed to restore the reputation of a forgotten hero, she describes herself shocked to discover that Hirschfeld maintained an ongoing and pseudo-scientific interest in the bodily markers of degeneracy. He kept a list of signs and symptoms, she said: anatomical evidence of unacceptability, betrayed by a helplessly exposing body. It was the opposite to his liberatory record of sex and gender difference. One argued for acceptance of diversity; the other for discrimination. Wolff records it with dismay, the minute, betraying stigmata of the Unfit: 'asymmetry of face and head, small eyes, nystagmus, squinting, too big ears, stammer, multiple lipomas, tendency to varicose veins.'

*

Ideas travel, morph, dwindle, resurge. The sex reformers had a dream of a better world, and a notion of eugenics to get them there. They believed in good and bad bodies, in a scale of human value that I personally find abhorrent. That their utopia – a world of pleasure uncoupled from the institutions of family, state and church – was founded on at best paternalistic and at worst coercive state involvement is one of the many ironies of middle-class socialism.

All the same, their version of eugenics is and must be kept distinct from what arose in Germany in the 1930s: eugenics not as a way of freeing sex from the reproductive imperative, but as a violent and obsessive programme of extermination; eugenics accompanied by a rolling back of freedoms and an installation of fascist laws concerned with controlling every aspect of bodily experience, towards the fantasy of populating the world with that pervasive impossibility, a pure 'Aryan' race. The grotesque, warped, pseudo-scientific project of white supremacy, everyone alike, the most hateful notion on earth.

Things changed very fast after the Reichstag fire on 27 February 1933. The next morning, there were mass arrests of communists and intellectuals. The absolute destruction – *Auflösung* – of the sex-reform movement was among the Nazis' immediate priorities. Sex might be a private act, conducted in seclusion and by night, but it is also the means by which nations are sculpted and maintained. Control of sexuality and reproduction is an absolute necessity in any totalitarian system, especially one with a collapsing birth rate. As Isherwood explained, the Nazi Party had been promising for years that 'it would stamp out homosexuality because "Germany must be virile if we are to fight for survival." '

That March was unseasonably mild. The porter's wife in Isherwood's building called it 'Hitler's weather'. His street, Nollendorfstrasse, was scarlet with swastikas. In the squares and parks, loudspeakers played speeches by Göring and Goebbels. Uniformed Nazis thronged the streets, bustling into restaurants to collect donations. It wasn't, Isherwood recalled, wise to refuse. Impromptu prisons and interrogation rooms sprang up across the city. The political prisoners were taken to the stormtrooper barracks on Papestrasse and rumours abounded about the dreadful things that happened behind its walls. Isherwood heard that people were made to spit on Lenin's picture, drink castor oil, eat old socks, that people were being tortured, that many were already dead. Even passing these rumours on was treason. Every day, the press announced new ways of committing treason. In April, he heard that three of his friends, all English, all gay, had been arrested. He was so frightened he started hallucinating swastikas in the wallpaper. Everything in his room seemed Nazi brown.

All across the city, the offices and clinics of sexual liberation groups were being searched. Books and documents were confiscated. Activists were arrested and interrogated. Organisations were banned, or forcibly taken over and run along Nazi lines. As a known Jew, communist and prominent sex reformer, Reich was in serious danger. Many of his allies in the movement were arrested and he knew the Gestapo was watching his apartment. Two of his friends were killed in Papestrasse, less than two miles from his own house. He spent weeks hiding in hotels under false names. After his book *The Sexual Struggle of Youth* was attacked in a Nazi newspaper, he finally left Germany, catching a night train to the Austrian border and escaping over the mountains with his wife Annie, disguised as ski tourists and carrying nothing but their passports. Then, perversely, mysteriously, he came back to Berlin – to get, he said, some clothes and underwear. Sneaking into his apartment, he discovered the Gestapo had stolen his copy of the Kamasutra, which added to his conviction that fascism was an outgrowth of sexual repression. None of his friends would lend him money. No one even wanted to be seen speaking to him. He packed a bag and fled again.

He spent that autumn in exile in Denmark, poring over *Mein Kampf* and writing *The Mass Psychology of Fascism*, his landmark analysis of the Nazi appeal in terms of sexual repression. It argues that the patriarchal family is the building block for fascism, and explores how Hitler's dehumanising of the Jews utilised a deep-seated terror of sexually-transmitted disease, especially syphilis, building a rhetoric of infection and inoculation that would swiftly move beyond the realms of the metaphorical.

Hirschfeld was still on his world tour when Hitler came to power. He never came home. The Nazis rescinded his German citizenship and he settled unhappily in Nice, dreaming of reopening the Institute in France until his death in 1935. Isherwood too went into exile, largely to protect his new lover, Heinz, a working-class German boy of eighteen, with big brown eyes and a broken nose. One of the last things Isherwood witnessed in Berlin was the Jewish Boycott on 1 April. As he pushed past the two stormtroopers guarding the door of Israel's department store to buy some small, defiant item, he recognised one of the uniformed thugs as a former hustler from the Cosy Corner.

Christopher and Heinz left Berlin on 13 May 1933, accompanied by a red-eyed Erwin Hansen, who had worked as a caretaker and general factotum at Hirschfeld's Institute and who would later die in a concentration camp. Heinz hadn't slept at all and Erwin was drunk. Their plan was simple. As Isherwood explained in a letter to his mother, 'as soon as Heinz has been formally called up and formally refused to return to that madhouse, he becomes, of course, from the Nazi point of view, a criminal. So he must get another nationality, either by adoption or by settling in some foreign country.'

At first exile was an idyll. Isherwood's old friend from the Institute, Francis, had rented a tiny island just off the coast of Greece and he invited the lovers to stay. Tucked up in a tent,

Isherwood was moved to write: 'Heinz is my one support. He makes everything tolerable. When he swims he says "Zack!" "Zack!" like the crocodile in *Peter Pan*.' He assumed he could bring Heinz to England, and travelled home alone, arranging to reunite at the port in Harwich. But when he and Auden went to meet the boat, Heinz wasn't there. Isherwood finally found him in the customs office, midway through what was clearly an interrogation. The problem, it transpired, was a letter from Christopher that Heinz was carrying. 'I'd say it was the sort of letter that, well, a man might write to his sweetheart,' the customs officer announced, eyeing them both. Heinz was denied entry. For the first time a furious, humiliated Isherwood understood why being gay is a tribal identity. From now on, his sexuality would trump any national loyalty.

The lovers spent the next four years shuttling around Europe, shifting countries whenever Heinz's visa or permit expired, trying all the time to buy him a new nationality. Thirty days here, thirty days there, fighting over money, locked together. They went to Czechoslovakia, Austria, Greece, France, England, Holland, Gran Canaria, Tenerife, Spain, Morocco, Denmark, Belgium, Holland again, Luxembourg, Portugal, Belgium again, France again, Luxembourg again. Jolly holidays that were like bad dreams, the permitted time draining inexorably away. They gambled and quarrelled, gathered menageries of animals that gave them a sense of rootedness but soon had to be abandoned.

In the end Heinz was expelled from Luxembourg as an undesirable. He was forced to return to Germany, where he was immediately arrested as a draft-evader, put on trial for homo-sexual liaisons, and sentenced in June 1937 for having committed reciprocal onanism in fourteen foreign countries and the German Reich. He was lucky: six months in prison, a year's hard labour and two years in the army. Miraculously, he survived the war.

During those final pre-war years, any gains in sexual freedoms in Germany were rapidly rolled back, replaced by eugenicist and frankly genocidal laws that gave the state unprecedented freedom to control what kind of sex people had and what sort of offspring could be born. On 26 May 1933, thirteen days after Christopher and Heinz took the train to Prague, Paragraphs 219 and 220, which banned education around abortion, were put back into the penal code. On 14 July 1933, the Law for the Prevention of Hereditarily Diseased Offspring made compulsory sterilisation legal in a variety of supposedly hereditary conditions, including epilepsy, schizophrenia and deafness. By the end of the war four hundred thousand people would be sterilised against their will. At the same time, birth control and abortion became increasingly restricted, except for racial or eugenic reasons. On 28 June 1935, Paragraph 175 was drastically extended (shamefully, it was not fully repealed until 1994). On 26 October 1936, Himmler established the Bureau to Combat Homosexuality and Abortion. On 4 April 1938, a Gestapo directive ordered that men convicted of homosexuality be imprisoned in concentration camps.

After the war began in September 1939, the restrictions became even more brutal. In 1941 a police ordinance banned 'importation, production, or sale of any material or instrument likely to prevent or interrupt pregnancy', with the exception of condoms, vital for preventing venereal disease in the army. In 1943, the death penalty for abortion was introduced 'if the perpetrator through such deeds continuously impairs the vitality of the German *Volk*', though secret directives allowed for abortions on prostitutes, non-Aryans and women pregnant by foreigners. Later that same year, non-consensual abortions began on foreign forced labourers carrying 'unworthy' foetuses.

It's all very well for Foucault to mock the sex reformers for believing that free access to sexual pleasure would automatically usher in a regime of liberty. The opposite, however, is unhappily certain. Sexual freedom is threatening, unruly. It's no accident that authoritarian regimes, then and now, crack down on homosexuality and abortion, returning each gender to their rigid, pre-ordained duties of procreation, or that these limitations occur as a prelude to more dehumanising acts, the purges and liquidations of genocide.

So many of the horrors that lay ahead were prefigured in the fate of the Institute itself. On the morning of 6 May 1933, trucks pulled up on In Den Zelten, accompanied by the incongruous sound of a brass band. Erwin Hansen ran to the window and saw a raiding party of around a hundred Nazi students, who had been recruited from the Institute for Physical Fitness. He called down that he would open the door, but instead they smashed it, pouring in under the inscription that read in Latin 'Sacred to Love and to Sorrow'.

There's a surviving photograph of the raiders that morning, lined up outside the Institute, all dressed identically in a neat uniform of white shirts and what look like culottes. There they are: the good, disciplined bodies, ready to mete out violence against the degenerate and perverted; what a Nazi newspaper described in a report of the day's activities as fumigating

Hirschfeld's 'Poison Shop'. Inside, they ran amok, pouring ink on manuscripts and playing football with the framed photographs of transvestites that had once so impressed Margaret Sanger with their dignity and poise. In the afternoon, SA stormtroopers arrived and made a more careful survey of the library. They loaded ten thousand books onto the trucks, along with a bronze bust of Hirschfeld, commissioned for his sixtieth birthday.

Four days later, after the sun had set, thousands of people gathered in Opernplatz, the great square between the Berlin State Opera and the University Library, for the first and most famous of the Nazi book burnings. There were thirty-four fires that night, in each of Germany's university towns, but the one in Berlin was the largest. Pyres had been built, made of pallets stuffed with Hirschfeld's vast collection of books on sexual expression, his volumes about transvestites and the gender indeterminate, his magazines on sexology and birth control and the free expression of love.

In the Pathé footage, you can see flag-wielding students silhouetted against the pyres, marching in unison to the accompaniment of another brass band. There are cheers as students and stormtroopers hand books along in human chains, lobbing armfuls into the flames, though when the camera pans to the crowd beyond they seem watchful and still. Goebbels spoke. Isherwood, who was there, called out *shame*, but quietly. Like everyone, he was afraid. Hirschfeld's bust was paraded on a spike. When Hirschfeld saw the newsreel in a cinema in Paris a few days later, he wept.

Eugenics regards the human race as a kind of library, some

# 4

# In Harm's Way

ON 13 MARCH 1973, a young woman was found dead in her dorm room at the University of Iowa in Iowa City. She'd been beaten in the face and chest, raped and suffocated. Her name was Sarah Ann Ottens and she was twenty. It was spring break, and nearly all the other women in the dorm were away. Ottens's body was discovered shortly before midnight by the only other student still in residence on the floor, after she came home from seeing a movie with her boyfriend.

It was a grim scene. Ottens's neck was grossly swollen. Her face and hair had been washed and she was lying naked from the waist down under a bedsheet. There was a bloody broomstick beside her and the sink was filled with bloody water. In the febrile days that followed, rumours began to circulate. Ottens had been raped. Ottens had not been raped while she was alive, but her corpse had been penetrated vaginally and anally with the same broomstick that had been used to choke her. 'An object had been used to mutilate her', the *Daily Iowan* confirmed during the trial. 'A broom was found nearby with faecal material on the handle and had apparently been used.'

The story, and especially this gruesome detail, lived on in people's heads. An arrest wasn't made until May and so for two months women lived in fear of a repeat attack.

The murder occurred at a moment when attitudes around gender and sexual freedom were once again in rapid flux. Ottens was killed less than two months after Roe vs. Wade was passed in the Supreme Court, securing a woman's right to legal abortion. The right to abortion had always been part of the sexual liberation movement fought by Reich and his colleagues in the 1920s. But the new women's liberation movement now gathering force around the world had a subtly different agenda. It wasn't focused so much on liberation *to* as liberation *from*.

Women's liberation in the 1970s meant liberation from violence, rape, structural sexism, exclusion, wife-beating, abuse, unwanted pregnancies, all the miserable apparatus that accompanies living inside a body gendered as female. Murder too, of course; stripped and harmed, discovered by a stranger. The fear was not abstract. It was driven by what happened to actual people: women you knew or heard about, stories you read in the papers that impacted directly on your own physical experience of living in the world, from what clothes you wore to what routes you travelled to what words you said to what voice you used.

The women's liberation movement broke into the mainstream in 1970 with the publication of Kate Millett's *Sexual Politics*: a revolutionary analysis of sexual dynamics in literature and psychoanalysis. Millett painstakingly revealed that the superstructure of patriarchy was not confined to economics or the law, but permeated even the furthest reaches of the culture, infiltrating and informing the domestic and erotic. She found in the novels of Ernest Hemingway, Henry Miller and Norman Mailer evidence of a communal misogyny so widely shared that it was assumed to be the natural texture of reality itself.

One of the few men to receive Millett's approval was Reich. Like many of this new generation of feminists, she drew on his work, not only for her title but also for her analysis of the patriarchal family. She quoted from his biting critique in *The Mass Psychology of Fascism*: 'The authoritarian state has a representative in every family, the father; in this way he becomes the state's most valuable tool.' A full-page review in the *New York Times* predicted *Sexual Politics* would become 'for lack of more inspired terminology – the Bible of Women's Liberation', which is exactly what happened. A copy sat on my mother's shelves all through the 1980s, bolstering a green armada of Virago paperbacks, likewise a legacy of feminism's turbulent second wave.

1970 saw an uprush of demonstrations. In March over a hundred women occupied the editor's office at *Ladies' Home Journal* in New York, demanding to put together a 'liberated' issue of the magazine while sprawling on his desk and helping themselves to his expensive cigars. In August, fifty thousand women marched down Fifth Avenue during rush hour as part of the first national Women's Strike for Equality. On 20 November, activists threw stink bombs and rotten tomatoes at the Miss World contest in London, causing the host, Bob Hope, to temporarily flee the stage ('Anyone who would try to break up a wonderful affair like this has got to be on some kind of dope,' he announced on his return to the mic).

In January 1971, radical feminists organised the first Rape Speakout at St Clement's Episcopal Church in Manhattan, breaking the silence on rape, and in March the first national demonstration of the Women's Liberation Movement assembled in the snow in London, marching behind a giant crucified mannequin, her outstretched arms burdened with a pinny, a pair of silk stockings and a string shopping bag. A chant of choice: 'Biology isn't destiny.' Enough of being reduced to a body, a dispensable object. That autumn, the world's first refuge for victims of domestic violence was established in London.

All this is to say that Ottens was murdered just as despair was shifting into rage, rage spiking into action. In the wake of her death, female students at the University of Iowa established one of the first rape crisis lines in the country, the Rape Victim Advocacy Program. It began that spring as a twenty-four-hour helpline, run by volunteers who spent restless nights on a camp bed, taking calls from a single landline in the Women's Center, which had itself been founded by the Women's Liberation Front two years earlier. Nothing was official yet. Everything was DIY, a trial run, makeshift, impromptu, improvised. You wanted things to change, but how? How could you communicate your distress, your fear, your refusal to participate in a society that so readily facilitated your destruction?

Among the students at Iowa that spring was Ana Mendieta, a twenty-four-year-old Cuban-American artist. The impression of her from snapshots is of enormous energy. She always seems to be turning away, impatient to get back to work, a tiny, scruffy, subversive beauty, smiling quickly at the camera in a polo neck and flared jeans. She arrived in America at the age

of twelve, one of more than fourteen thousand children air-
lifted out of Cuba as part of Operation Pedro Pan, a programme
spearheaded by the Catholic Welfare Bureau and the US State
Department in response to widespread fears about the new
Castro regime (her parents hoped to follow, but her father was
arrested and imprisoned for eighteen years for supporting the
failed American invasion of the Bay of Pigs). She spent a traumatic adolescence in brutal Catholic orphanages and foster
homes before coming to the university to study art.

In 1972 she gave up painting, literally destroyed all her
canvases, saying they weren't real enough for what she wanted
an image to convey – 'and by real I mean I wanted my images
to have power, to be magic.' That same year she graduated
from her master's and joined the Intermedia MFA, a cutting-
edge interdisciplinary course founded four years earlier by the
artist Hans Breder. It was a space for experimentation, and she
began to work with her own body, playing with her gender,
dressing herself up in moustaches and beards. The performance was the work, art as physical transformation, though like
many of the emerging category of body artists she also documented the temporary things she did, leaving behind a visible
residue in the form of photographs and films.

A few weeks after Ottens's murder, she invited her Intermedia
class to her apartment in the Moffitt building. The door was
unlocked, as doors in Iowa City in 1973 tended to be. Inside,
her friends found Mendieta tied face-down to the table. She
was wearing a plaid shirt, and was naked from the waist, her
knickers round her ankles. Blood was smeared over her but-
tocks, thighs and calves. Her arms were tightly bound with

white cord and her face was pressed into a pool of blood. A light was on directly overhead, casting the periphery into shadow, though it was possible to make out signs of a struggle, including torn and bloodied clothing and smashed crockery. *Untitled (Rape Scene)*, 1973: her first serious attempt to mould reality, to seize and shape it.

Mendieta's classmates stayed for almost an hour, discussing the scene and what it might mean. They were unsettled, but they were still art students, practised at analysing visual material, no matter how graphic. For the entirety of their visit, Mendieta didn't move a muscle. Her performance was ephemeral, existing in a single place for a single afternoon, but she also asked a friend to document it. In these disturbing photographs, her body is exposed ankle to waist, smeared lavishly in blood. You can't even see her head, let alone her face. The flash has blasted her calves and the rim of the table with light, throwing looming fairy-tale shadows up the wall. Little moons of broken crockery, bloodied moons of ass, a sticky red patch of something on the floor.

Critics often say *Untitled (Rape Scene)* is a recreation of what happened to Ottens, but it clearly isn't, even judging by what was being reported in the local press at the time. Mendieta has given the events her own grotesque flourish, introducing the table and the cord (that same year she'd made a work in which she was tied up with rope and then writhed painfully across the gallery floor). Nor is it a reconstruction from the point of view of the attacker. The explosion of cold white light immediately frames it as a crime scene, not incident but aftermath, casting the viewer not only as voyeur but as investigator, even cop.

Incorporated into the moment of image-making, the viewer becomes complicit in the queasy pornographic framing, the way a woman's body can't even be just a corpse.

Years later, Mendieta said the work came out of her own fear about what happened to Ottens. She couldn't get it out of her head, not just the violence but the toxic atmosphere, the way newspapers wrote salacious accounts of the 'slaying of Iowa co-ed', speculating about Ottens's sexual partners instead of reporting on the city's abysmal rape statistics. 'I think all my work has been like that,' she said, 'a personal response to a situation . . . I can't see being theoretical about an issue like that.' In an interview in 1985, she added: 'A young woman was killed, raped and killed at Iowa, in one of the dorms, and it just really freaked me out. So I did several rape performance-type things at that time using my own body. I did something that I believed in and that I felt I had to do. I didn't know if it was alright, or if it wasn't, or it didn't matter. That's what I did.'

All summer, she kept making work about the murder. She constructed a crime scene with a mattress drenched in blood. She arranged herself in the middle of Clinton Street in Iowa City as if she herself was a corpse. She poured a bucket of cow blood and animal viscera onto the pavement outside her apartment, a meaty stain that a janitor eventually scraped into a cardboard box, and secretly filmed people's reactions to it. But though she always used her own body, if she included a body at all, these pieces were not just about victimhood, and nor were they primarily designed to arouse empathy or mourning. Instead, they're powerfully punitive. Whether Mendieta was in them or not, she remained aggressor and perpetrator as well as prey: the ringmaster of sadistic tableaux that confronted the viewer – and especially the random, non-art student passer-by – with evidence they could never quite decode, that lingered uneasily in their imagination.

Each culture has blind spots and I think what Mendieta was doing in Iowa City was not unrelated to Kate Millett's agenda in *Sexual Politics*. Each time she assembled one of her nightmarish scenes, she was making it apparent that a crime had been committed, a bloody stain that would not wash out. By recreating the unnamed region in which violence happens to women she kept forcing it into visibility, making it indelible, impossible to ignore. This motivation situates her work amid the collective struggle of the period, since one of the many things the women's movement was trying to do was expose sexual violence, a cultural blind spot so pervasive that it had almost escaped the attention of the sexual liberationists.

★

The same year that Mendieta was collecting her buckets of blood from the butcher at Whiteway Supermarket (she kept the receipt in case she was questioned by the police), two other women were also trying to get to grips with sexual violence, to drag something damaged and unpleasant out of the dark. Both were writers who were unusually idiosyncratic and forthright in their visions, and both chose to conduct their enquiries, Kate Millett-style, by interrogating books and films to reveal the political ideology embedded in cultural artefacts. Strangely enough, although their conclusions ran counter to each other, Angela Carter and Andrea Dworkin even focused on the same set of texts. They looked at *The Story of O*, that staple of female abnegation, at European fairy tales like 'Snow White' and 'Cinderella', and in particular at the eighteenth-century theatre of cruelties dreamt up by the Marquis de Sade from his prison cell in the Bastille.

Andrea Dworkin was twenty-six in 1973, and frantic to finish her first book. She'd grown up in New Jersey, in a left-wing, lower-middle-class Jewish family haunted by raw, undigested memories of the Holocaust, the horrors of which were in the 1950s still walled up in agonised silence. She was molested for the first time at nine by a stranger in a cinema, and though this trauma never left her she was powerfully determined to follow her own erotic and intellectual appetites, to escape the suburbs and taste the world. She went to the liberal arts college Bennington in Vermont, was briefly imprisoned for protesting the Vietnam War, and after graduation slipped the traces and ran away to Europe, a passionate young hippie with a soft, open, laughing face and a mass of dark curls.

In 1969, she married a Dutch anarchist she met in Amsterdam while researching an article on the anarcho-left group Provo. He was so gentle at first, the man who almost killed her, who hit her with an iron bar, burned her with cigarettes, punched her in the breasts, smashed her head repeatedly into a concrete floor. Two decades later, she described this experience in an essay titled 'What Battery Really Is'. The worst thing, she said, was the absolute isolation of the battered wife, the way that neighbours – *her* neighbours, *her* family, *her* friends – had turned a blind eye to her bruises, her visible injuries.

No one would believe her. No one would intercede or get

her out or even acknowledge the reality of what was happening. Even her own beloved father refused to help, and there was no institutional assistance either. Hospitals, the police: everyone she went to disbelieved her, or thought she was being paranoid and hysterical, accusations that would follow her right to the end of her life. It wasn't just the pain or the fear of pain that made her want to die. It was the fact of becoming invisible, severed from the world by her abject status.

Reality itself began to degrade. 'You become unable to use language because it stops meaning anything', she wrote. 'If you use regular words and say you have been hurt and by whom and you point to visible injuries and you are treated as if you made it up or as if it doesn't matter or as if it is your fault or as if you are stupid and worthless, you become afraid to try to say anything. You cannot talk to anyone because they will not help you and if you talk to them, the man who is battering you will hurt you more. Once you lose language, your isolation is absolute.' (In an ironic and no doubt acutely painful testament to the ongoing truth of what she was saying, lawyers at *Newsweek* halted publication of 'What Battery Really Is' in 1989 because they needed either independent verification like hospital or police records, self-evidently unavailable, or for Dworkin to publish anonymously to 'protect' the identity of her attacker. She published it in the *Los Angeles Times* instead.)

She ran away from him in 1971, but for a year her husband kept pursuing her, catching her, trapping her, punishing her again. She hid in empty or derelict places on the outskirts of Amsterdam, moved around a lot, tried to stay beneath the threshold of visibility. A houseboat infested with mice, someone's kitchen, a deserted mansion, a commune on a farm, a movie theatre, the basement of a nightclub called Paradiso. Part of the nature of the trap was that she couldn't afford the flight home to America, though she tried to save up money by working as a prostitute.

During this fugitive period, she met a woman, Ricki Abrams, who helped her hide and brought her books, the core texts of second-wave feminism. *Sexual Politics. The Dialectic of Sex* by Shulamith Firestone. *Sisterhood is Powerful* by Robin Morgan. It wasn't surprising she became so interested in fairy tales. Her life already had the bare, stripped outlines of the Brothers Grimm, where malevolence is structural and kindness erratic. But even though she was in the middle of an emergency, it still took her months to get her head around Millett's argument: that what was happening to her, Andrea, was not personal or individual. It was not her fault. This humiliating and painful episode was in fact systemic, shared and culturally ordained. It was the central revelation of her life: that violence against women is political, and therefore capable of being communally resisted and overturned.

Like Mendieta, Dworkin was propelled by a sense of outrage and horror. She wanted to be safe, but she was also driven by a need to testify, to haul the ruined body into the light. It was as if she had come across evidence of a crime that was somehow simultaneously everywhere and completely invisible. (Later, as one of the most visible and radical figures of the women's movement, she frequently compared violence against women to an unreported, unpunished, transhistorical, globally sanctioned genocide.) On the run, homeless and displaced, she began to write a book with Ricki, an account that would tear back the veil, exposing the secret, deforming nature of misogyny.

She finally made it back to New York in 1972. Someone asked her if she'd take a suitcase on the plane, for a payment of $1,000. The suitcase, which she knew contained heroin, never materialised, but she had the money and the plane ticket, a rare piece of luck in a long run of terror. Back in the city, she made contact with the women's movement and finished her book – now called *Woman Hating* – alone, writing an impassioned foreword in July 1973, just as Mendieta was recreating rape scenes in the Iowa woods.

What Dworkin was trying to do was to find a language for sexual violence. The task wasn't easy, either emotionally or stylistically. Violence occurs when one person treats another as expendable, an object, garbage, but part of the violence, and the abiding horror of the violent transaction, is that their humanity does not vanish, but is made to coexist with being an object; 'just some bleeding thing cut up on the floor.' Back in 1940, Simone Weil wrote in her essay *The Iliad, or The Poem of Force* a much-quoted line defining violence as that which 'turns anybody who is subjected to it into a thing', but what she goes on to say is much stranger and more accurate.

From its first property (the ability to turn a human being into a thing by the simple method of killing him) flows another, quite prodigious too in its own way, the ability to turn a human being into a thing while he is still alive. He is alive; he has a soul; and yet – he is a thing. An extraordinary entity this – a thing that has a soul. And as for the soul, what an extraordinary house it finds itself in! Who can say what it costs it, moment by moment, to accommodate itself to this residence, how much writhing and bending, folding and pleating are required of it? It was not made to live inside a thing; if it does so, under pressure of necessity, there is not a single element of its nature to which violence is not done.

Bottom line, the body becomes its own inescapable prison, its needs turned against it, reduced to unbearable, unignorable sensation. This is the true horror of violence, that the you of you is still inside.

As Dworkin knew from her own experience, it isn't easy to speak from this place. When the rape victim Lavinia in *Titus Andronicus*, tongue cut out, hands chopped off, writes the name of her attackers in the dirt with a stick held in her mouth, she might be said to be enacting a metaphor, surmounting what Jacqueline Rose once described as the 'obstacles that litter the path between sexual violation, indeed all sexuality, and language', and of which scorn and denial are by no means the least difficult to overcome. Years later, introducing yet another room of college students to the concept of rape, Dworkin fantasised about standing on a stage and screaming instead of speaking: a communal scream that contained embedded in it the silence of all those women who had not been able to find language, or who had not survived long enough to tell their story.

How do you convey the systemisation of violence against women if there is a conspiracy of silence around it, if it is so tolerated and sustained as to have merged with the fabric of ordinary reality? Dworkin's tactic was to amplify. To go hard. To find a language 'more terrifying than rape, more abject than torture, more insistent and destabilizing than battery, more desolate than prostitution, more invasive than incest, more filled with threat and aggression than pornography.' It's this strident, stylish, uncanny voice that makes *Woman Hating* and the dozen books that followed so exhausting and estranging, but also impossible to unhear.

Writing about misogyny did not, unsurprisingly, make her enough money to live on, and so the lecture circuit became a way to survive. In 1975, the year after *Woman Hating* was published, she started giving a speech called 'The Rape Atrocity and the Boy Next Door'. In an era in which, as Dworkin's brilliant biographer and editor Johanna Fateman points out, marital rape was still legal in fifty states, this marked one of the first attempts to articulate the pervasive and everyday nature of rape.

It was hard enough just giving the speech, but the more Dworkin revealed, the more she discovered. 'The Rape Atrocity' made her the repository of thousands of women's stories: 'women who had been sleeping, women who had been with their children, women who had been out for a walk or shopping or going to school or going home from school or in their offices working or in factories or in stockrooms . . . I simply could not bear it. So I stopped giving the speech. I thought I would die from it. I learned what I had to know, and more than I could stand to know.' While I do not always agree with Dworkin, I wish that every one of her detractors stopped for a minute to imagine what it might be like to hold that kind of information inside their own bodies.

These communal experiences of misogyny, gathered personally and stored at a high cost, fuelled all her later books, especially her third, 1981's terrifying and incantatory *Pornography: Men Possessing Women*. I can still remember where I was when I first read it. In the mid-1990s, I started an English degree at Sussex University. One of my courses was on feminism, and one of the set texts was *Pornography*. I read it in the library in a state of mounting physical horror. That library was a strange place. It was a marvel of brutalist architecture, shaped like a camera, but in those days every desk in every reading room was covered in a dense scrawl of pornographic graffiti, a palimpsest of fantasies and jokes. Working in the remoter regions, at the end of some dark avenue of stacks, it often felt almost overpoweringly erotic. As I read Dworkin, this pervasive atmosphere became more sinister, the pleasure of being able to inhabit a sexual body shifting into the horror of never being allowed to be anything else.

Like Weil said, the reduction of person into thing is the base equation of all violence, and in *Pornography* Dworkin presents it over and over again, naked, unadorned and, unlike Mendieta, from the perspective of the person to whom it's happening: how it feels, what it looks like, how it smells. She recreates by way of words the ongoing, annihilating, manifestly non-consensual depersonalisation of women, their transformation into literal or metaphorical meat. Her intention is inoculation, the homeopathic dose of poison that cures, and yet this aspect of her writing is – in means if not in ends – reminiscent of no one so much as the Divine Marquis, the Madman of Charenton, Citizen Sade: aristocrat, revolutionary, prisoner, and the figure against whom *Pornography* is organised. Sade was famous as a libertine, an icon of sexual freedom. But freedom for whom, Dworkin asks. Her attack on Sade was about nothing less than the nature of freedom itself.

★

What Dworkin found in Sade was the playbook of misogyny, the source text that spliced sex and violence together, revealing them not as opposites but as the twin devices by which male supremacy is enforced. Too often, she thought, Sade had been let off the hook because admiring critics, from Baudelaire to Barthes, had argued that his crimes were purely textual, confined to the bloodless realm of the imagination. But for Dworkin there was no material difference between what he did and what he dreamt up. Just as the staged scenes of pornography laid bare real misogynistic ideology, so Sade's fantasies were acts he had attempted, or would have tried to carry out had he not been locked away in the Bastille, his demonic career as seducer and sadist – 'sexual terrorist' – checked only by being confined to a cell for nearly twenty-nine years. 'In him,' she writes with grim relish, 'one finds rapist and writer twisted in one scurvy knot. His life and writing were of a piece, a whole cloth soaked in the blood of women imagined and real.'

They were there, the women; she knew they were, as shadows, footnoted names, scraps of gossip. She went back through time and found them, not as a scholar or historian, but as a prosecutor tracking down witnesses in hiding. She once wrote that if a reader lifted up the words on the pages of her books they would see – 'far, far under the surface' – her own life, and that if the print turned to blood, it would be her own blood, from many times and places. She wasn't a memoir writer. She used that energy, that physical investment, to animate the dead, painstakingly disinterring Sade's women from centuries of neglect and contempt.

The first of the three crimes she investigates is the case of Rose Keller, to whom *Pornography* is dedicated. Keller was a baker's widow encountered by Sade begging on the streets of Paris on Easter morning, 1768. He persuaded her to come to his house, where he attacked her and cut her with a knife. She escaped by climbing out of the window, seeking assistance from the village women, who summoned the police. She was paid off and Sade was arrested the following day, imprisoned for seven months and banned from living in Paris. Four years later, he engaged in an orgy with a group of prostitutes in Marseilles, giving them sweets laced with the aphrodisiac Spanish fly, which made several of them violently sick. This time he was sentenced to death for sodomy and poisoning, both capital crimes. He fled the region, but was caught and imprisoned again in December 1772, escaping after four months.

Dworkin was a polemicist. Writing was shock therapy, a way to jolt the world out of its treads. Ambiguity, uncertainty, doubt did not suit her purpose. If there were six versions of a story, she took the worst and lit it with the most lurid filter, even if this meant underplaying women's agency to make her case. She had sworn to tell the truth, but she also knew that the truth of her own experience and that of women like her wouldn't be found in the official apparatus of police or hospital or legal records. It happened in the margins, unrecorded. Lean back through the centuries, listen for a struggle in the dark.

All the same, it is a matter of court record that none of the prostitutes in Marseilles were, as she claimed, forcibly sodomised, and all but one of the women refused anal sex entirely. Their own testimony suggests there was robust negotiation over what acts would be performed. As for Keller, the detail about the knife was not in her first testimony and Dworkin declines to record that it was she who negotiated a settlement with Sade's mother-in-law, asking for an enormous 3,000 livres and eventually compromising on 2,400 livres.

This is not to say that Sade was innocent of all Dworkin's charges. The final and most distressing act of his libertine years occurred in 1774, when he and his wife holed up in their chateau at Lacoste, procuring five teenaged girls as servants and sealing the castle for the winter. There is no surviving record of what happened inside, but Dworkin regarded it as indisputable that the focus was 'sexual extravaganzas'. Whether this is true or not, the girls were held prisoner, despite entreaties from their parents; one received unnamed injuries and another died. When he was finally imprisoned three years later, Sade explained in a passionate letter that he had committed no crime, since under French law it was the procuress who was punished and not the purchaser, who was after all 'only doing what all men do' – Dworkin's argument summed up in six words.

Sade's casual attitude is matched by his biographers. They speak cheerfully of giving 'a spanking to a whore', 'a sore behind', 'a rather disagreeable hour or two'. In 1953, Geoffrey

Gorer remarked disbelievingly of Keller: 'a woman so badly wounded would surely have had some difficulty in climbing walls.' And in 1999, nearly two decades after *Pornography* was published, Neil Schaeffer observed of Sade's behaviour in Lacoste: 'the sort of girls . . . and the sort of parents such girls were likely to have, made Mme de Montreuil's suspicions about blackmail rather more plausible.' In these accounts, the poor are untrustworthy and prostitutes manifestly fair game.

Dworkin casts off this pervasive way of thinking. In all her books, she demonstrates a refined ability to think her way into the reality of violence, to locate her account from the position of the person with the least power, and to detrivialise the experience of hurt and terror. A former sex worker herself, she refuses the pervasive fallacy of regarding those who work as prostitutes as automata, not people; insensate and disbarred from saying no. Furthermore, she sees that what is supposedly transgressive and radical about Sade's writing is actually business as usual, that 'advocacy and celebration of rape and battery have been history's sustaining themes.'

What she is not skilled at is separating actual from imaginary wounds. Dworkin's entire argument in *Pornography* is that there is no such thing as a purely imaginary sphere. As she says in her introduction, her work is distinguished from other books on pornography 'by its bedrock conviction that the power is real, the cruelty is real, the sadism is real, the subordination is real: the political crime against women is real.' What is imagined always impacts on someone's body, either literally or by creating a climate of possibility. This is why it was so necessary to prove Sade's actual crimes, and why years later the actress Linda

Lovelace's testimony about being abused on the set of *Deep Throat* would become the prime exhibit in Dworkin's case against pornography. A classic pro-censorship activist, she regards Sade's novels – *The 120 Days of Sodom, Justine, Juliette* – as a direct extension of his lived experience, the pen stroke equal to the multiple instruments of torture wielded by his fictional libertines. The life stains the work. It is a totalitarian model of reading, in which no ambiguity or complexity can be allowed.

Not all women agreed. In the summer of 1973, around the time that Dworkin was writing the introduction to *Woman Hating* and Mendieta was spilling pig's blood on the streets of Iowa City, Angela Carter put together a proposal for a book about 'de Sade and sexuality as a political phenomenon and the myth of gender.' She was thirty-three, newly divorced, recently returned to London from Japan, the author of five strange and entrancing, aggressively sexual novels. Unlike Dworkin, she wrote as happily for the soft-porn magazine *Men Only* as *Spare Rib*, the feminist bible, both of which emerged in the early 1970s.

Although Carter was far too individual and independent ever to be a doctrinaire feminist, she took her Sade idea to Virago, the new women's publisher whose books my mother loved so much. She pitched it over lunch at the glamorous San Lorenzo in Knightsbridge (a favourite of Princess Diana, it's not where one imagines the machinations of the women's movement taking place). The proposal was accepted at the very first Virago commissioning meeting, in September 1973.

Carter warned her new editor, Carmen Callil, that she'd need 'as long as a year to complete it'. In the end it took her five difficult years to construct an argument out of her gut feeling that there was more to Sade than misogyny, that there might even be something useful for women to discover in the interminable prison cells and torture chambers of his unhappy imagination. For all its elegance and erudition, *The Sadeian Woman: An Exercise in Cultural History* is a sleek anatomy of hell. Each time I read it I have an image of Carter swinging her long legs above an abyss, undeceived as to the horrors on display but formidably certain there's a way out; protected, like the wise children of her own fictions, by her curiosity, her intelligence, her strong stomach and her interest in reality.

Her take on Sade, finally published two years before *Pornography* and criticised in it as a work of pseudo-feminism, is far more willing to assign agency to women, even if the system in which they are trapped offers few opportunities for independent action. She doesn't entertain female victimhood, or consider it an empowering foundation for feminist futures. Her Rose Keller flipped a nasty situation on its head, using her ingenuity to get one over on the aristocracy. As for Sade himself, his misogyny is counterweighted by his advocacy for a full female sexuality, unchecked by reproductive obligations (he was as vocal an advocate of abortion as Reich, though the grotesque things that happen to pregnant women in his books suggests that liberation was not his only motivation).

For Carter, fantasy is not the same as fact. She regularly points out the gulf between the real and the imagined, observing that while Sade invented multiple horrific fictional ways of killing, as a judge on the revolutionary tribunal he was so adamant in his opposition to the death penalty that he was imprisoned yet again, this time for being too moderate (Dworkin, on the other hand, believed in the death penalty for rape, once arguing that if the first woman attacked by Sade had killed him, many lives would have been saved).

What's more, Carter doesn't believe Sade's fantasies are primarily about sex at all, and nor does she regard misogyny as the driving force of his novels. She thinks they are actually about power and the lamentable, hateful consequences of power imbalances. Gender and genitalia are relevant, of course, but so too are class and money. Even more radically, she argues that the aim of Sade's fiction is to expose this abhorrent system, even if in the pre-incarceration years of his libertinage he profited abundantly from it. For her, Sade's subject is not the joy of freedom, but its obscene price.

In *Pornography*, Dworkin decried the way Sade was perpetually celebrated as someone in pursuit of freedom, by Sartre and de Beauvoir among many others.

> Throughout the literature on him . . . Sade is viewed as one whose voracious appetite was for *freedom*; this appetite was cruelly punished by an unjust and repressive society . . . Sade's violation of sexual and social boundaries, in his writings and his life, is seen as inherently revolutionary. The antisocial character of his sexuality is seen as a radical challenge to a society deadly in its repressive sexual conventions . . . The imprisonment of Sade is seen to demonstrate the despotism of a system that must contain, control, and manipulate sexuality, not allow it to run free toward anarchic self-fulfilment.

But what Carter saw was Sade's deep ambivalence about total freedom. She doesn't regard the novels as revelling in depravity, but rather as a *reductio ad absurdum* of the nightmarish consequences of unchecked appetite. Her Sade is sceptical, even paranoid, about freedom, and obsessed in particular with weighing and calculating its cost. Part of the pain of his novels is that they peel back the myth of liberty, exposing the multiple ways in which any individual's sexual and political freedom depends upon the servitude and abasement of others. A connoisseur of mutilations, Carter calls him, meaning the mutilations that arise out of inequalities of every kind.

The people who have the power in reality – the bankers, judges, bishops, law-makers, financiers and politicians – are the people who have the power in Sade. The libertines in *The 120 Days of Sodom*, say, spending their profits from the Thirty Years War on a murderous blow-out, 'leeches always lying in wait for the calamities they provoke rather than quell in order to profit from them all the more.' Disaster capitalists, we call them now. Likewise, the people who don't have power in reality suffer its lack here. Wives, daughters, women, girls, boys. The poor, the badly educated, the innocent, the young. Freedom in Sade's universe is a zero-sum game: you either have it or you don't, which is one of the reasons he continues to resonate in a twenty-first century of rape camps and Me Too. Neither the sexual practices of Harvey Weinstein and Jeffrey Epstein nor the dehumanising effect they had upon their many victims would have surprised Sade, and nor would the ascent of Trump. As Carter puts it: 'One of Sade's cruellest lessons is that tyranny is implicit in all privilege. My freedom makes you more unfree, if it does not acknowledge your freedom, also.'

Part of the reason her interpretation seems to me so accurate is that it attends, as very few people do, to the actual experience of reading Sade: what it feels like on a sentence by sentence level, in the body of the reader. Although Dworkin talks about Sade's novels as gratifying lust, they aren't comparable to other pornographic literature, and not simply because they contain scenes of extreme violence. Unlike S&M classics like *Story of the Eye* and *The Story of O*, they're fundamentally untitillating.

To say, as people often do, that the sex is like a complicated formal dance or the action of machines in a factory is to catch at the immense tedium and mechanisation of the Sadeian debauch, while failing to convey its horror, which is not just that of observing a grisly spectacle. Sade's fantasies and the way he writes about them have a capacity to perform a kind of internal severance, a spectacle of absolute nihilism that makes you at once reduced to and a stranger in your own body. One gets a brief, immolating whiff of what it might be like to be, as Simone Weil put it, a soul housed within a thing, a ruin with a human face.

Pleasure is not the point, either for the reader or for the libertines who control and operate the devilish machinery. The meticulous rituals that may or may not culminate in their difficult orgasms rest almost entirely on two things: forcibly assuming control over other bodies, including their involuntary or semi-voluntary functions, and the associated power to inflict serious pain, to wound and to kill. But this does not result in satisfaction. The more they seek gratification, the more empty, repetitive and tortuous their world becomes. The problem with creating hell is that you have to live there, too. Meanwhile, the bodies of their victims pile up, drained of blood, burned, cut apart and stitched back together, subject to atrocities that recall the work of Idi Amin or the Khmer Rouge.

A libertine himself, Sade embodies the complexities of the word *liberty*, which contains sinuously opposed meanings. From the Middle Ages on, it has meant freedom from bondage, slavery or imprisonment, from arbitrary control or dictatorship, but also the faculty or power to do as one likes without hindrance or restraint; freedom from fate or necessity; freedom of will; permission, leave; unrestrained use or access to a specific thing; action beyond the bounds of custom; licence; a privilege, immunity or right.

What this reveals, and what Sade is at pains to tell us, is that taking liberties is not the same as bestowing them. It's no accident that the libertine's paradise is a prison camp, walled and sealed, from which no one whose liberty is taken or who is taken at liberty will escape. Total liberty to act can and does have hellish consequences for the bodies unlucky enough to be acted upon. Absolute freedom, Sade warns, is closer to Auschwitz than Eden.

*

Sade's unwavering scepticism about the nature of sexual freedom is especially interesting in the light of reading Reich. Both imagine a society organised around the orgasm. But while Reich's vision is utopian, Sade's is an even more apocalyptic version of the vision of unbounded violence and rape imagined by Freud in *Civilisation and its Discontents*. Reich thought that sexual expression was a route not just to individual freedom but also to a freer world, composed naturally of equals. Sade, on the other hand, knew – indeed Sade's own name attaches to the knowledge – that sex is not just about pleasure, connection, intimacy or transcendental joy. It's an act that has multiple different intentions and imperatives, among them to hurt, to subdue, to humiliate, to punish, even to destroy.

The evasion of this darker aspect of sex was one of Sontag's many criticisms of Reich. In her interview with *Rolling Stone* in the autumn of 1979, the year *The Sadeian Woman* was published, she talked about the naivety of his vision of sex. 'I think that he really didn't understand the demonic in human nature,' she said, 'and that he had a picture of sexuality only as something wonderful. And of course it can be, but it's also a very dark place and a theatre of the demonic.'

This is typical of Sontag's selective approach to facts. Reich was well aware of the possibilities of the demonic. It's just that he regarded it as a symptom of damage, a warping of what he termed natural sexuality, which he believed could only ever be equable and benign (you can practically hear Foucault snorting from the grave). In *The Mass Psychology of Fascism*, he specifically uses the word 'demonic' in a bravura account of how sexuality becomes distorted under patriarchal capitalism, that binding and pervasive system of submission and control. The limitation of sexual freedom for women and children – Sade's perennial victims – makes sexuality into a commodity. As for men, they undergo so much shaming and repression in childhood that gentleness turns into rage. 'From now on,' he writes, 'sexuality is indeed distorted; it becomes diabolical and demonic and has to be curbed . . . That this dirty sexuality is not natural sexuality but patriarchal sexuality is simply overlooked.'

Like Dworkin, Reich's analysis was bedded in personal experience. When he was a boy of eleven, he realised his beloved mother Cecilia, a woman so unassuming she was nicknamed *das Schaf*, the sheep, was having an affair with his tutor. He saw them kissing. He heard the bed creak when they were together. Finally he watched them through a door, fascinated, disgusted, jealous. Part of him wanted to take the tutor's place, and he fantasised about using the threat of telling his father as Oedipal leverage into his mother's bed.

Reich's father Leo was a jealous man. By the time Reich was twelve, Leo had become convinced his wife was having an affair, though he didn't know with whom. One evening, he saw her standing alone with the tutor. He dragged her upstairs and accused her of being a whore. From his own room, Reich could hear 'only (!) the sound of someone being pushed around and landing on the bed', followed by his father's voice, full of rage, threatening to kill her. Moments later, his father burst in and made Reich confess to what he'd seen. This fraught conversation was interrupted by a 'deep groan' from the bedroom. Cecilia had swallowed Lysol and was writhing on her bed.

Leo saved her life by forcing an emetic down her throat, but for the next year he subjected her to vicious beatings, until her hands and face and body were permanently marked by his attacks. In his memoir *Passion of Youth*, Reich remembered 'ghastly scenes and ever increasing violence. Mother become completely numb and apathetically allowed the blows to rain down upon her.' To his unending shame, he failed to protect her. Worse, he turned away from her too, even shouting at her himself (the pain of this confession always reminds me of Dworkin, who wrote of her shame that at the peak of her husband's attacks, she kicked and beat her beloved dog). Eventually Cecilia tried to commit suicide again. This time she only managed to destroy her stomach lining. Like a character in a fairy tale, she had to take a draught of poison for a third time before she was successful, though even then it took her two days to die.

I don't think it's an exaggeration to say that what his mother underwent drove Reich's work as a sexual liberationist, opening his eyes to the dreadful consequences of patriarchal models of ownership as well as restrictive attitudes to sex. When he talked about the Sexual Revolution, he didn't mean a fantasia of endless orgasms so much as a world in which women could experience sexual pleasure without fear of retribution, violence or death. It was this interest in and sympathy for women that made Reich such a touchstone in the 1970s, for feminists of many different persuasions. His ideas about politics and gender are right at the heart of Shulamith Firestone's *The Dialectic of Sex: The Case for Feminist Revolution*, published the same year as *Sexual Politics* and far more radical in its demands. He's a major and not uncontroversial figure in Juliet Mitchell's 1974 weighty re-examination of psychoanalysis, *Psychoanalysis and Feminism: Freud, Reich, Laing and Women*, while the eco-feminist and gender essentialist Susan Griffin drew on him for her work on pornography and rape.

Dworkin too read him avidly. In 1987, she published

*Intercourse*, her harrowing interrogation of the sexual act in terms of power. It's here that she describes Reich as the most optimistic of sexual liberationists, 'the only male one to abhor rape *really*.' At first glance they seem unlikely comrades, but though it isn't easy to square Reich's celebration of orgiastic potency with Dworkin's scepticism around the act of hetero-sexual penetration, her call for men to embrace the limp dick, there is a shared bedrock to their visions. They both regard pornography and sexual violence as unnatural cultural symp-toms, at once the product and enforcer of patriarchy. They both believe the family is where this ideology is instilled, training people from infancy to submit to the authority of the father. More importantly, they both retain faith in a different kind of sex, and though the details of this utopian act remain hazy they are both certain it isn't founded in the desire to do harm, but in absolute equality.

In the 1980s, Dworkin was vocally and controversially opposed to certain kinds of sexual practice, particularly BDSM, which she regarded as a kind of Stockholm syndrome re-enactment of abuse. As with her attack on Sade, she refused or was unable to separate the imaginary from the actual. Though I find many of her arguments convincing, I must admit my own scepticism overwhelms me here. It isn't necessary to believe there exists in each of us a pure, unsullied self to deplore the damage that the iniquitous and ineluctable structures we live inside do to our sexual imaginations. But I don't agree, as Reich and Dworkin did, that sex is necessarily dysfunctional or expressive of misogyny just because it involves consensual acts of masochism or sadism.

Like literature, sex is a space of imaginative play, in which dangerous forces can be encountered and sampled. And like illness, sex is a descent into what Edward St Aubyn once described as 'the darkness of the pre-verbal realm', where uncertain ecstasies and terrors lurk. BDSM, the volitional version of the Sadeian revel, is one of the ways of getting there, a route back to the immense feelings of infancy, to the body before language intervened. It's not, as Dworkin argues, simply and always a replication of the habits of misogyny. One only needs to leaf through Tom of Finland's drawings to be convinced of that.

I'm sure I wasn't the only pre-teen who took *Sexual Politics* off my parents' shelf and found the opening account of a woman being fucked in a bathtub not horrifying but arousing. Wasn't there something else going on in *The Story of O* too, a possibility of submitting not to male supremacy (those interchangeable dick-swinging men, so naked in their desire to be called Master) but to the body itself, its frightening, consuming realms of speechlessness? What was exciting was what Dworkin objected to most strongly: O's pleasure at being reduced to a body, parts and a hole. Isn't that the point of sex, to relinquish the speaking self, to be tumbled into infinity?

Not long after I read *Pornography* in the library at Sussex, I saw Dworkin speak at the International Conference on Violence, Abuse and Women's Citizenship in Brighton. It was 1995 and she was nearly fifty, dressed in her famous uniform of plimsolls and dungarees, 'the *ur*-figure', as Johanna Fateman puts it, 'of so-called anti-sex feminism, a contentious term used to characterize feminist opposition to pornography, prostitution, and S&M.' In addition to her activism against certain types of sex, she'd spearheaded a controversial attempt to pass civil rights ordinances in American cities that would allow women to sue pornographers for damages.

The mood at the conference was fractious. There were walk-outs and stand-up fights. I'd gone with a lesbian friend of my mother's who I'd always liked, but over the course of the weekend we found we were on opposite sides of a painful gap, combatants in different armies of what were known as the porn wars. Was censorship the way to roll? Many feminists agreed with Dworkin that it was a route to liberation, but many, me included, dissented, especially after she made tactical alliances with right-wing anti-obscenity campaigners.

Angela Carter was dead by then (she died of lung cancer in 1992, at the age of fifty-one), but she too had been a dissenter. As her biographer Edmund Gordon explains in *The Invention of Angela Carter*: 'Angela's socialist consciousness meant she believed that pornography *was* an expression of power relations, but only in so far as everything else was, and like everything else it was capable of expressing those relations differently.' 'I think some of the Sisters make too much of a fuss about porn,' she'd told *The Face* back in 1984. 'They imply also that women who don't make a fuss are in some way in complicity. I think that's bananas.' At the time, she was still smarting over feminist attacks on *The Sadeian Woman*. The paperback cover, which featured a surrealist painting by Clovis Trouille of semi-clad women being whipped, had been stickered by the British Federation of Alternative Bookshops as being offensive to women, never mind its liberatory contents.

Was pornography – the display of genitals and body parts;

the description of sexual acts – really so harmful, or was anti-porn feminism reinforcing the ancient, puritanical commandment against female desire? Where was freedom situated: in the struggle for a world without sexual violence, or in the right to engage in any kind of consensual act? By the time I saw Dworkin, these questions were tearing second-wave feminism apart. She seemed a lonely, embattled figure that day, still carrying her painful message, still preaching her extreme, unfashionable solutions.

The problem, as I experienced it that afternoon, was that Dworkin made you feel bad for wanting sex at all. The problem wasn't just that she legislated against certain strains of desire, but that she left no room for the possibility of arousal at all. The problem – but it was me and my erotic imagination that were apparently the problem. Though I find much of her writing electrifying now, what Dworkin made me feel then was shame.

★

I studied *The Bloody Chamber* for A-level, but I didn't realise for another two and a half decades that it was an arrow fired in the same debate. Carter wrote it alongside and much more easily than *The Sadeian Woman*, and it was published by Gollancz in May of the same year. Though the plots are lifted from fairy tales like 'Beauty and the Beast', 'Snow White' and 'Bluebeard', the dynamics are recognisably Sadeian in descent. She drags out the moth-eaten sets, chivvies forward the sinister old cast – the isolated chateau, the cruel marquis, the doomed and pliant ingénue – and then she disrupts the machinery, opening unexpected doors and windows everywhere.

In the title story, the pallid young bride of a serially wid-
owed nobleman breaks into his locked chamber of horrors,
only to discover her embalmed, decapitated and exsanguinated
predecessors inside. 'I had played a game in which every move
was governed by a destiny as oppressive and omnipotent as
himself, since that destiny was himself', she says regretfully,
certain she is next, but it's no longer true. These lost girls only
submit when it pleases them to do so. They have a destiny of
their own. 'The blade did *not* descend, the necklace did *not*
sever, my head did *not* roll.'

One of the things that makes *The Bloody Chamber* so invig-
orating is that it doesn't shut the door on sexuality, or try to
clean it up. Red Riding Hood fucks the wolf; Beauty chooses
to become a Beast, her skin tongued off to reveal beautiful fur.
If Dworkin could only find evidence of misogyny in fairy tales,
Carter unearths the polymorphous perversity that Freud speculated formed the very earliest phase of human sexuality. Her
answer to misogyny is not to refuse sex, but to transform it.
You don't have to foreclose on erotic possibility just because
you'd like to leave the bedroom with your limbs intact.

The violence that does occur is often situated within the
wild framework of the natural world, its turbulent seasons and
many small deaths. In the bleakest story, a count conjures his
heart's desire, a beautiful naked girl, out of a hole in the snow
filled with blood. She dies, he penetrates her, comes, she melts
away, leaving a bloody smear on the icy ground. It's the Sadeian
story in miniature, use and discard, but it's also a time-lapse
version of life itself, the violent passage from birth to death.

After the rape works of 1973, Ana Mendieta too shifted

away from documenting specific, gendered acts of violence to works that have odd, pervasive parallels with Carter's bloody chambers and metamorphosing girls. That summer, she travelled with Hans Breder, the director of the Intermedia course and her then-lover, to Yagul, an archaeological site in the valley of Oaxaca in Mexico. Early one morning she went to the Oaxaca market and bought great armfuls of flowers with long green stems and an abundance of tiny white petals. She and Hans drove to Yagul, and there Mendieta removed all her clothes and climbed inside an open Zapotec tomb, its sides great lumps of rock. Following her precise instructions, Hans covered her body with the flowers, until her naked body was almost entirely effaced. In the photograph he took, also at her direction, the flowers rise up from between her arms and legs, blooming exuberantly from the grave.

The next work she made in Oaxaca, a year later, has even stronger Carterian echoes. This time she bought blood from a butcher at the market. She and Hans went to the Palace of the Six Patios and she lay down in the ruins of the labyrinth while he traced round her body. Then she scooped out the earth and filled the hollow with blood, a perfect illustration of Carter's bitter little fable. In a photograph now owned by the Tate, you see first the massive stony ruins, set among damp green mountains almost obliterated by cloud. It is only slowly that the eye discerns the small, ragged shape of a body, arms upraised, composed of saturated sand, a wounded arterial red.

These images mark the beginning of Mendieta's famous Silueta series. Between 1973 and 1980, she would make over a hundred Siluetas in Mexico and Iowa. In the earliest versions, like those she made at Yagul, she used her own body, but she soon replaced it with a surrogate, a plywood cut-out of her not-quite-five-foot form that she'd strap to the roof of her VW Beetle. She took it to marshes and creeks on the outskirts of Iowa City, most often Old Man's Creek and Dead Tree Area. There she impressed it into the mud, the snow, the sand, filling the human-sized hollow with pigment or flowers or blood. She burned it into the earth, tipping in paraffin or gunpowder and lighting it like a candle.

Though the Siluetas were deliberately left to be reclaimed, interfered with and eventually annihilated by nature, Mendieta preserved them by way of photographs and film. These sublime, eerie images foreground the body's vanishing. They look like graves, obviously, or murder sites, but they also suggest more ecstatic or miraculous translations: fables by Ovid in which a girl transforms herself into a tree or deer, leaving behind the tangled evidence of her departure. In their attentiveness to decay, they likewise recall kusozu, the medieval Japanese paintings produced for the purpose of Buddhist meditation, which reveal the nature of impermanence by depicting the nine stages of decomposition of the corpse of a noblewoman.

I was introduced to the Siluetas by the same boyfriend who made the film about boarding school. I found them captivating, even exhilarating. There was something immensely freeing about seeing those bodily forms melt or be washed away, as if some knot in my own body was also being eased apart. They attested to fluidity and they also made a distinction, a gap, as Dworkin never could, between the native violence of bodily existence and the violence of misogyny. 'I don't think that you can separate death and life,' Mendieta explained in an interview with Linda Montano. 'All my work is about those two things – it's about Eros and life and death.' The Siluetas in particular are about cyclical time, contextualising violence in a much larger frame of material impermanence. Mendieta's own body, small, female, Cuban, pitches for universality, and it's up to the viewer whether they accept it or not.

What she captures is the certainty of bodily change, everything shifting and dissolving, matter on its dance through time. The abiding power of her work is that she used violent material in ways that feel full of liberating possibility, but that doesn't mean she herself was out of harm's way. She died in violent and uncertain circumstances, and in the murky aftermath her work was used as evidence in court that she was culpable for her own death.

Mendieta moved to New York in 1978. There she joined the women's gallery A.I.R., on 97 Wooster Street in SoHo. Established in 1972, A.I.R. was the first not-for-profit, artist-directed and maintained gallery for women in the United States. Like Virago, it was an attempt to tackle the exclusion of women in the arts by seizing control of the means of production. As the gallery's 'Short History' explains, the name stood for Artists in Residence, 'announcing that women artists were now permanent residents in the art world.' Mendieta loved it at first, but she resigned after two years, declaring her frustration with the white, middle-class nature of American feminism.

In 1983, she won the Rome Prize, spending a joyful year at the American Academy, a beautiful complex of buildings set high on the Janiculum. It was a relief to be back in a Latin culture and she stayed on in the Eternal City after the fellowship ended. In January 1985, she got married there, to the American minimalist artist Carl Andre, with whom she'd had an on-off relationship for the past five years. He continued to be unfaithful and by September she was telling friends that she planned to divorce him.

Love aside, her life was going well. In Rome, she'd made a significant shift from the Siluetas and other transient outdoor works to studio sculpture, physical objects that could be exhibited or sold. She had a major show coming up at the New Museum in New York and she'd also been commissioned to make a permanent public installation in MacArthur Park in Los Angeles, her largest work to date. In August she came back to New York for a few weeks, staying at Andre's penthouse at 300 Mercer, a luxury high-rise in Greenwich Village, while she dealt with evicting a problematic subletter in her own more modest apartment on Sixth Avenue, near the Spring Street subway.

At around 5:30am on Saturday 8 September, Mendieta fell thirty-four storeys from the bedroom window at 300 Mercer, smashing so heavily into Delion's grocery on Waverley Place that she left the indentation of her body in the tar-paper roof. She was naked except for a pair of blue bikini pants. The impact of the fall broke all her major bones. Her head was smashed in, the skin of her upper right arm ripped off, every organ in her body damaged. She was thirty-six years old.

When Andre called 911 at 5:29am, he said to the operator: 'My wife is an artist and I am an artist, and we had a quarrel about the fact that I was more, uh, exposed to the public than she was and she went to the bedroom and I went after her and she went out the window.' When the police spoke to him at dawn, after they'd found the body, he said: 'You see, I am a very successful artist and she wasn't. Maybe that got to her, and in that case, maybe I did kill her.' Nobody had asked him if he had.

Later he said that she had jumped and later still that she had fallen while trying to close or perhaps open the bedroom window. He was arrested and tried for her murder, waiving his right to a jury trial and choosing not to testify. With very few exceptions, the art world closed ranks around him, just as the literary world had closed around Mailer during his trial for stabbing his wife a generation earlier. In February 1988, nearly three years after Mendieta's death, he was acquitted by the judge, who concluded that there was insufficient evidence to convince him beyond reasonable doubt of Andre's guilt. Because of a peculiarity of New York State Criminal Procedure Law, the trial records were then permanently sealed, which means the only way to access the police and court proceedings now is via contemporary newspaper reports or by reading Robert Katz's 1990 book *Naked by the Window*. Katz attended the trial and conducted exhaustive interviews with all the main participants. Despite its schlocky title, his book is the most detailed record of the trial now in existence.

It's never going to be possible to ascertain what happened from the messy and contradictory fragments that have survived. A doorman on the street heard a woman screaming, *No, no, no, no*. The bedroom was very disordered. There were raw scratches on Andre's nose and back and arm. Mendieta was terrified of heights, so scared that when she was invited by the Vatican to view the Sistine Chapel ceiling, an honour very rarely offered, she wasn't able to climb the ladder. The marriage wasn't going well. She was planning on leaving him. She was so small that 73 per cent of her body height was beneath the window sill. To fall, she would first have had to leap into the air. She was drunk. He was drunk. She had been mixing her wine with soda water. When Andre rang 911 for the second time his voice was so high-pitched the operator thought she was talking to a woman. *Calm down, ma'am*, she said. The doorman suffered from auditory hallucinations. Ana had discussed her husband's affairs on the phone with a friend that night, sometimes in Spanish, which he couldn't speak, and sometimes in English. Yes, she said *divorcio*, a word even a non-Spanish speaker can understand. Yes, he was in the room.

During the trial, Jack Hoffinger, the lawyer for Andre's defence, tried to build an argument that Mendieta was suicidal, deputising her own work against her. 'Do you know the art where she used her own body to make impressions on the ground?' he asked a witness. He asked about the photographs in which there was blood running down her face, in which her body impacted on earth, in which she was melding into earth, 'in which she depicted the body of a woman lying face down with blood coming out.'

Maybe he'd seen a photograph of Mendieta taken in Mexico in 1973, where she's lying on a rooftop, covered by a sheet that is drenched, truly flooded in blood, an ox heart lying at the place on her chest where her own heart would be. I have read

repeatedly, by critics as well as lawyers, that this is a prefiguration of what would come to pass in New York City a decade
later, but this is a tautology, since part of what her work was
constructed to reveal was the certainty of violence and death,
as well as the probability of violent death being gendered. As
Chris Kraus says in *I Love Dick*: 'Why does everybody think
that women are debasing themselves when we expose the conditions of our own debasement?'

This was Dworkin's question too, and though she lost the
porn wars, it hasn't yet been solved. But Dworkin said something as well. In the preface of *Intercourse* she wrote: 'Submission
can be refused and I refuse it.' Isn't Mendieta's work also about
that refusal? About the certainty of destruction, and the certainty too of abiding, resisting, fertilising the future. A woman
turning into flowers, a woman rising from the dirt. Like Sarah
Ann Ottens, like Rose Keller, like everyone who has been
subjected to violence, she was a person, not a thing, bursting
with possibility until the end.

Mendieta left a gap in the world, and her absence has served
as rallying point for resistance against both the exclusion of
women in the arts and the ongoing failure to stamp out what
remains an epidemic of violence against women, both of which
disproportionately affect women of colour. In 1992, the
Women's Action Coalition organised the first protest in
Mendieta's name. Five hundred women gathered outside the
opening of the new Guggenheim Museum, holding a banner
that announced: 'Carl Andre is in the Guggenheim. Where is
Ana Mendieta?' In 2015, a new generation of activists, the No
Wave Performance Task Force, protested Andre's retrospective

at Dia: Beacon, leaving chicken blood and guts outside the gallery's Chelsea outpost. In the intervening years, and in part because of this ongoing activism, Mendieta's astonishing body of work has finally begun to achieve the recognition it deserves.

Whether she was murdered or not, the fact of her death continues to expose entrenched layers of misogyny. In a hagiographic profile of Carl Andre in the *New Yorker* in 2011, twenty-six years after her death, the interviewer described Mendieta's work as morbid. Imagine believing that we brought it on ourselves, that we desired, coveted, longed for our own destruction. Now turn to her notebook, full of what she called, conscious of her own value, Important Ideas. They'll never be realised now, but a phrase keeps recurring: the essence of Mendieta, the antithesis of morbidity. 'Do it with a size 5 feet . . . Do it outside . . . Do it with a structure . . . Do a *volcano*.' She knew that the body was many things at once, that it is always in flux. 'Document over a long period of time the eruption of the figure', she scribbled. 'Make a figure so that it shines like when water runs down a mountainside.'

# 5

# A Radiant Net

IT ISN'T EASY FOR a solid body to slip the net. The women's liberation movement addressed the things that happened to a category of bodies, proposing ways of resisting and fighting back. But what if there was another route to freedom, a way of evading categorisation altogether?

In the sweltering September of 1967, when she was fifty-five, Agnes Martin renounced her life as an artist and left New York for good. She cut off her long hair, gave away her brushes and paints, hitched an Airstream to a Dodge pick-up and lit out for the territories, pausing only to park outside a Howard Johnson's restaurant and sleep for two days. For more than a year she lived on the road, camping in deserted national parks, swimming wherever there was a river or a lake, looping west, crossing north into Canada and then plunging south nearly all the way to Mexico.

She reached harbour in 1968, pulling into a cafe in the small town of Cuba, New Mexico and asking if they knew of any land with a spring to rent. For the princely sum of ten dollars a month, the manager's wife leased her fifty acres on a remote mesa, one thousand feet above sea level. There was no electricity or phone, water came from a well and the nearest neighbour was six miles away. To get into town meant driving twenty miles on unmarked dirt roads. Martin was undeterred. The wide-open space and corresponding sense of going unwatched were more than compensation for the toughness of the life.

She slept in her camper while she built a one-room house out of adobe, followed by a log-cabin studio made from ponderosa pines. She lived up there alone, a stocky, red-cheeked pioneer. But even high on the mesa, with her back to the world, Martin was still a person moving between obstacles, braking and cornering in search of empty space. Her retreat to the desert was tightly bound up with a need to escape the body – to manage illness, to sidestep gender, to outrun sexuality. 'Now I'm very clear', she wrote in 1973, 'that the object is freedom.'

She'd long been trying to leave the figure behind, never mind all the heavy weather it drags with it. By the time she left the city, Martin was famous for the frugal revelation of the grid, a mode of abstraction that goes as far from form as it is possible to travel. She made the first grid at the age of forty-six, initially scratched into paint and then pencilled onto primed and painted six-foot canvases coloured white, burlap brown, deep-water blue, even gold. They were deliberately the size of a person, she explained, so that the viewer would feel as if they could step right into the shimmering ocean of her lines.

To look at one of Martin's grids is to receive an object lesson in the illusory nature of physical form. Close up, it is plainly a net, composed of thousands of rectangular cells: little boxes that sometimes house small incumbents in the form of dots or dashes. Step away, and the lines abruptly dissolve into a wavering, pulsing mist. There is nothing to hang on to. No one line matters more than any other and so the eye is free to move, an ocular liberty that induces a kind of rapture in the viewer, an experience of being temporarily untethered from the material realm. Because you can only have one of the available viewing experiences at any given moment, there is a sense that the painting always has more to give, that it's pulsing at a frequency that cannot be fully grasped or comprehended.

Despite its liberatory effects, the grid is manifestly about control; though it induces an experience of abstraction, even borderlessness, it is an art composed of fixed and rigid boundaries. The grid represented a new artistic horizon for Martin, an aesthetic territory grab, as well as a moral and spiritual declaration, humility as the path to happiness. But there was also the psychological dimension of what it meant to spend day after day, year after year drawing lines that are boxes that dematerialise. Duck/rabbit: a grid is always two things at once, a door onto empty space and a mesh or cage. Does it let you out or hold you in? Both might be appealing, needful, or then again alarming, even dangerous.

When Martin left New York in 1967, it wasn't that she'd run out of ideas. The year before, she was photographed by Diane Arbus for an article on the American art scene in *Harper's Bazaar*. She sits on a wooden chair in her near-empty studio, dressed in quilted overalls, thick white socks and paint-splashed moccasins, testament to the chill her Acorn wood-burning stove could never quite dispel. Her thin hands are clutched in her lap, and one foot turns inward, pressing anxiously against its fellow. An immensely capable person, who could build a house from scratch and also wire it, she looks through Arbus's lens worn, fearful, eager to please and dangerously undefended.

There are subtle technical means by which Arbus has generated her mood of apprehension and foreboding. Martin's chair is set at a diagonal, right at the front of the frame. The shot is constructed so the lines of the floorboards seem to converge behind her, giving a sense that she is being drawn on tracks towards a region of mysterious darkness at the rear of the room. Arbus was almost supernaturally attuned to currents of anxiety and unease, sometimes conveying them when they weren't actually present in her subjects, and the track lines could also be read more prosaically as a nod to Martin's grids. But the disquiet she was picking up did in this case stem from a real source. Though the existence of the picture is in itself a testament to Martin's new-found fame, she was right on the verge of a precipice. In the months after the shutter's click she suffered a psychotic break.

She wandered the city in a fugue state, unable to speak. After a day or two, she was picked up by the police and taken to Bellevue, a public hospital and place of last resort for New York's homeless and uninsured. She didn't know or wasn't able to give her own name or address and so she was confined on the locked public ward, alongside violent and disturbed patients. While she was there she was restrained, heavily medicated and given electro-convulsive therapy. In this controversial procedure an electric current is applied to the brain, inducing a fit or seizure. It can relieve depression and catatonia, though it doesn't always work and often has a side-effect of memory loss.

Later, Martin told a friend she had shock therapy over a hundred times. These days patients are routinely anaesthetised and given a muscle relaxant before the electric current is applied, but in the 1960s, and especially in underfunded hospitals like Bellevue, they were often fully conscious and strapped down in a brutal process known as unmodified ECT. Sylvia Plath, who was given two courses of ECT, the first unmodified, described the process in her semi-autobiographical novel *The Bell Jar*. The first is terrifying: the narrator feels something split and shake her until she believes her bones might break. The second course, based on Plath's treatment at McLean Hospital in Massachusetts, is administered more gently, and the metaphors are correspondingly softer: 'the darkness wiped me out like chalk on a blackboard.'

Martin had been in the grips of what she called a trance, an acute episode of the schizophrenia diagnosed in her early adulthood. Schizophrenia is generally not a constant condition, but tends to involve unpredictable cycles of acute episodes punctuated by longer chronic phases. Like many patients, Martin was broadly sane and capable much of the time, though subject to ongoing symptoms that included auditory hallucinations she called voices, logorrhoea and mild catatonia. These basically steady periods were punctuated by acute episodes of psychosis, frank breaks with reality in which she became paranoid and delusional, beset by fear and dread.

★

Visiting the Agnes Martin Gallery at the Harwood Museum in Taos in 2007, three years after Martin's death at the grand old age of ninety-two, the critic Terry Castle deployed an unusual metaphor. The gallery was designed by Martin herself. It's octagonal, and houses seven paintings, all made of horizontal layers of softly glowing blue and pink. Castle described this unusual space as 'a tiny orgone box of a room, full of faintly pulsing energy currents, but also strangely full of grace, a promise of contact.' When I first read that sentence, I was filled with pleasure. When people write about Reich's doomed invention they almost always concentrate on its failings as a medical or scientific device. By comparing it to Martin's paintings, Castle opens up the possibility of a whole new spectrum of meanings.

Though they seem at first glance poles apart, there are many odd parallels between Martin and Reich. Both were driven by that promise of contact, which they longed to make available to humanity at large. They wanted to connect people to a kind of universal love, and at the same time they both suffered from a paranoia that inhibited their capacity to achieve it, which might explain why their liberation devices – the grid, the orgone box – took the paradoxical form of cells, cages, closets.

In his fifties, Reich too found himself overwhelmed by paranoia in the wide-open spaces of the American south-west. He believed he could control the weather using a giant home-made gun made of metal pipes, a sci-fi weapon he called a cloudbuster, which he used to fight a 'full-scale interplanetary battle' with alien spaceships he thought were attacking the Earth. He wrote frequent letters to Eisenhower about his revelations, talked of formulas so secret he had never confined them to paper, identified publicly and in print with Jesus and Galileo, speculated that he would be put in prison for his own protection, but also told family members and his few remaining supporters that he believed he would be killed there. A letter to Eisenhower written on 23 February 1957 closed plaintively: 'I am doing my best to keep in touch w an at times elusive and complicated reality.'

How could the lucid, politically engaged figure of the 1930s have become so thoroughly unmoored? What happened to Reich after he left Berlin in 1933 is a tragedy that perversely bears out the truth of his belief that all bodies are continually assailed by larger forces, sometimes too powerful to withstand. Though his enemies began whispering about schizophrenia that year, he never accepted the diagnosis, and nor was it confirmed by any doctor he saw. In 1957, by which time he was convinced that aliens were patrolling above his house, two psychiatrists concluded that though he was prone to paranoia and could become psychotic, he was not insane. He had delusions, but like Martin that doesn't mean the fact of his paranoia was in itself unjustified or lacked an intelligible source.

During the run-up to war, Reich lost his home, his clinic and his country. His marriage to Annie broke up and he was separated from his two daughters. But the worst blow was his expulsion from psychoanalysis. Reich had his last private conversation with Freud in September 1930, just before he moved to Berlin. Freud had a holiday house in Austria, by the beautiful lake in Grundisee, and Reich went to call on him there. In a photograph taken that summer, Freud looks old and fragile and very thin, leaning heavily on the arm of his daughter

Anna, who is wearing an airy green dress with short sleeves. Her father, by contrast, is in an immaculate three-piece suit and tie, his beard neatly shorn, a small dark object – perhaps a glasses case – protruding from his waistcoat pocket. He was seventy-four, and suffering badly from the cancer in his jaw.

In 1923, he'd been diagnosed with a malignant ulcer. The right side of his jaw and palate were removed, a major operation conducted under local anaesthetic. It turned his mouth and nasal cavity into a single gaping hole and destroyed the hearing in his right ear. He couldn't eat or speak without his horrible prosthesis, nicknamed 'the monster' by his family, which caused constant pain and irritation, distorting his voice so that it sounded as if he'd been gagged. Over the years, he'd had dozens of operations (thirty-three by the time of his death). It's worth bearing in mind that during his conflict with Reich, Freud inhabited a body in serious pain.

The orgasm theory had irritated him, but Reich's shift into politics troubled Freud more deeply. Reich had come to discuss his new ideas and the conversation quickly stalled. 'Freud wanted nothing of politics . . . He was very sharp and I was very sharp too.' Neither man shouted, but it was clear that they had reached their parting place. Reich stayed perhaps an hour and a half, and when he left he looked back and saw Freud in the window, pacing 'up, down, up, down, fast, up-down, up-down in that room.' Reich had spent his whole adult life observing and interpreting bodies. His overwhelming impression was of an animal in a cage.

The two men never saw one another alone again, but over the next few years Freud kept a close eye on Reich's political activities. He thought total political neutrality was the only way psychoanalysis could survive under Nazi rule, and Reich's very public activism and Communist alliances struck him as dangerously inimical to this strategy. As Anna Freud explained in a letter written on 27 April 1933, a month after Hitler's frightening Enabling Act confirmed the powers of the new regime: 'what my father finds offensive in Reich is the fact that he has forced psychoanalysis to become political; psychoanalysis has no part in politics.'

That spring, the new Nazi government gave the Berlin Psychoanalytic Institute a choice: submit to Aryanisation or close down. Reich fought for closure but was outvoted. Most of the Jewish analysts went into exile (this is when Reich fled over the mountains disguised as a ski tourist) and the Institute stayed open under the leadership of Nazi sympathisers. Within a few years, Freud's surviving books would be locked in a 'poison cupboard', while the famous free clinic itself was transformed from a seedbed of left-wing idealism into what Elizabeth Ann Danto describes as 'a horrible triage centre where psychoanalysts condemned their patients to death.'

Reich had known it wasn't possible to stay neutral under fascism, but Freud was adamant psychoanalysis must take the middle way. If Reich couldn't be silenced, he'd have to go. Freud was too ill to attend the annual congress of the International Psychoanalytic Association in Lucerne in 1934 but he authorised what happened there, an indication of how cold and ruthless he was capable of being. Reich, who had made a difficult journey by boat from Denmark to Belgium to avoid Germany, was summoned to a private hearing by Anna

Freud and Ernest Jones, the English President of the IPA. They informed him that his political work was damaging psycho-analysis and asked him to resign. At first he refused, accusing them of accommodating fascism, but when it became clear that they were serious he finally agreed. He spent the rest of the congress raging and storming to anyone who'd listen, a wild, isolated figure. His colleagues speculated that he'd gone mad, though if I were served up as scapegoat to the Nazis I might lose my temper too.

At the age of thirty-seven, he'd been cast out by Freud, the difficult, beloved father. The rejection was painful and shock-ing, and it also fundamentally damaged his work. 'I lost literally all of my friends in professional circles', he noted in *People in Trouble*, but it was more than that. He'd lost his context, the profession that had been his home since his early twenties. For the rest of his life he'd work in isolation, outside of any insti-tution or system that might have checked or countered his more wayward or aberrant beliefs.

Some analysts had breakdowns or even killed themselves after being rejected by Freud, but Reich was determined to prove himself right. He knew there must be a reason that people chose fascism over freedom. What made them so com-pliant? His political work in Berlin had achieved so little, in the end. People were too repressed, too rigid, terrified by the pos-sibilities of liberation. Their vital energy was all dammed up. The mistake he'd made was to try to fix the structures they lived inside. But what, he thought, if the problem was biolog-ical in nature? Forget revolution. What he needed to do was find a way of working directly on the libido, the life energy.

Damaged people made damaged worlds. Only those with unbound vital energy would be able to handle real freedom.

In the summer of 1939, he left Europe for America, travelling alone on the SS *Stavangerfjord*, the last ship out of Norway before war was declared. Thanks to two former students, he'd been offered a post as associate professor of medical psychology at the New School in New York City, part of its University in Exile. This programme was established to provide a haven for European academics and intellectuals fleeing Germany (among the 180 scholars given visas and jobs in the run-up to war was the philosopher Hannah Arendt).

A few days after Reich arrived in New York, German soldiers marched into Poland, beginning the Second World War. Three weeks later, on 23 September 1939, Freud died in exile in London, in his beautiful new house in Maresfield Gardens. He'd asked his doctor for an overdose of morphine, no longer willing to tolerate the agony – torture, he called it – caused by his inoperable cancer, though in the preceding weeks he'd refused anything stronger than aspirin and a hot-water bottle. There was no possibility of a rapprochement now.

Depressed and subdued, Reich rented a house in Forest Hills in Queens, a popular suburb that Susan Sontag's family also moved to two years later. Cancer obsessed him. He believed Freud's tumour was a physical manifestation of his resignation and despair, a consequence of the same process of withdrawal that had led him to reject Reich. Cancer was a turning away from life, Reich thought, the biological analogue of the wave of violence and authoritarianism sweeping across Europe. He converted his dining room and basement into laboratories, carrying out experiments on cancerous mice. His diaries of the period are full of feverish speculations about cancer cells, rotting tissue, tumours. As Sontag observes in *Illness as Metaphor*, 'as a theory of the psychological genesis of cancer, the Reichian imagery of energy checked, not allowed to move forward, then turned back on itself, driving cells berserk, is already the stuff of science fiction.' (I'm not sure if she ever realised it, but the theories that so troubled her in later life were invented a couple of blocks from PS144, while she was sitting at her fifth-grade desk.)

On holiday in Maine in the summer of 1940, Reich had what he regarded as the great revelation of his career, which drew all his speculations and intimations together. He was staying with a new lover, Ilse Ollendorff, in a rented cabin in the remote region of the Rangeley Lakes. The air was very clear up there. Gazing at the sky over the lake one night, he thought he saw something flickering between the stars. Suddenly, he realised that the life force he'd been searching for was everywhere, a radiant energy that hummed and buzzed amid the grasses and flowers, the colour of St Elmo's fire. He'd been standing in it all along, 'at the bottom of an ocean of orgone energy.'

What Reich saw in Maine sounds like a mystical vision, but he believed that orgone energy, as he called it, was the same thing as Freud's libido. It wasn't metaphorical at all, but a real, tangible, measurable force. It was orgone that got blocked as a result of trauma; orgone that caused the sensation of streaming. Orgone was the force that drove the orgasm. Orgone was the energy that propelled all life. Back in his lab in Forest Hills, he built a machine to harness this free-flowing interplanetary resource. Based loosely on the design of a Faraday cage (a gridded enclosure that blocks electromagnetic fields), the orgone accumulator was a wooden cabinet just large enough to house a single person, made of pine panels packed with alternating layers of steel wool and sheep's wool, lined on the inside with galvanised steel. It functioned something like a rarefied sunbed, charging the occupant with a blast of orgone energy, which would have the effect, or so Reich claimed, of enlivening their own energetic resources and making them more resilient to illness, infection and stress.

There's something immensely sad about the image of Reich that year, sitting in a device that exemplified his isolation and sense of being under attack. The orgone accumulator betrayed far more about his mental state than he perhaps realised: a liberation machine like a closet, in which you sat alone, protected and sequestered from the outside world. If it worked, it didn't matter that he was no longer a member of the International Psychoanalytic Association or that Sex-Pol had failed, that Freud was dead or that he was in exile from everything he'd once loved. His machine could automate the communal work he'd been doing back in Europe, obviating the need for both hands-on, person-to-person therapy and the massed bodies of activism. It meant he didn't need to collaborate with other people, or risk being rejected by them. One of the biggest ironies of Reich's life is that this passionate advocate of bodily contact developed a device designed to dispense with it altogether.

But just because he'd invented a new tool didn't mean

Reich had lost his appetite for changing the world. He believed the orgone accumulator could reverse the process of stasis and repression that was at the root of cancer and fascism alike, and as such it was his duty to make it available to a wider audience than the patients and supporters who comprised his inner circle. In the early 1940s, he founded the Orgone Institute Press to self-publish translations of his work, liberally rewritten to incorporate the pulsing blue light of his new discovery. *The Function of the Orgasm* came out in 1942, followed by *Character Analysis* and *The Sexual Revolution* in 1945. These books carried his ideas about sex, politics, sickness and the body to a new generation of thinkers and intellectuals, among them Paul Goodman, William Burroughs, Jack Kerouac, J. D. Salinger, Saul Bellow and Norman Mailer.

Allen Ginsberg was so beguiled that he wrote to Reich, explaining that he was homosexual and requesting help with his persistent melancholy and depression. Reich refused to treat gay patients, but Ilse, who served as secretary as well as lab assistant, replied with a list of three Reichian substitutes. Ginsberg chose Alan Cott, who treated him with twice-weekly sessions in the orgone box, a literal closet from which he emerged at a dash to come out to his father in the winter of 1947.

Though Burroughs told Ginsberg that he didn't trust 'those straight genital Reichians from here to Benny Graff', he too was fascinated by Reich's ideas about cancer and character armour. He built the first of many orgone boxes in an orange grove in Pharr, Texas in the spring of 1949, after reading Reich's *The Cancer Biopathy*, which had been published the previous year and included building instructions. He meditated in it naked, enjoying a series of spectacular orgasms. 'I tell you Jack,' he wrote enthusiastically to Kerouac, 'he is the only man in the analysis line who is *on that beam*.' A few months later he wrote worriedly to Kerouac again, asking if he could find out what an accumulator was meant to look like, and especially if it required a window? (Reich's instructions had neglected to describe shape.) In 1957, Burroughs was building one in Tangier. Ensconced in a SoHo loft twenty years later, he covered his newest model in rabbit-fur coats – 'very organic, like a fur-lined bathtub'.

As James Baldwin observes in 'The New Lost Generation', his disabused account of this period and its overwrought participants, Reich's ideas had fallen on fertile ground. The war had obliterated people's enthusiasm for political activism and sharpened their appetite for pleasure. The idea that sexual liberation was a route to social change was immensely seductive. 'It seemed to me', Baldwin recalled, 'that people turned away from the idea of the world being made better through politics to the idea of the world being made better through psychic and sexual health like sinners coming down the aisle at a revival meeting.' The free-love crowd exuded euphoria, but to Baldwin it was as if they'd turned inward, becoming more closed, less generous, incapable of listening, shrink-wrapped in their own self-regard – something one could also say of Reich himself.

To his abiding dismay, Reich's ideas were providing the theoretical underpinnings for a hip, sexually loose counter-culture that he regarded with suspicion, if not active dislike. He was never at home among the bohemians of Greenwich Village, and in 1950 he transferred operations once again, moving with Ilse, their infant son Peter, his adult daughter Eva and a few acolytes to land he'd bought on the outskirts of Rangeley, the small town in Maine where he'd first seen orgone energy.

He christened his new kingdom Orgonon (hence the first bubbling line of Kate Bush's 'Cloudbusting', 'I still dream of Orgonon'). He envisaged it as the command centre of the bold new discipline of orgone energy, which might in time end cancer and put a stop to war (endearingly, he also observed that he put on less weight up there than he had in New York). He planned to build a university, a hospital, even an orgone accumulator factory, but in the event the buildings that he'd envisaged didn't extend beyond the high modernist Orgone Energy Observatory, which doubled as the family home, and a laboratory at the bottom of the hill, where students and colleagues engaged in research. In photographs from its bustling heyday, Reich is in a plaid shirt holding forth to a room full of clean-cut young people, the lab equipped with shiny, enigmatic machines.

Orgonon might have looked like a Bond villain's holdout, set high above the icy blue waters of Dodge Pond, but it didn't protect him from scrutiny or invasion. In 1947, a beautiful journalist and self-styled consumer activist called Mildred Edie Brady interviewed Reich for what he didn't realise would be exposés in *Harper's Magazine* and the *New Republic*. She declared him the leader of 'the new cult of sex and anarchy', though he was never an anarchist and regarded the pornography and promiscuity of the Beat generation as symptoms of chronic sexual dysfunction, not goals to be achieved. Worse, she accused him of peddling a quack cure, a box that could cure everything from cancer to the common cold.

These articles and the many copy-cat versions that followed introduced Reich to a massive mainstream audience (according to Christopher Turner, *The Mass Psychology of Fascism* was the most requested book in the New York Public Library in 1949), but they also drew him to the attention of the Food and Drug Administration, the body responsible for verifying medical devices. While the FDA was right to question the orgone accumulator's medical efficacy, it substantially overestimated the danger posed to the public. There were only about three hundred orgone boxes in existence by 1950, some self-built and some sold or rented out by Reich. What's more, the FDA's campaign against Reich was driven by a prurience that ran far outside its remit. Throughout the course of their investigations, its inspectors never quite relinquished their belief that orgone accumulators were a cover for some more illicit activity. Perhaps Reich was running a porn ring, or trafficking prostitutes, or teaching children how to masturbate. Even if he was just facilitating the orgasms of beatniks and intellectuals, he was still driving a sexual movement that was dirty and dangerously immoral.

Over the course of the next decade the FDA spent an eye-watering $2 million on its pursuit of Reich, a quarter of its total budget. Inspectors watched his mail, read his bank records and illegally obtained copies of telegrams he sent to friends. They got doctors and university medical departments to test out orgone accumulators, but they also gathered up unfounded local gossip about nudity at Orgonon and asked women in his employ if he talked to them about sex. As *The Chemical Feast*, Ralph Nader's inculpatory account of the FDA's multiple failings and inconsistencies, observes of Reich's treatment: 'when faced with the relatively minor transgressions of individuals it particularly dislikes, the agency has managed to exhibit a frightening vigour.'

On 10 February 1954, he was served with a complaint for injunction that accused him of claiming he could cure a range of diseases so broad as to constitute a dictionary of the afflictions of the human body. This list was assembled from around twenty-five case histories in several of Reich's books. In their original context they often illustrated failures, and so could hardly be described as claims of cures, but these sections were deliberately excised. Paranoid and balky, Reich refused to appear in court. He didn't even point out the inaccuracies of the complaint, instead writing an arrogant four-page statement asserting his freedom as a scientist. (More powerful by far is a note in his diary, written on 13 December 1947: '*I request the right to be wrong.*')

The statement didn't help. The judge issued an injunction under the Federal Food, Drug, and Cosmetic Act, banning him from shipping orgone accumulators across state lines or promoting them in print. It ordered the destruction of all books, pamphlets and journals published by the Orgone Institute Press, including *Character Analysis* and *The Sexual Struggle of Youth*. Furthermore, it barred Reich from ever again discussing the existence of orgone energy ('perpetually enjoined and restrained from'), thereby demanding the wholesale demolition of his intellectual life.

It was that winter, as large forces closed in around him, that he fled to Arizona with his ten-year-old son, Peter, armed with two cloudbusters. Peter, nicknamed Peeps, grew up a soldier in a paranoid private army, a sergeant in what his father, always a fan of grand titles, dubbed the Corps of the Cosmic Engineers, 'the first human beings to engage in a battle to the death with spaceships.' In the miserable wake of the injunction, father and son spent each night driving out into the desert to fight pitched battles against flying saucers.

★

Reich was always exceptionally sensitive to the mood of his times, and his obsession with an enemy that must be defeated, from alien invaders to cancer cells, reflects the cultural and political climate of America at the time: the post-atomic age of blacklists and Red Scares, nuclear tests on Bikini Atoll and McCarthyite persecutions, when paranoia soaked through the fabric of national life, rank and pervasive as cigarette smoke.

He might have acted out his own version of that paranoia, out in the desert with a home-made gun, but he was also a victim of it, at least in part because of the nature of his ideas about sex. This was an era in which fears around subversion and degeneration collected in the twinned figures of the communist and the pervert, and though Reich had long since repudiated communism ('Red fascism', he called it) and was by now a Republican voter, he remained an object of suspicion because of the threat his vision of sexual liberation posed to the increasingly repressive and reactionary new order of Eisenhower's America.

Although Agnes Martin was fifteen years younger than Reich, she too lived in this oppressive environment and she too deployed a kind of closet to survive it. Moving to a mesa in New Mexico was not the only way she ensured her privacy and freedom. She also created a formidable barricade of silence around the difficult zones of gender and sexuality, refusing or evading the existence of the body. In interviews, she often denied being a woman at all, declining to be pinned down by categorical identities that others at the time were finding it liberating to claim. She cropped her hair like a Roman emperor, dressing in an androgynous uniform of farm-store overalls and T-shirts, part pre-schooler, part stone butch. In 1973, the year that Mendieta was re-enacting rape scenes in Iowa and Andrea Dworkin was finishing *Women Hating*, she shut down a question about the divergent reputations of male and female artists by announcing, 'I'm not a woman and I don't care about reputations', adding even more unanswerably: 'I'm not a woman, I'm a doorknob.'

Though her relationships were with women, she resisted being pinned down by the label of lesbian too, and her sexuality was only publicly acknowledged by her lovers after her death. No one has to leave the closet, of course. We're all free to refuse burdensome identities or to insist on privacy, but the public screen of silence and concealment that Martin set up around the subject of her sexuality is too often taken at face value, without enquiring into the forces against which it was raised.

In 1950, the year that she turned thirty-eight, a witch-hunt began in America that was in many ways more aggressive and pervasive than Senator McCarthy's attack on communists, though it's far less well historicised. As David K. Johnson explains in his revelatory history, *The Lavender Scare*, the purge began the same year as the Red Scare, and in the same way: as a rumour about State Department infiltration that sparked a national moral panic. Between seven thousand and ten thousand federal workers lost their jobs in the 1950s alone because of suspicions of homosexuality. Many struggled to find work again, and there were many suicides. One of the most formidable components of the purge was Executive Order 10450, signed by Eisenhower on 27 April 1953, three months into his presidency. It barred homosexuals ('sex perverts') from federal employment, along with drug addicts, alcoholics, anarchists and anyone else bent on undermining the project of America.

This document enshrined in law the belief that to be homosexual was to be innately subversive and immoral, an individualist who was by nature disloyal to the national family, not to mention a security threat because of what was regarded as a susceptibility to blackmail. A failure to conform to gender norms was seen as particularly suspicious, as an anonymous memo written by a clerk-secretary to the head of State Department security on 13 March 1953 demonstrates. It denounces eighteen co-workers as potential security threats. Reasons include women having a 'deep voice' or 'very little in the way of hips', while a male co-worker is accused of having 'a feminine complexion, a peculiar girlish walk'. These observations were added to each suspect's personnel file, and all were subject to further investigation.

During this period, many states either passed new laws or

reinforced existing statutes to criminalize homosexual acts. Sentences ranged from fines to decades in prison simply for having sex with someone of your own gender in your own home. When Martin received a Wurlitzer grant in 1955, she 'was terrified', her girlfriend at the time, Kristina Wilson, recalled. 'She thought it would ruin her career if it got out of the closet . . . In those days it was a project to keep it absolutely as undercover as you could.' Secrecy was an armour against the prevailing atmosphere of suspicion and contempt, in which a muttered rumour about fairies or bulldaggers could scupper a whole life.

Homophobia also infiltrated the domain of medicine. In 1952, the American Psychiatric Association published the first edition of the *Diagnostic and Statistical Manual of Mental Disorders*, *DSM-I*, an immensely powerful tool for designating which behaviours were considered normal and which cast as aberrant. Among the disorders listed was homosexuality, categorised as a 'sociopathic personality disturbance'. In California, men convicted of consensual sodomy could be imprisoned for life in a mental hospital, subject to electric shock therapy, castration and lobotomy, 'treatments' that were widespread elsewhere too. In 1968, homosexuality was reclassified as a sexual deviation and in 1973, after years of activism and resistance, it was finally removed from the manual, though 'sexual orientation disturbance' and then 'ego dystonic homosexuality' lingered into the late 1980s.

What this means is that for the entire decade in which Martin lived in New York, 1957 to 1967, her sexuality was formally designated as pathological. Whether she concealed it during her involuntary institutionalisations or had the luck to encounter sympathetic psychiatrists, it was officially categorised as a sign of sickness: a symptom like catatonia or auditory hallucinations, and just as liable to shock treatment. In 1959, the young Lou Reed was given twenty-four sessions of ECT, spaced three days apart, at Creedmoor Psychiatric Hospital in Queens, in part because of his sexuality.

During those years, Martin lived down by the waterfront in Lower Manhattan. A queer community of artists, including Robert Rauschenberg, Jasper Johns, Robert Indiana and Ellsworth Kelly, had taken up not-quite-legal residence in the abandoned nineteenth-century sailmakers' lofts and warehouses of Coenties Slip, a haven in the most literal of terms. Martin's first studio was on the Slip itself, followed by a beautiful, cathedral-like space on South Street. It might not have had heat or hot water, but there were vaulted ceilings and huge windows that looked straight onto the East River. She told an interviewer that they all sang when they came back from the city to this watery, cat-haunted place, adding: 'You feel as if you've climbed a mountain above the confusion.'

She had relationships with at least two women during the Coenties Slip years, the sculptor Chryssa and the weaver Lenore Tawney, who occupied a neighbouring studio and whose extraordinary creations riff on some of the same plain and exultant notes as Martin's grids. They read Gertrude Stein to each other, surely the antecedent for Martin's curiously burbling literary style. As Martin's biographer Nancy Princenthal rather carefully puts it, 'the Slip, like Taos, was distinguished as a place where homosexual men and women could be comfortable, even if the constraints of the time prohibited the openness acceptable today. In fact the tension between gay and straight artists during the years Martin was in New York erupted, at times, into open hostility.'

Little wonder you might prefer to be a doorknob. But prejudice wasn't just enacted at the Cedar Tavern, the aggressively macho watering hole patronised by straight artists. Even after the end of the McCarthy era, it was still enshrined in law. In the 1960s cross-dressing was illegal in New York, a crime known as gender impersonation. Anyone who didn't conform to gender stereotypes was a potential target, and the law was used to limit and frustrate queer sociability as well as sex. Drag queens, butches, effeminate men and transsexuals were regularly rounded up at the city's gay bars, arrested and imprisoned for the crime of wearing fewer than three articles of clothing appropriate to their gender.

It was this prohibition against cross-dressing that kick-started the modern-day gay liberation movement. On 28 June 1968, police raided the Mafia-run Stonewall Inn on Christopher Street, one of the few bars in New York where dancing between same-sex couples was permitted, making it a romantic as well as erotic refuge. During these raids, cross-dressing patrons would generally be taken to the bathroom by female officers to have their gender humiliatingly verified. This time, they refused. A crowd began to gather in the street outside. When a butch lesbian fought back after being violently rammed into a patrol wagon, they erupted.

That night and the next, thousands of people were out on the streets of Greenwich Village, fighting running battles with riot police. Allen Ginsberg lived a few blocks away and for the first time in his life he ventured into the Stonewall Inn, where he was beguiled into dancing. On the way home, he commented to a friend, 'the guys there were so beautiful – they've lost that wounded look that fags all had ten years ago.' When they parted company on Cooper Square, he yelled in salutation: 'defend the fairies.' A sea change was underway, but Martin wasn't there to see it. While the drag queens lobbed bricks and garbage cans, she was out on the highways of America, escaping encounter altogether.

*

To be born at all is to be situated in a network of relations with other people, and furthermore to find oneself forcibly inserted into linguistic categories that might seem natural and inevitable but are socially constructed and rigorously policed. We're all stuck in our bodies, meaning stuck inside a grid of conflicting ideas about what those bodies mean, what they're capable of and what they're allowed or forbidden to do. We're not just individuals, hungry and mortal, but also representative types, subject to expectations, demands, prohibitions and punishments that vary enormously according to the kind of body we find ourselves inhabiting. Freedom isn't simply a matter of indulging all material cravings, Sade-style. It's also about finding ways to live without being hampered, hobbled, damaged or actively destroyed by a constant reinforcement of ideas about what is permitted for the category of body to which you've been assigned.

The realisation that embodiment is more dangerous or

oppressive for some people than others is what drives liberation movements, but it might also have formed part of the lasting appeal of Buddhism for Martin. Zen and Taoism were enormously popular in the counterculture of the 1950s, and Martin was an ardent student, practising in her own idiosyncratic way for the rest of her life. In the 1970s, she started giving lectures and writing essays that focused not so much on her paintings as the spiritual lessons she wanted them to convey, a cross between Buddhism and the rigid Presbyterianism of her childhood. Her reputation as a desert mystic stems from these hypnotic, repetitive homilies, which return again and again to the freedom that comes when you turn your back to the world.

Buddhism teaches that the material realm is an illusion and that servicing the body's clamorous demands leads only to suffering. As Martin put it in 'The Untroubled Mind', her long essay on art making and inspiration: 'the satisfaction of appetite happens to be impossible' (itself Freud's argument against the absurdity of sexual pleasure as a guiding impulse). In this vision of the world, renunciation, silence, denial – themselves the watchwords of the closet – are not ways of avoiding life but of entering the liberating dimension of the spiritual, where, in the lovely words of the Heart Sutra, 'form is only emptiness, emptiness only form.' Freedom is a consequence of relinquishing the material world. It's the same magical dematerialisation her paintings enact – painful categories abolished, dangerous bodies left behind.

In August 2015 there was an exhibition of Martin's work at Tate Modern, the old power station transformed, just as Terry Castle had suggested, into a vast orgone box. When I went it was raining. My friend was late and I waited in the vestibule by the white birches, looking out over the river as a tide of damp people filtered gratefully through the doors, many of them dressed in transparent macs. No one stood out. Everyone had been anonymised by the weather.

Walking into the gallery was like stepping off a ledge into deep water. The paintings hummed. They were like windows into how the world would be if all the architecture was removed, the language gone, the concepts dispensed with, the forms melted away. What if you stopped wanting, I wrote in my notebook, what if you gave in and let the moment seize you. A few days earlier I'd had sex with an old lover, unexpectedly, and my body was still ringing with pleasure and confusion.

I stood for a long time in front of a painting called *White Stone*. From across the room it looked wet and gleaming, rain over an ocean, endlessly receding. I'd met the man back in the 1990s, when we were practising Buddhism, with a similar combination of scepticism and intensity. The relationship between us had been dangerous and ecstatic. Looking back at it now, we were in search of some kind of abandon, only each time we went out over the ledge we got caught in a vicious undertow, strange objects smashing into us in the dark. Aversion, ignorance and craving, the three poisons that lead to suffering. We used to go on camping retreats and at night there'd be pujas in the shrine tent and in the wavering candlelight people would rise one by one and throw themselves down in front of the altar. It was called full prostration practice, and people did it maybe twenty or a hundred times. People meaning me. The ecstasy of self-effacement, surrendering the ego, letting everything go. You weren't bowing to a God, you were just bowing.

The sex we had was like that too, like you could fall out of the world altogether. He was a physicist and sometimes he'd tell me about the atomic level of reality, where nothing was as solid as it looked, not trees or buildings or our two bodies, one of them at least an animal that didn't want the gender it had been given. Animal meaning me. There were no hard edges, not really, just particles falling through empty space. It was like the Heart Sutra said: 'No eye, ear, nose, tongue, body, mind. No colour, sound, smell, taste, touch, or what the mind takes hold of.' Or as Virginia Woolf put it in *The Waves*: 'Everything falls in a tremendous shower, dissolving me.' Imagine the relief.

The painting was a grid on a gessoed white surface. You had to stand pretty close for its glow to resolve into two closely placed sets of pencil lines, one graphite-grey and the other rose-red. The whole thing shimmered, tender and diffuse, the hand-made quality counteracting any potential rigidity or coldness. It was good to look at. Reviewing a Martin retrospective in the *New Yorker* in 2004, Peter Schjeldahl speculated that her paintings produced what he described as a 'conceptual traffic jam', adding: 'My analytical faculties, after trying to conclude that what I'm looking at is one thing or another, give up, and my mind collapses into a momentary engulfing state that is either "spiritual" or nameless.'

I was certainly feeling something. The paintings unlatched a whole suite of emotions, among them pleasure, sadness, longing, even gratitude. I didn't think it was the product of a perceptual trick, though. It was something to do with the architecture of the grid itself. The point about a grid is that all the disparate tensions are in balance. There are four sets of opposing forces, and they're all ratcheted equally. We feel this instinctively, since a line that isn't tensioned will simply sag. The paintings were so large, and so evidently the product of long, meticulous, repetitive labour, that they begged the question of what forces were being mastered, what kind of longings assuaged.

Martin herself often said that her paintings were about innocence, by which she meant a kind of pristine openness that she associated with childhood. 'My paintings are about merging, about formlessness', she told her friend the artist Ann Wilson. 'A world without objects, without interruption.' I thought about that statement as I stood there, and for a long time afterwards. Most of us experience merging as a product of love or sex, which has the power to flood or obliterate the ego's defences – the dizzy, oceanic high of falling in love or fucking, until the boundary between self and other turns foamy and dissolute. What would you merge with in a world without objects? Nothing?

In a way, yes. The kind of merging Martin was advocating was not to do with other people. It was the product of stringent self-denial, designed to facilitate access into a far richer spiritual reality. 'Solitude and independence for a free mind', she wrote in 1972. She'd always been an advocate of self-reliance, maintaining tight control over her needs and resources long after she became very rich indeed. She never allowed herself to depend on anyone else for fulfilment or care, and quickly banishing them if she did let down her guard. In New Mexico, her renouncement of worldly things seems to have included roman- tic and sexual relationships. 'Fifteen minutes of physical abrasion', she once said to an interviewer, though she may have been laughing at the time.

Withholding pleasure from herself was a route to freedom from the ego, a monkish practice of self-denial. But if the years of living off coffee and bananas were a kind of spiritual auster- ity measure that brought manifest rewards, they were also a safeguard against the omnipresent danger of being flooded by the outside world. People, animals, music, even food had the capacity to capsize her. 'I can't deal with distraction,' she said. 'I don't have a dog because they demand love.'

In the 1940s and 1950s, while Reich was building his orgone accumulators and cloudbusters, a group of his former col- leagues formulated a set of ideas that casts a rather different light on Martin's world without objects. Before the war, Reich had worked closely with two of the people who would go on to develop object relations theory, practising with Melanie Klein at the Ambulatorium in Vienna and with Edith Jacobson at the Berlin Poliklinik. He and Klein had never been close, but Jacobson was a friend and political ally as well as colleague.

In psychoanalytic terms, object relations refers to an indi- vidual's capacity to form connections with other beings, the so-called object world. As Jacobson explains in her 1954 essay 'The Self and the Object World', in very early infancy there is no differentiation between self and other. The infant experi- ences itself as part of the mother. Through repeated experiences of minor frustration, of being hungry or wet or wanting com- fort, it comes to realise that the mother is a separate, independent being. This process of differentiation – of realising that the world is composed of many people, each with their own needs – begins the hard road to maturity.

But the longing to re-establish total union never quite goes away. We all share a desire to recover the lost paradise of uterine existence, when we were warmly housed inside the body of another, when there was no differentiation between the loved object and the self, no separation and therefore no possibility of need or loss. In the late 1990s, when she was in her eighties, Martin began a series of paintings that celebrate this primitive, devoted state. *Little Children Loving Love. An Infant's Response to Love. A Little Girl's Response to Love. I Love Love, Loving Love, Lovely Life.* They were nearly all formed of horizontal stripes in what Terry Castle once tartly called Sippee Cup colours, the watery pinks, yellows and blues with which the infant realm is furnished.

To leave this paradise for the object world, the world of other people, other bodies, other needs and desires, means experiencing inevitable rejection and lack, but there are abundant compensations. When Sylvester sings 'you make me feel mighty real' (and you might want to take a minute to call him up from the world of the dead that is YouTube to listen to the message again), he is taking an objects relation position. As Klein, Jacobson and their British colleague Donald Winnicott all taught, one of the major rewards of the separation process is the feeling of reality conveyed by being apprehended by another, starting with the smiling face of the mother, the first good object.

That's assuming, of course, that the mother is a good object.

Though Martin was reticent about many elements of her life, she was garrulous in telling the story of her own mother, Margaret, who didn't love her and who she believed wanted to destroy her. She remembered being kept locked out of the house all day, playing alone in the dirt, telling an interviewer for the *New Yorker*:

> My mother didn't like children, and she hated me, god how she hated me. She couldn't bear to look at me or speak to me – she never spoke to me . . . When I was two, I was locked up in the back porch, and when I was three, I would play in the backyard. When I came to the door, my sister would say, 'you can't come in.'

In the same interview in which she described a world without objects, Martin also talked about how she wanted the viewer to be able to enter her paintings. 'Nature', she said, 'is like parting a curtain. You go into it. I want to draw a certain response like this . . . that quality of response from people when they leave themselves behind.' There are so many ways to read her work, but one of them is surely as a permanent opening of that closed door. All of her canvases stand ajar. Anyone can pass in. Anyone can experience what it feels like to let go of the things they carry, to be incorporated, just for a moment, into a world of love.

★

Martin found a way of keeping herself afloat, but not everyone is so lucky or determined. In Jacobson's experience a retreat from the object world suggested two things: substantial damage or neglect in the earliest stages of infancy, or a traumatic experience that plunged the psyche back to its most primitive phase. She also thought that if supported by constitutional factors – what we would now call genetic predisposition – this neglect could predispose a child to psychosis. 'Reality may be denied, and magic, infantile convictions sustained forever.'

The extent to which these forces can capsize a life was not quite evident to me until the first autumn of the Trump administration, when I went to Washington to look at Reich's papers, a cache of which were housed at the National Library of Medicine. They'd been assembled by his last girlfriend, Aurora Karrer. She met Reich in 1954, just after Ilse left him, and always described herself as his wife, though they were never actually married.

It was strange being in Washington. The library was part of a compound of buildings belonging to the National Institute of Health. There was hardly anyone around, and in my hotel I read newspaper stories about gutted government departments, the deserted offices filled with empty desks. The network was humming with paranoia. It was the aftermath of Hurricane Maria, and Trump was on Twitter giving favourable reports on his own progress. At 5:25am he'd tweeted: 'A great day in Puerto Rico yesterday. While some of the news coverage is Fake, most showed great warmth and friendship.' An hour and four minutes later, he'd added: 'Wow, so many Fake News stories today. No matter what I do or say, they will not write or speak truth. The Fake News Media is out of control!'

The library too was almost empty. By the door a screen was

playing a black-and-white film loop of a man being dragged away by two policemen. I sat alone in the panelled reading room and worked my way through the Karrer archive. Though the folders were neatly catalogued – *Correspondence, Notes & Miscellany, Litigation* – the impression was of startling confusion. Many of the papers, which included legal documents, newspaper articles and letters from Reich's family, had been annotated by Karrer in looping red biro. 'Wilhelm Reich was living in a dream world', she'd scribbled in huge letters on a report entitled 'The Jailing of A Great Scientist in the USA'. It wasn't clear to whom these notes were addressed, but because she signed them all with her full name, Aurora Karrer Reich, it gave the uncanny impression that it was the reader who was being petitioned in what increasingly seemed like a battle over sanity.

What Karrer was keen to convey was Reich's mental state during his final years, the unravelling period in which she was involved with him. 'In 1956 WR believed himself a spaceman', a typical entry ran. 'WR had massive delusions of grandeur. People believed him because their own lives were empty.' Interspersed among these pages were transcriptions of the messages he'd apparently concealed all over his property at Orgonon, anticipating an invader of some kind. A note inside a locked steel cabinet in the treatment room read: 'You, are you not deeply ashamed of your own rotten nature. You cannot reach my realms.' Another, on the door to one of the cabins, warned: 'Watch out. Want to make it kind of look like suicide? Don't you, LM? By Proxy!!' The last line was underlined three times.

He wasn't just being paranoid. That year, 1956, one of his

associates was caught breaking the terms of the injunction by an FDA inspector posing as a customer. On 7 May, Reich was found guilty of contempt of court, fined $10,000 and sentenced to two years' imprisonment. On 5 June, a US marshal and two FDA inspectors appeared at Orgonon, dressed in dark suits. They ordered Reich to destroy all his accumulators, as demanded by the injunction, and he in turn told the twelve-year-old Peeps and their caretaker Tom Ross to do the job. They took the accumulators apart, screw by screw, and then they carried them to a triangle of land beneath the observatory, where they smashed them up with axes. It took a long time. 'The pile', Peter wrote in his heart-breaking memoir, *A Book of Dreams*, 'was crumpled and broken, and steel wool was hanging out of the panels, all frothy and grey.'

The net was closing in. A few weeks later, the FDA returned to Orgonon to oversee the burning of two hundred and fifty-one of Reich's books. Reich watched the bonfire being assembled but refused to help, telling one of the inspectors that his books had been burned by the Nazis, and that he did not think it would happen in America. The bonfire was the prelude to a still larger conflagration. At the end of August, FDA inspectors went to New York to supervise the destruction of all the stock still held by the Orgone Institute Press in Greenwich Village, along with many of Reich's own papers. Six tons of books and printed matter were loaded into a truck and driven to the Gansevoort Street incinerator on the edge of the Hudson River, close to where the Whitney is now. Several of the works being burned were outside the terms set by the injunction, including *The Mass Psychology of Fascism*. Though plenty of books have been banned, before and since, it remains the only nationally-sanctioned book burning in American history. Until 1960, the FDA was still engaged in hunting down and burning copies of Reich's dangerous books.

Reich's response to these shattering events was to sever himself still further from the world. According to Karrer's papers, that summer he degenerated into a drunken bully, who hit his favourite dog Troll with an iron bar, breaking his hind leg, and then blamed it on a mysterious invader, perhaps from space. Tuesday 14 August 1956: 'Willie violent and threatening. Said he felt the need to kill someone – might as well be me. He had been drinking heavily. Didn't remember his threats and violent flailing around the next morning when sober.' Later on the same page: 'What gets passed off as the effects of Oranur [a negative version of orgone energy, which Reich claimed to have discovered in the early 1950s] is really violent temper outbursts by Wilhelm Reich!' A letter, perhaps undelivered, from October 1956 added: 'I do not plan to sit calmly and be hit, slapped or beaten by you under the influence of alcohol.'

I read my way through these pages in horror, not just because of what they revealed about Reich but because it seemed that Karrer too had become increasingly delusional in the years after his death. In one of the folders, I found a pile of newspaper articles she'd cut out and kept, many of them dating from 1984. Two of the pages had features on Reich, but the others didn't mention him at all. I flicked through them, puzzled. There was a horoscope, a TV preview in the *Washington Post* of *Aurora*, an NBC movie starring Sophia Loren, and an article in *USA Today* about an Aurora Dye Laser that was

designed to kill cancer cells. On each page, Karrer had underlined the word *Aurora*, as if mysterious messages were being sent
to her by way of the medium of her own name.

To be paranoid is to be certain of conspiracy, to know that
one is caught in a giant net of connections, extending out in
all directions. Nothing and no one can be trusted. The threat
might come from anywhere, at any moment of the night or
day, and so the paranoid person must remain vigilant, poised to
renounce and retreat. This retreat can occur physically, like
Reich's move to Orgonon or Arizona, or it can mean a descent
into fantasy, like his belief in alien invaders. Even more dam-
agingly, it can mean the severing of emotional relationships, as
Reich did with almost all his friends and colleagues in the
1950s, cutting himself off not just from affection and love but
also from the anchoring to reality that other people provide.

It was evident from the notes Reich hid around Orgonon
that he'd long since lost faith in the world around him, experiencing it as a place of attacks and hidden dangers, in which
he was right and everyone who disagreed with him was not just
wrong but wicked and rotten. To be the partner of someone in
this state of mind is to be permanently at risk of physical harm,
since dissent and even ambiguity can no longer be tolerated.
One is either good or bad, angel or betrayer.

Karrer was not the only person to see this side of Reich.
His second wife Ilse Ollendorff left him in 1954 after he
became violent and possessive, drinking heavily and once hit-
ting her so hard that he perforated her eardrum. He accused
her of conducting secretive and sordid affairs, which she denied
('Absolutely NOT true,' she told Christopher Turner shortly

before her death). Reich forced her to write out confessions, and locked these documents in the official Orgone Institute archive alongside his own reports on her sexual behaviour and denouncements he'd bullied his followers into composing. It was as if he was re-enacting the dynamics of the investigation against him, but this time in the role of perpetrator, not victim. The champion of women's sexual liberty had become a prurient, vindictive spy, the McCarthy of his own domestic realm.

But this wasn't the only dynamic he was re-enacting. He was also playing out his father's hated role. In her biography of Reich, published in 1969, Ilse observed that he'd never come to terms with the tangled circumstances of his mother's death. It was he who'd told his father about the affair, albeit under coercion, and for the rest of his life he felt responsible for the year of violence that followed, not to mention his mother's increasingly grisly suicide attempts. Even in his thirties, he still woke abruptly from the nightmare that he'd killed her. He went into analysis three times before leaving Europe, but he was never able to deal with her death. It was too painful. Each time the subject arose, he shied away or terminated the analysis. Ilse thought his guilt added something obsessive and relentless to his personality, a need to be right at all costs. Difficult as it was to admit, she suspected that in the 1950s her husband had begun to lose contact with reality, and though he kept hauling himself back, 'the continued pressure forced him to seek escape into the outer regions, into a more benevolent world.'

It was all so unutterably depressing. As a young man, Reich had seen how a net of social forces and past traumas shapes and affects every individual's behaviour, and yet he seemed incapable of grasping what was happening to him now. He had been so brave, so stalwart in those early years, so concerned to change the conditions that affect the most vulnerable among us. Had he lost his mind under the accumulated burden of loss and grief and guilt, or was it just that men, even the most progressive, cannot unlearn the cultural lesson that a woman's body is always a suitable receptacle for bad feelings? 'Not', as Andrea Dworkin once said, 'because biologically they are men but because this is how their social power is organized.'

Reich was among the people who taught her that, but just because he knew how power functioned didn't mean he was immune to its effects. The biggest mistake he made was to think you can isolate yourself from the outside world. You can't. Our past stays with us, embedded in our bodies, and we live whether we like it or not in the object world, sharing the resources of reality with billions of other beings. There is no steel-lined box that can protect you from the grid of forces that limits in tangible, tormenting ways what each private body is allowed to be or do. There is no escape, no possible place to hide. Either you submit to the world or you change the world. It was Reich who taught me that.

# 6

# Cells

In 1976, the singer Kate Bush was browsing the shelves in an occult bookshop when she came across a copy of Peter Reich's memoir, *A Book of Dreams*, published two years earlier. She was so captivated by the story of his strange childhood that it inspired 'Cloudbusting': an anthemic admixture of hope and loss, its weird, spacy optimism cut through with thick currents of grief and unease. 'I still dream of Orgonon,' it begins. 'I wake up crying.'

In the 1980s video, she took the part of Peter herself, dressed in dungarees and a ragamuffin wig. She wanted Donald Sutherland to play Reich, calling unannounced at his London hotel to persuade him into the role. He agreed as soon as he realised what 'Cloudbusting' was about. He was obsessed with Reich. He'd just finished filming *Novecento*, Bertolucci's epic history of the twentieth-century Italian struggle between communism and fascism, in which he'd played the brutal fascist foreman Attila Mellanchini, who rapes a boy and then beats his brains out against a wall. He'd used *The Mass Psychology of Fascism* as a guide to his character, much to Bertolucci's irritation.

'Cloudbusting' was filmed on Dragon Hill in Oxford, not Maine. They couldn't find a real cloudbuster, so they commissioned a model from the designers who'd worked on *Alien*, which looks like a vast steam-punk trombone. Bush and Sutherland haul and shove this absurd contraption to the summit, pointing it at the clear blue sky, which starts to fill with streaming clouds. Then Bush spots a black car, just as Peter did at Orgonon all those years before. It's the men from the government, come to take her beloved father into custody. Stabbing strings. Her voice drops to a growl, splits into multiple yelping Kates. There are deep chanting voices, then children's laughter, libidinal joy pitted against oppression and threat. The men arrive, in their shiny black shoes, to arrest Sutherland, who's kitted out as a rumpled, tweedy scientist (Reich actually preferred plaid shirts). They root through his files, smash test tubes, force him into the car. Racing back up the hill, Bush grabs the cloudbuster controls. As Sutherland looks back through the rear windscreen, an ecstatic rain sluices from the sky.

'Cloudbusting' is a lightly fictionalised version of Reich's life, but the entire album, *Hounds of Love*, has a compelling Reichian atmosphere. All the songs seem to struggle over the same dynamic, fretting ambivalently back and forth between repression and surrender, pleasure and withdrawal. My favourite is the hypnotic, unearthly title song, in which love is conveyed as a terrifying force. The protagonist struggles to escape, begging for help, before hurling herself down with that amazing, rejoicing line about taking her shoes off and *thrrrrrr-rowing* them in the lake. In the video, which riffs on Hitchcock's *The 39 Steps*, the lover is once again stalked by government agents, as if desire itself is an anarchic, dangerous force. Bush ends up handcuffed to him, desperate to escape, longing to submit, caught up in competing waves of fear, desire and shame. Pleasure and love aren't just alluring possibilities, but annihilating states, places you can reach but perhaps can't come back from.

I love those songs. They seem to clarify something about why Reich's work was so endlessly controversial, long before he built the orgone box. His vision is frightening. Pleasure is frightening, and so too is freedom. It involves a kind of openness and unboundedness that's deeply threatening, both to the individual and to the society they inhabit. Freedom invokes a counter-wish to clamp down, to tense up, to forbid, even to destroy. Understanding this pervasive dynamic helps to explain why Reich, who longed to help people unlock the prison of their body, ended up locked in a prison cell himself.

On 20 March 1957, he was sent to the Federal Correction Institution in Danbury, Connecticut (the basis for the prison in *Orange is the New Black*). Two days later, he was moved to Lewisburg Penitentiary in Pennsylvania to serve his two-year sentence. In the social worker's report conducted during processing, he was described as a '60-year-old divorced white offender, does not embrace any religion nor is he a member of any church.' Perhaps because of his mental state or some lingering suspicion around his communist past, he was assigned a private cell. For the last six months of his life, he lived alone in a space not all that much bigger than the orgone box itself.

He told Peter, who was away at boarding school, that he cried often. Crying was a way for the body to release feeling.

The great softener, he called it. He'd suffered from psoriasis since boyhood, and after his imprisonment it flared up, as it often did in times of stress, leaving him covered in painful red sores. He asked for Vaseline to soothe it, and for permission to bathe several times a week. He made no friends. The other prisoners watched him shuffling along the corridors or standing alone in the yard and exchanged gossip about him: the sex box man, who must be onto something, judging by the attractiveness of his much younger girlfriend.

Aurora applied to visit as soon as Reich was taken away, but she had to wait the standard thirty days before she received written permission. The warden's letter was accompanied by a page of rules, setting out the terms by which her relationship with Reich would henceforth be controlled. I'd read them in the library in Washington, claustrophobia mounting in my own body. Visits were limited to three hours a month. There was no bus service between Lewisburg town and the prison. No packages, gifts, or written messages could be exchanged. When the session was concluded, all visitors must immediately leave the grounds.

Peter was also given permission to visit, and in *A Book of Dreams* he describes what Lewisburg was like back then, from the perspective of a child. You entered through two sets of locked doors, so that wherever you looked, you looked through bars. The entrance hall had display cabinets full of the cheap combs and wallets the prisoners made and sold for pocket change. In the visiting room, Reich sat on a plastic chair and Peeps sat opposite on a red and green couch. There was a table between them, and guards stood watching around the walls

(Malcolm X, incarcerated a decade before Reich, remembered dozens of prisoners telling him that their first act of freedom would be to waylay these guards, who policed the tattered remnants of their outside lives). Reich was wearing a blue denim uniform and his face looked sad. He asked Peter about school. At the end of the visit they were allowed to hug on a black rubber mat: 'a runway for hugging'. Then he was led back to his cell.

That was the last time Peter ever saw his father. In October there was a flu outbreak at his school, and he was sent home to Ilsa's house in Sheffield, Massachusetts. On 3 November, the phone rang. When he heard his mother crying, 'Oh my God, oh my God!' he knew at once what had happened. Reich had been found dead on his bed, fully dressed. 'His heart had stopped', Peter wrote. 'I wanted to know if it made him wake up or if it just happened.' They played 'Ave Maria' at the funeral and afterwards poor Peeps lay on the floor in his father's study and whispered into the carpet a child's prayer: 'Come back, come back.'

★

The saddest element of Reich's life is surely that he died alone in a prison cell. But the fact that his lifelong struggle for freedom culminated in imprisonment is hardly a tragedy confined to him. Anyone who attempts to enlarge the freedoms of the body has to reckon with the institution of the prison, one of the state's most formidable weapons for limiting and curtailing emancipation movements of all kinds, and itself the focus of centuries of activism and reform.

To say that Reich was in Lewisburg because he'd broken an injunction explains the reason for his confinement but not its aim, a much more complex and contested issue. Should prison serve as a painful punishment or a deterrent, as a container to seclude dangerous individuals from society at large or as a space in which wrongdoers can be rehabilitated? And does it have a relationship with freedom, apart from to take it away? Is there any truth in the pervasive belief that confinement can serve, like Reich's paradoxical box, as a space of transformation, or does the institution of the prison only compact the forces of oppression that already make so many bodies into prisons in themselves?

The odd thing about prison is that, as Foucault famously observed, it is already the result of a substantial reform in how nations discipline and punish their citizens. Prior to the eighteenth century, imprisonment was not considered a punishment in its own right. The gaol was simply a holding bay, generally crowded and unpleasant but only a precursor to true retribution, which was often corporal, enacted on the body. (*Discipline and Punish* opens with a grisly twelve paragraphs detailing the sort of physical horrors this might entail; further stomach-churning examples drive Hilary Mantel's Thomas Cromwell trilogy.) It wasn't until the Enlightenment, when the rights of the individual were first articulated, that prison could be understood as a viable punishment in and of itself. As soon as liberty is regarded as a human right, it becomes a possession that can be confiscated or rescinded. It's the same basic dynamic of Sade's libertine novels, which were written in this moment of seismic change.

In the 1770s, as Sade himself was repeatedly incarcerated in French prisons, the British prison reformer John Howard visited hundreds of correction houses, mad houses, debtors' prisons and gaols across Europe. He was appalled by the conditions of the British prisons in comparison to their counterparts abroad. Fees governed every aspect of life, and abuse and extortion were endemic. Men and women mixed freely, rich prisoners could purchase food and alcohol, while the poor were tortured and starved, often to death. In 1777, he published *The State of the Prisons*, an account that brought about a major shift not only in how prisons were designed and maintained, but also in what they were configured to achieve.

Howard thought the purpose of prison should be repentance and rehabilitation, not punishment, and he was concerned that the crowded, debauched conditions served as a breeding ground for vice. His advocacy, along with campaigners like Jeremy Bentham and Elizabeth Fry, helped to transform and restructure the corrupt, chaotic, disease-ridden edifice of the past into the highly organised, rational, surveilled space of modernity. Over the next seventy years, nearly every prison in England was torn down and rebuilt.

One of the fundamental features of Howard's vision was that inmates should not be held together but kept in individual cells. These days we think of solitary confinement as the ultimate punishment, but Howard was a Quaker and his insistence on solitude arose from a belief in the necessity of direct, unmediated contact with God. He imagined the prisoners in their cells like monks in a monastery, silence and seclusion driving the work of moral renewal. He thought work too was a route to liberty, giving people a future outside of crime. One of the many ways of reading Sade's novels is as a satire of these supposedly liberatory Enlightenment ideas, exposing the modern prison as an authoritarian system for generating docile bodies: a disciplined, biddable new workforce servicing capital without choice or recompense.

The systems of imprisonment that arose in the nineteenth century preserved the rigours of Howard's vision but dispensed with the uplifting ideals. In the Pennsylvania or separate system, formally inaugurated at Eastern State Penitentiary in 1829 and quickly taken up in Britain too, the prisoner was kept in total isolation, labouring and living alone. When Oscar Wilde was sentenced to hard labour for gross indecency in 1895, all three of the gaols in which he served his time – Pentonville, Wandsworth and Reading – were designed and run on the separate system. In his letters to the *Daily Chronicle* and in his poems, Wilde testified to an existence of unrefined misery.

Each man was kept in a tiny cell with a hard plank bed and no plumbing. The air stank of sewage, and the food was likewise rancid, a near-starvation diet that in Wilde's case induced life-threatening diarrhoea. Days were spent on pointless, painful, repetitive activity. For the first month he was tied to a treadmill for six hours a day, with five minutes' rest after each twenty-minute uphill slog. After that he picked oakum, unravelling strands of old tarred rope until his unaccustomed hands split and bled. When he exchanged a few consoling words with a fellow prisoner in the exercise yard, he was punished with three days on bread and water. Stripped of all contact, it wasn't surprising that people's sanity began to erode. The main reason the separate system fell out of use was because under its uncompromising rule, prisoners lost their minds.

The alternative was not much better. Founded in 1818 in Auburn Prison in New York State, the silent system established a mode of confinement that would become endemic across America and Europe right up to the present day, including the wearing of uniforms and the architectural innovation of double lines of cells off a main corridor, so that inmates couldn't see their fellows. Convicts lived in solitary and spent the entirety of their time in silence, as Howard had enjoined, but worked 'in congregate', making products for the prison to sell for profit; not as a form of rehabilitation, as Howard had hoped, but explicitly as punishment. They were watched constantly, living under what one approving contemporary commentator described as 'unceasing vigilance' – humiliated bodies in grey striped uniforms, marching in lockstep, eyes averted, under constant threat of the whip.

In 1825, a female prisoner in solitary confinement at Auburn became pregnant and was subsequently flogged to death by a male guard, prompting a public scandal. The grand jury trial that followed made whipping for female prisoners illegal and paved the way for housing incarcerated women separately from men, as Howard had enjoined. But the problem with arguing against the morality of punishment, overcrowding or squalid conditions was that many people didn't think prisoners deserved the rights of human beings. By the early twentieth century, reformers were trying a different tack. Just as the sexual liberationists of the 1920s used eugenic arguments to make their case palatable to conservatives, so the prison reformers began to focus on the failures of punishment in terms of recidivism rates. What if rather than brutalising criminals, they could be converted into upstanding, fiscally useful citizens? Perhaps education was the royal road to ending crime.

The institution in which Reich served his time was the embodiment of this new reform movement. Built in 1932, Lewisburg was the most modern and influential prison of its day, and the standard in American design for the next forty years. It was set high above the Susquehanna river, its cloisters and tree-lined courtyards giving it the impervious, slightly sinister appearance of a de Chirico painting. A monastery, you might think, or a small, exclusive college. Shortly after it opened, the Bureau of Prisons issued a booklet celebrating Lewisburg as the epitome of its changed vision of incarceration, observing that 'in prison, all work and no play leads to brooding, plotting, perversions and riots. Deprived of recreation even the normal individual becomes morose and irritable, his nerves dangerously on edge.'

The lavish facilities, unthinkable in today's stark carceral landscape, included a theatre, a baseball diamond, ten classrooms and a library. Because of his heart condition, Reich was assigned to work in here, borrowing Emerson's essays and Sandburg's four-volume biography of Lincoln to pore over later in his cell. If he'd happened to glance up, he would have seen a ceiling decorated with stucco reliefs of open books, meant to symbolise the liberatory power of education, though not perhaps to a man whose life's work had just gone up in flames.

The progressive prison was designed to change lives and there's no greater testament to its possibilities than *The*

*Autobiography of Malcolm X*, though the transformations it charts were not quite those envisaged by the Bureau of Prisons. In 1946, a young hustler and pimp called Malcolm Little was sentenced to ten years in Charlestown State Prison in Boston for fourteen counts of crime, including larceny and breaking and entering. Not quite twenty-one, not even shaving yet, self-declaredly so evil-tempered and aggressive that his nickname inside was 'Satan', he might have spent the entirety of his sentence getting high on nutmeg and smuggled Nembutal, cursing guards and starting fights if it hadn't been for Bimbi, an old-time burglar, tall as Malcolm, who refused to kowtow to anyone and whose alluring self-possession was plainly the fruit of education.

Although he was clearly bright, Malcolm had dropped out of high school in eighth grade, the legacy of a childhood annihilated by racism. His father, the Reverend Earl Little, had been an organiser for Marcus Garvey's Universal Negro Improvement Association, and was a target for Ku Klux Klan attacks. When Malcolm's mother Louise was pregnant with him in Nebraska, Klansmen on horseback had come to the house with flaming torches to drive the family out of town, smashing all the window panes with rifle butts ('His welcome to white America', the civil rights activist Bayard Rustin observed drily in his review of *The Autobiography* for the *New York Herald Tribune*). The Littles' next home in Lansing, Michigan was torched. Malcolm's earliest memory was of waking to pistol shots and the smell of smoke. The family managed to escape just before the structure collapsed, only to discover white police and firemen were standing by, looking idly on as it burned to the ground.

In 1931, when Malcolm was six, his father was killed in what was almost certainly a lynching, his skull staved in and his body dragged to the streetcar tracks, where it was cut nearly in two. Five of Reverend Little's six brothers had also been killed by white men. Louise was left alone with eight children to feed. Her husband had life insurance, but the company refused to pay out, insisting he had killed himself. There was little money, and Louise became entangled in a long-running battle with the welfare service, who wanted to put her children into foster care. She refused to accept charity, and they began to call her crazy when she turned down a gift of pork, though it was prohibited by her religion as a Seventh Day Adventist. After she fell in love things became more stable, until the man in question jilted her and her sanity unravelled.

She talked to herself and stopped cooking or cleaning. 'Our anchor giving way' was how Malcolm described it as an adult, during a long night of pacing back and forth, remembering all the buried details of Louise Little's unhappy life for his book. In the end she had a breakdown and was committed against her children's will to the state mental institution in Kalamazoo, Michigan, seventy miles from the family home, where she would remain for the next twenty-six years. After she was taken away, the Littles were made wards of court and scattered among foster homes by a local judge. 'A white man in charge of a black man's children! Nothing but legal, modern slavery – however kindly intentioned.'

In the wake of this shattering, Malcolm was expelled from school and sent to a detention home in Mason, twelve miles from Lansing. He was so helpful there and so obviously intelligent that he was allowed to attend Mason Junior High rather than going to reform school with all the other detention home kids. He was one of only two or three non-white students, and though he was top of his year and the class president, he always understood that he was a mascot, 'like a pink poodle'. The cheery, relentless racism wore away at him and when a favourite English teacher balked at his idea of becoming a lawyer and told him he should find a more realistic goal – a carpenter, perhaps – he left school for good, moving to Boston and drifting into a 'groovy, frantic' life of small-time crime.

In prison, he had time to realise what had been sacrificed. With Bimbi's encouragement, he took correspondence courses in English and then in Latin, recovering the basic knowledge that had grown fogged and foxed during his years on the streets. Several of his siblings had become involved with the separatist Nation of Islam, and they introduced him by way of letters to the electrifying ideas of its leader, Mr Elijah Muhammed, who preached that the white man was the devil and the black man had been brainwashed to forget his true history. Later, Malcolm would become disenchanted with Mr Muhammed, but at that moment his teaching represented the salvation of mind and soul alike.

In 1948, his sister Ella managed to secure his transfer to the progressive, experimental, rehabilitative Norfolk Prison Colony, thirty miles south of Charlestown. Built five years before Lewisburg, Norfolk likewise possessed an extraordinary library, which had been the personal collection of a local white millionaire, Lewis Parkhurst, who had a special interest in history

and religion and who had collected an abundance of abolitionist and anti-slavery materials. It was in this room that Malcolm
X became a reader, driven by his frustration at being unable to
convey and discuss Mr Muhammed's astounding teachings with
the limited street slang he possessed. He gained a vocabulary by
the simple expedient of copying out the dictionary in its
entirety, though at first he was so unaccustomed to writing that
he could barely scrawl the letters. A page each day, each new
word unlocking another portion of the world, until he had two
hundred thousand of them and for the first time felt truly
emancipated by knowledge. Now the books he borrowed made
sense. He no longer needed to skim or skip or guess. He read
constantly, insatiably. Will Durrant's *Story of Civilization*, H. G.
Wells's *Outline of History*, Gregor Mendel's *Findings in Genetics*,
W. E. B. Du Bois's *Souls of Black Folk*, Fanny Kemble's *Journal
of a Residence on a Georgia Plantation*. Kant, Schopenhauer,
Nietzsche.

The prison placed so much faith in the rehabilitative power
of reading that any prisoner who showed an interest was
encouraged to borrow extra books. Day after day, Malcolm X
lay on his bunk, reading his way through the past. He read
about slavery ('I never will forget how shocked I was when I
began reading about slavery's total horror'), Nat Turner's revolt,
Herodotus, the Opium Wars, the British in India, Mahatma
Gandhi. Was the white man a devil? The history of the world
attested: yes. After lights out at 10pm, he would sit on the floor
by the cell door, using the glow from the corridor to carry on
through the night in fifty-eight-minute increments, jumping
into bed as the guards made their hourly patrol. He was so

absorbed that he never once thought about his sentence. 'Months passed without my even thinking about being imprisoned', he wrote two decades later. 'In fact, up to then, I never had been so truly free in my life.'

What had set him free was knowledge. Each book he read revealed another aspect of the entrenched, occluded history of racism. His entire life had to be reconsidered in this stark new light. What had once seemed like tragedies or missteps, from the loss of his parents to his own presence in a cell, were emerging as consequences of the global, trans-historical system of white supremacy, the grotesque, forced dominance of one kind of body over another. It was the same type of revelation that Andrea Dworkin had when she read *Sexual Politics* for the first time. Confined to a cell, Malcolm was able to see that he had been in prison since he was born, and to consider the possibilities of fighting back.

A revolutionary analysis of racism was not the kind of rehabilitation the Norfolk Prison authorities had in mind, and Malcolm was returned to Charlestown for the final year of his sentence. The diminishment of privileges didn't bother him. He spent the time passing on the knowledge he'd acquired to every black prisoner he thought might be capable of receiving Mr Muhammed's ideas. Already he'd made the transition from student to teacher that would become so emblematic of civil rights organising in the decades ahead.

★

Prison was where Malcolm X became free, but that didn't mean he approved of it as an institution. On the contrary,

Any person who claims to have deep feeling for other human beings should think a long, long time before he votes to have other men kept behind bars – caged. I am not saying there shouldn't be prisons, but there shouldn't be bars. Behind bars, a man never reforms. He will never forget. He never will get completely over the memory of the bars.

What do those bars actually do, in the memory or the mind? What is the effect of prison, not on recidivism rates, but on the person held in a cage? While Malcolm X was reading his way through the library at Norfolk Prison Colony, an essay was published by Reich's old friend and colleague, Edith Jacobson. It's one of the first attempts by a psychoanalyst to discover what the psychological effects of incarceration were on the prisoner – certainly the first to be written by an analyst who had herself been in prison.

Jacobson was part of Reich's inner circle in Berlin in the 1930s, and was particularly close to his wife Annie. Before she arrived in the city she'd hardly given politics a thought, but at the Berlin Psychoanalytic Institute she encountered the *Kinder*, the second-generation analysts who'd become politicised while treating working-class patients. She joined Sex-Pol and was part of the splinter group that met at Reich's apartment on Schwäbische Strasse to discuss the future of psychoanalysis in the face of fascism. They even spent weekends at the beach together.

After the Aryanisation of the Berlin Psychoanalytic Institute, most of the Jewish analysts, Reich included, went into exile.

Jacobson was the only one to stay on in Berlin, at least in part because her parents refused to see the danger ahead (they hadn't read *Mein Kampf*, she later said grimly). With Reich in Denmark and the rest of the *Kinder* scattered, she joined the socialist resistance group Neu Beginnen, which met in private houses and apartments to share foreign news, raise funds for political prisoners and smuggle people and money across borders. Her alias was John and one of her activities was hosting group meetings in her own home, an illegal act under the new Nazi government.

On 24 October 1935, Jacobson was rounded up by the Gestapo, along with several other members of Neu Beginnen. Dozens more were arrested the following month. In her booking photograph, Jacobson looks ill and resolute, her hair untidy, her clothes mussed, black smudges that could be bruises ringing her dark eyes. Her colleagues were frantic, and in letters that crisscrossed Europe they discussed the possibility that she was being tortured, though it was also understood that she was lucky not to be in Dachau, where people were already being systematically murdered.

She was held for almost a year while the Gestapo prepared their case. During this period she kept a diary, recording her feelings of loneliness and terror. She was tormented by guilt over her mother and fear of the judgment ahead. 'Who will still be there, when I eventually come out, who will still exist to love me', she asked herself. 'Who will have forgotten me?' She missed her dachshund, and in solitary confinement spent her days training a fly with sugar water to come to her finger, a sad remnant of the object world she'd lost.

One of the reasons for her arrest was that she'd been treating a fellow activist, Liesel Paxmann, a student of the philosopher Adorno who'd served as a courier for the group and who was murdered or committed suicide after being arrested on the border. Despite repeated interrogations, Jacobson refused to break confidentiality and give up information on her patient's political work. On 8 September 1936 she was sentenced to two years and three months' imprisonment for 'preparation for high treason'. Her other crimes included giving a sum of five marks a month towards food and clothing for political prisoners and treating patients who opposed the Nazis, an act that was both illegal and expressly forbidden by the newly Aryanised German Psychoanalytic Society.

In the wake of Jacobson's imprisonment, the Vienna Psychoanalytic Society went even further in its attempts to ensure the survival of psychoanalysis under the Nazis, ruling that no member could engage in illegal political activity, which included any act of anti-fascist resistance. Anna Freud in particular was furious that Jacobson 'had put the analytic movement in danger', and her expulsion was discussed, another example of the appeasement policy that had brought about Reich's ejection the previous year.

In the Berlin-Moabit remand prison and later in Jawor prison in Silesia, Jacobson was able to observe the effects of imprisonment on around a hundred women. By a heroic act of will, she wrote a paper that she smuggled out to a friend, who read it at the annual International Psychoanalytic Association Congress in Marienbad in 1936 (Reich was in the audience). The next year she became seriously ill with Grave's disease and diabetes, and was moved to a hospital in Leipzig, from which she managed to escape in 1938. She made her way to America with the help of Annie Reich's new husband, and in New York City established herself all over again as a psychoanalyst. In her new apartment on West 96th Street she rewrote her prison essay, the first draft of which had been made without access to any books. 'Observations on the Psychological Effect of Imprisonment on Female Political Prisoners' was finally published in 1949.

Plenty of people had examined the psychology of the criminal, right back to Cesare Lombroso and his theories of degenerate throwbacks, but what Jacobson was trying to do was more radical. She wanted to turn the equation on its head, looking not at the psychology of the person in prison, but the psychological effect of the prison on the person. It was only by doing this, she argued, that one could properly assess whether incarceration could achieve any of its supposed effects. She wanted to know what happened to ordinary humans when they were subject to the bodily conditions of incarceration. The fact that the observer had also been a participant might be an advantage, she thought: 'a rare opportunity to observe first-hand and to watch the psychic reactions to prison confinement more closely than is possible under any other circumstance.'

Her account begins with a description of conditions and personnel. The women were between twenty and sixty years old. Most were the wives or daughters of labourers, artisans and craftsmen. Perhaps ten per cent were the wives or daughters of professional men, and a very few had professions in their own right. Before her trial, the conditions were very poor, with tiny cells, a bad diet, rare opportunities for exercise and constant interrogations, including beatings. The state prison where she served her sentence was a marked improvement. Visitors, lawyers and letters were permitted, the cells were larger, and prisoners had the choice of manual or intellectual work. Most of the women were held collectively, spending their days in workshops and sleeping in overcrowded dorms. Intellectuals might spend a stint in solitary, but only those accused of high treason were in isolation for the entirety of their term. As per the Auburn system, conversation was not permitted, and inmates were expected to work in silence except for half an hour of recreation. Under the Nazis, recreational evenings had been abolished and most people spent the ten-hour work day picking oakum, just as Oscar Wilde had in Reading Gaol forty years before.

The arrest, with its 'sudden violent attack on the narcissistic safeguards of the captive', was followed by a series of shocks and deprivations. The dreadful new surroundings, the restriction of day-to-day activities, the loss of personal belongings like clothes and glasses, the severing of familiar relationships and the isolation or horribly enforced contact had, Jacobson thought, a dramatic effect on the prisoner's psyche, bringing about a catastrophic breach in object relations. Abandoned and utterly helpless, the prisoner underwent an intense regression, the structures that sustain the personality eroded as if by a giant wave.

The signs were everywhere. Prisoners suffered from phobias, panic attacks, anxiety, irritability, insomnia. They forgot names and places. They developed physical symptoms as a consequence of what we would now call traumatic stress: racing hearts, clammy hands, urticaria, thyrotoxicosis, amenorrhea. Many, Jacobson included, were racked with guilt over their friends and relations, though prisoners from families with a tradition of political activity were far better protected against the travails of their situation.

One of the most distressing symptoms was depersonalisation, and in June 1958 Jacobson presented a second paper exploring it in more depth; one of the first attempts to understand what is now regarded as a defining feature of post-traumatic stress disorder. Prisoner after prisoner complained of feeling as if their body or some part of it – a limb, the genitals, the face, the bladder – was no longer theirs. These 'estranged body parts' might feel bigger than they really were, or tiny, numb, foreign, even dead. People described a sensation of being outside themselves, of watching someone else altogether go through the motions of movement and speech. Under the crushing pressure of the prison, body and psyche had come unhitched.

It wasn't just a consequence of being locked behind bars, trapped in the physical environment of the prison. One of the most important aspects of Jacobson's argument – and one that continues to resonate in a twenty-first century of mass incarceration – is that what happens to prisoners psychologically is the consequence of an interpersonal dynamic. Primed by her own experience, she understands what many commentators cannot: that no matter what system a prison is built on or ethics it claims to uphold, the most important element in creating and sustaining its emotional atmosphere is not the warden, the architect or even the law, but the guards. Uneducated, unprepared, untrained, it is they who decide day-to-day policy, maintain discipline and mete out punishment. They favour or persecute individuals, creating a sadistic framework that makes it very hard for even the most sturdy of inmates to resist regression, with all its dismal, desolating consequences.

The example that Jacobson gives is familiar from prison narratives right through to the present day, resonating particularly sharply with accounts of the treatment of immigrant families in American detention centres under Trump. It concerns what she describes as 'the contradictory educational system of cleanliness and order' in place at Jawor. The guards maintained a strict regime concerning objects associated with the body. Blankets had to be exactly straight, towels folded in a particular way, the tin covers of slop buckets polished until they shone. Any infraction of these rituals was severely punished. But the obsession with neatness did not extend to the bodies of the prisoners, which were equally deliberately kept in a state of filth. Prisoners were only permitted to wash the upper parts of their body, and complete undressing was punished. Showers were weekly and scant, soap was scarce and the entire prison was infested with bedbugs. There was no drainage, and only two toilets for a hundred women. They had no doors and the constant waiting led to chronic problems with constipation, cystitis and diarrhoea, heightened by the impossibility of ever washing properly. It was a system of bodily humiliation and its effect was to estrange the body from itself.

In her landmark work on torture, *The Body in Pain*, Elaine Scarry points out that torture does not necessarily require violence but can be carried out simply by setting the body against itself, making the most ordinary and modest of habits and obligations an occasion for shame, discomfort or pain. In confinement, as in infancy, the body's needs quickly become unbearable if they aren't met. Removing toilet or washing facilities, denying sleep, food or water or requiring prisoners to hold fixed positions are all techniques that rapidly induce intense physical as well as emotional distress, without any need for force.

This was Wilde's experience, too. Sentenced to 'hard labour, hard fare, and a hard bed', Prisoner 4099 was tortured by the basic needs of his own body. He suffered from crippling insomnia because of being forced to sleep on a plank bed without a mattress or pillow. He wasn't capable of digesting the food, which, as he wrote later, 'in a strong grown man is always productive of illness of some kind.' He lost twenty-eight pounds in the first three months of his confinement due to dysentery and malnutrition. Forced to attend chapel while ill with an ear infection, he collapsed and the abscess in his eardrum ruptured. The prison doctor refused to institute even basic hygiene measures and in the end Wilde wrote a petition to the Home Secretary, saying that his ear was running continually with pus and that he had gone almost totally deaf.

★

Confinement, humiliation, pain, brutality, obsessive control over bodily functions, especially eating and shitting: the connection between sadism and the prison is by no means coincidental. The Marquis de Sade spent a total of twenty-six years in prison, sometimes in lavish accommodation but more often in spaces that were no better than dungeons. Like Jacobson, he experienced terror, loneliness and deprivation on a daily basis. Reading his prison letters, it's impossible to ignore the way they writhe with desire for the satisfaction of physical needs, for exercise, food and rest.

Like Wilde he longed for good ventilation, warmth and light. He asked over and over again to be able to walk outdoors for an hour a day ('I have the most urgent need of fresh air'). He requested a fire in winter, candles, a camp bed, sheets and fur-lined slippers. He begged for a 'rump cushion' stuffed with horsehair for his agonising piles, an oversized pillow to prevent his constant nosebleeds, beef-marrow ointment in winter. Most of his requests were not fulfilled, or not fulfilled to his satisfaction.

Some of the things he most ardently desired were sexual, like the hyper-specific glass dildos, eight and a half inches long, that he bullied his humiliated wife into having commissioned. Others were more like the cravings of a greedy child, a cornucopia of Blyton-esque delights. The pleas for chocolate cake, marshmallow syrup, Breton butter, jam testify to a type of regression that Jacobson thought especially common in prisoners held in long-term solitary. The consequences that seem most pertinent to Sade include loss of contact with reality, dangerous daydreams of freedom and a crude, even perverse obsession with sex. As Agnes Martin once said, 'the panic of complete helplessness drives us to fantastic extremes.'

But Jacobson's analysis of the psychological consequences of imprisonment doesn't just help explain the state of Sade's mind. It also provides an optic through which to look again at his novels. In the context of prison, they seem less driven by misogyny than with the problem of the incarcerated body itself. This is especially true of *The 120 Days of Sodom*, which was produced in what must fairly be described as a frenzy over thirty-seven consecutive evenings in the Bastille in the autumn of 1785, between the hours of seven and ten at night. Sade wrote his abysmal fantasy in a minuscule hand on a narrow twelve-metre scroll he'd created by gumming tiny scraps of parchment together, rolling it up and hiding it each night in a crack in his cell wall. In it, he created a mise en abyme, a prison vision of a prison: the locked and sealed castle of Silling, from which no victim will ever escape.

The acts he imagined taking place in the cells and chambers of Silling form an encyclopaedia of bodily terror, by which I don't just mean the abundant bad things that can happen to bodies, but rather the fears that having a body, being trapped in a body, can engender. Sade's novels are about being able to gratify desire, yes, but they're more powerfully animated by a compulsion to punish the body for needing anything at all, for having so many relentless, insufferable demands. To eat, to shit, to breathe: all the functions that are the source of ongoing pain in prison become in his fiction systematically abased and denied. This is at least one path through the Sadeian labyrinth, to read it as a fantasy about being inviolate, untouchable; a fantasy of solipsism and mastery that is itself the product of helplessness and deprivation. It's not just that prison is sadistic; it's that the historical concept of sadism was born in a prison cell, a place of deprivation that served to reveal how the body itself is a kind of prison.

In the conclusion of her essay, Jacobson returns to the question she posed in the first paragraph: does prison work? Bearing in mind its deleterious psychological effects on even the most sane inmates, can it serve any purpose? Ever scrupulous, she admits that there are some rare cases in which it can provide benefit. In an example that recalls Malcolm X, she acknowledges that prison can inspire 'truly constructive development' in particularly strong and intelligent people, if they're given richer resources than were available in childhood. But, she adds, these 'exceptional' cases should not lead to the idea that prison confinement is of psychological benefit for the majority.

For everyone else, prison is an abject failure. The only thing it reinforces, she argues, is delinquent tendencies. The sadistic world in which the prisoner is immersed results in a collapse into infantile behaviour. It doesn't work as a corrective or as a rehabilitative institution, not without a profound shift in the relationships between prisoners and guards, and not without an end to the deprivation of bodily needs for food, light, exercise, hygiene, companionship, sex and free movement. No, Jacobson concludes: 'social and cultural development of criminals cannot be obtained by privations, sadistic measures and senseless hard labour, nor by means of ethical and religious exhortation alone.'

★

Prison can't improve the inmate, but perhaps the inmate can improve the prison. There was even a moment when it was hoped that prison could be used as a lever to change the world. On 3 August 1945, a young conscientious objector was moved to Lewisburg from the maximum-security prison of Ashland Federal Correctional Institution in Kentucky, where he'd been for the past sixteen months. Bayard Rustin was a gay black man of thirty-one who'd been sentenced to three years' imprisonment as a consequence of refusing to fight in the Second World War, or to take up any of the non-combative activities available to pacifists.

Born five days before Agnes Martin, raised, like John Howard, as a Quaker, and inspired by Gandhi, he was fundamentally opposed to violence. As the youth secretary for the pacifist Fellowship of Reconciliation, he'd spent the early years of the war travelling across America, spreading the message of non-violent direct action to thousands of young African-Americans, among them Martin Luther King's future wife, Coretta Scott. In his letter to the draft board, he wrote unambiguously: 'War is wrong . . . Segregation, separation, according to Jesus, is the basis for continuous violence . . . Though joyfully following the law of God, I regret I must break the law of State. I am prepared for whatever might follow.'

Rustin had been fighting Jim Crow laws since his teens. Like Reich, he spent a youthful spell in the Communist Party before becoming disillusioned. He knew that racism turned bodies into prisons, and he wasn't afraid of incarceration if it would help to change the crisis of oppression. In the early 1940s, the mass imprisonment of conscientious objectors had turned prisons like Lewisburg and Danbury into hot zones in the struggle against segregation. As Michael Long, the editor of Rustin's collected letters, observes: 'There is little doubt that Rustin would have seen the federal prison system as the centre

of some of the most exciting work undertaken by radical pacifists in World War II.'

A couple of weeks after he arrived at Ashland, this young
black man demanded a meeting with the white prison warden,
R. P. Hagerman, to discuss the problem of racial injustice in
the prison. He followed it up with an extraordinary letter,
which set out a calm opposition to segregation, followed by a
series of proposals for instigating an educational programme to
end racism in the prison community. Perhaps he could teach it
himself?

Hagerman was stunned. The next day, he wrote a rather less
coherent letter to the director of the Bureau of Prisons, claiming that his 'plausible, smooth and ingratiating' new prisoner
was planning to instigate an uprising and asking that this
'extremely capable agitator' be transferred to Danbury. The
letter was accompanied by a report from a junior officer, who
said Rustin had sung a strange, subversive song through the
prison pipe system, which began by describing 'the lovely natural scenes and the scented air from the flowers of Louisiana',
but culminated 'in a tragedy of a human body with bulging
eyes being hanged and the air filled with the stench of burning
flesh.' He'd evidently never heard 'Strange Fruit' sung by Billie
Holiday before.

Hagerman's feelings about Rustin changed a few weeks
later. He'd been persuaded to experiment with desegregating
cellblock E for a few hours on Sunday afternoons. Rustin was
the only black prisoner to enter the white area, and his presence infuriated a man named Huddleston, who attacked Rustin
with a mop handle. His friends tried to break up the fight, but

Rustin asked them to stand aside and allowed Huddleston to beat him until the stick splintered, at which point Huddleston broke down and collapsed shaking on the floor. Rustin's wrist was broken but his spirits were buoyant. In a letter to a friend a few days later, he was far more excited about the operetta he'd organised than the attack, which, he explained, had strengthened his position with the warden by demonstrating the moral authority of non-violent resistance. Can you find me a second-hand mandolin, he finished by asking. He wanted to learn to play sixteenth-century ballads.

All the time, he kept chipping away. Even the movie theatre was segregated. Fine, he wouldn't watch movies. His letters were censored, or not delivered at all. Very well, he would write more of them and lose his privilege altogether, rather than sink to censoring himself. He wouldn't ask permission for specific books to be sent to him, either. 'I shall not help them rob me', he wrote to his white lover, Davis Platt. 'They are obstructing justice; they stand between the inmate and his basic rights . . . One ought to resist the entire system!'

He was on the brink of succeeding in his campaign to desegregate cellblock E when a devastating incident occurred. An assistant warden told Hagerman that two inmates had seen Rustin engaging in oral sex. A report was filed, and the prison disciplinary board ordered Rustin into solitary confinement. Insisting it was a frame-up, he clung to his chair until three officers managed to drag him away. A few days later the prison psychiatrist assessed him as 'a constitutional homo', adding: 'the high voice, the extravagant mannerisms, the tremendous conceit, the general unmanliness of the inmate frame a picture . . .

that it does not take a Freud to diagnose.' Though the Lavender Scare was not yet underway, signs of gender transgression were already regarded as official markers of sexual deviancy.

It was the beginning of a dynamic that would recur right through Rustin's life. In the pacifist and civil rights movements alike, his homosexuality was regarded as an unexploded bomb, capable of jeopardising or even destroying the campaigns in which he played such an outsized role. Unlike Martin, he had no desire for a life of secrecy or self-confinement, and nor was he interested in monogamy. As his colleague Rachelle Horowitz once observed, 'he never knew there was a closet to go into.' While his colleagues in the Fellowship of Reconciliation wrote him coercive, distressing letters, begging him to curb his objectionable desires, perhaps even marry a woman, he was in the library, reading the history of non-cooperation, strikes, sit-ins and civil disobedience.

'For these are our only weapons', he wrote to a friend. In June 1945, he led a mixed group who refused to eat in the dining room until it was desegregated. 'We are willing to pay a price for freedom', he wrote in an open letter to all inmates. That price was transfer to Lewisburg, where he promptly went on hunger strike to desegregate the dining room there, becoming so emaciated that he was tube-fed in the prison hospital. It wasn't until he was told by Muste about the atomic bomb dropped on Hiroshima on 6 August that he decided to stop resisting and serve his remaining time quietly. 'I am needed on the outside', he explained in a letter to the warden in which he formally resigned from his acts of agitation (Reich too was horrified by the atom bomb, writing furiously in his diary

about the impossibility of such a menacing weapon ever bringing peace, and describing it strangely as a prisoner that kills).

Lewisburg was by no means the last prison Rustin saw.
Almost as soon as he returned to New York, moving into an
apartment with Platt, he began to plan the Journey of
Reconciliation, a precursor to the famous Freedom Rides of
1961. The Journey was an attempt to enforce *Morgan v. Virginia*,
a recent Supreme Court ruling that had declared segregation
on interstate buses unconstitutional. 'Unjust social laws and
patterns do not change because supreme courts deliver just
verdicts', Rustin wrote emphatically in the *Louisiana Weekly*.
'Social progress comes from struggle.'

There's a photograph of some of the team that went into
the South in the spring of 1947, led by Rustin and his white
colleague George Houser. They're smartly dressed in suits,
coats over their arms, cases in their hands. Rustin is at the back,
taller than the rest, looking dandyish and handsome in a bowtie.
They planned to travel for two weeks to Virginia, North
Carolina, Tennessee and Kentucky, in interracial pairs or threes,
the black rider sitting in the white section at the front, and the
white rider sitting in the black Jim Crow section at the back.
If they were arrested, they were instructed to go peacefully to
the police station and there contact the nearest lawyer from the
National Association for the Advancement of Colored People,
which promised to provide legal support for the campaign.

Rustin sang on the buses, and gave impassioned talks each
night in whatever small town the freedom riders found themselves. There were fewer violent incidents than they'd expected
until they reached North Carolina. At Chapel Hill bus station

they were arrested for violating the local Jim Crow law against integrated travel. A lynch mob of white taxi drivers assembled and the riders had to be rescued by a sympathetic local reverend. The taxi drivers followed, throwing rocks through his windows and threatening to burn down his house. None of the mob were arrested, but despite the best efforts of the NAACP lawyer, the charges incurred by the riders could not be overturned.

On 21 March 1949, while Malcolm X was reading the history of slavery in the library at Norfolk Prison and Reich was being pursued by the FDA, Rustin began a twenty-two-day sentence on a chain gang in Roxboro, North Carolina. His harrowing account, published that summer in the *New York Post*, mirrors Jacobson's argument of the same year. The men lived in filth. Each week, they were given a pair of trousers, a shirt, a pair of socks, a single set of undergarments and a towel, which had to last a week of heavy labour in the rain and mud. Everything else – comb, brush, razor, toothbrush, pencil, paper, stamps, cigarettes – they either had to buy, steal or do without. The ten-hour days, punctuated by two fifteen-minute smoking breaks, were physically hard, but often just as pointless as picking oakum or slogging on a treadmill. Rustin's crew spent one day digging holes they knew another road crew would be ordered to fill.

As Jacobson had observed, the prisoners existed in a sadistic environment controlled in every respect by the guards. The chain gang worked under the aggressive scrutiny of a boss and a guard, the latter armed with a revolver and a shotgun. On his first day, Rustin watched the boss punch several convicts in the face. When a prisoner swore at the convict next to him, the boss suggested the guard shoot at the feet of the next offender and cripple him. 'Hell no,' the guard replied. 'I ain't aimin' fer no feet. I like hearts and livers. That's what really learns 'em.' Often the guards got so bored they selected a victim to torment. On several occasions, Rustin watched as the guard trained his rifle on a boy named Oscar's chest, insisting that he dance, and grin as he did it.

Formal punishments were just as unpleasant as they had been back in Wilde's day. For major offences, men were beaten with a leather strap or placed in 'the hole' – solitary confinement in an unlighted cell on a diet of water and three soda crackers a day, from which they emerged pounds lighter but still expected to resume their exacting labours. For minor crimes, prisoners were 'hung up on the bars', which meant being cuffed to the vertical bars of a cell in a standing position for days at a time, with short breaks to use the toilet. The men's feet and wrists would swell, as would their testicles. A horizontal version of this procedure, known as four-pointing, is widespread in American prisons today, particularly in Lewisburg, which has long since abandoned its reformist ideals and is now distinguished by the double-celling of occupants in spaces no larger than the average parking space.

What was the point, Rustin wondered. It was plain no one would be improved or cured by this kind of treatment, but it also left society unprotected, since 'these men and thousands like them return to society not only uncured but with heightened resentment and a desire for revenge.' The prison was plainly an inescapable system for generating free labour, continuing the practices of slavery under the guise of punishment. Many of the men left without a cent and were back within days, arrested for the crime of vagrancy.

Rustin's experiences led him to the same conclusion as Jacobson: that retribution or deterrence was not only inhumane, but pointless too. Violence perpetuated violence, maintaining a cycle of limitless revenge and robbing people of the capacity to behave like human beings. The only principle on which a successful prison could be founded was rehabilitation. What would happen if the men among whom he'd been confined were given meaningful work and education, medical care and proper food, he asked his readers. 'If the law of cause and effect still operates in human relations, the answer seems clear.'

★

But nothing is clear in human relations. We all want many things, and those things do not always correlate or align. While Rustin's account of his experiences on the chain gang did bring about a reform of North Carolina's penal practices, the next time he entered a prison was not as a consequence of his political beliefs, and it did not enlarge his or anyone else's freedom. On 12 January 1953, he was giving a lecture in Pasadena. Later that night he was walking through the city when he encountered two white men in a car, both twenty-three. Perhaps he propositioned them, or some flirtation occurred, but the upshot was that he was found by the police in the car, in the act of giving the passenger oral sex. All three men were arrested on a morals charge and sent to Los Angeles County Jail. It was reported in national newspapers and Rustin was forced to resign from the Fellowship of Reconciliation. Right to the end of his life, he still swore he'd been the victim of entrapment.

If you haven't heard of Bayard Rustin, this arrest is the reason. It served to destroy his reputation, casting a long and inescapable shadow over the remainder of his career. He went on to become one of the great architects of the civil rights movement, but though he made alliances with multiple organisations and ran some of the movement's most significant campaigns, he never held a major leadership role. Because of the prejudice that attached to his sexuality, this brilliant strategist and tactician had to operate beneath the threshold of visibility, subject to ongoing exclusion and erasure even as he sought to liberate other bodies from the prisons they were in.

In 1955 Rustin was invited by activists in Montgomery, Alabama to help engineer a planned boycott against segregation on the city's buses. If the Journey of Reconciliation had established a working method for the civil rights movement, the Montgomery bus boycott ignited it, creating an unstoppable wave of resistance across the nation. While he was in the city, Rustin was introduced to a charismatic young preacher, only twenty-six but with a striking gift for public speaking. Though Martin Luther King Jr. had read Gandhi, he didn't fully understand non-violent direct action. It was Rustin who served as his mentor, introducing him to the principles and practices of pacifism. At the time King still had guns and armed guards in his home, and Rustin encouraged him to dispense with them, explaining that violence could only ever kindle more violence (this belief would form a major point of contention with

Malcolm X and the Nation of Islam, who believed that the state-sanctioned ultra-violence of white supremacy made self-defence essential).

Before he started work with the King family, Rustin laid out his personal history, explaining the circumstances of his arrest and how it made him a potential liability. King, he thought, had never met a gay person before but nor was he willing to dispense with this charismatic source of experience and guidance. During the late 1950s, the two men worked closely together to establish the Southern Christian Leadership Conference, a network of community groups that fought segregation, with King as its first president.

It wasn't until the turn of the decade that their relationship was brought up short. One of the many ways the civil rights movement was undermined was a concerted campaign to discredit its leaders through revealing evidence of sexual infidelities. King, who had many extra-marital affairs, was particularly vulnerable to this mode of attack. In 1960, the African-American Congressman Adam Clayton Powell tried to shut down a demonstration that Rustin was organising at the Democratic convention by threatening to announce Rustin and King were lovers. It wasn't true, but King's advisors warned him it would be wise to distance himself from Rustin and cancel the protests, rather than risk evidence about his own sexual history leaking out to a hostile press. Aware that King was 'torn', 'distressed', 'uneasy', and sensible of the higher purpose of their work, Rustin resigned from the SCLC.

He was brought back into the fold in 1963 to run the March on Washington, 'the greatest demonstration for freedom in the history of our nation' (Malcolm X saw it rather differently, decrying 'the Farce on Washington', which he thought was rapidly taken over and controlled by the white establishment). The ongoing controversy around Rustin's sexuality meant he was swiftly demoted from official organiser to deputy. Despite this more discreet position, the white segregationist Senator Strom Thurmond still tried to use Rustin as a tool to discredit the march. On 13 August, with fifteen days to go, he launched an attack in the Senate, reading out the entirety of Rustin's police record and jail booking log. 'The conviction', he bellowed, 'was sex perversion.' By reciting it inside the Senate, he ensured it was logged in perpetuity in the Congressional Records, where it can still be read today, a malevolent memento of an era that has only just passed.

This time, at least, the organisers stood by Rustin. It was he who insisted that King speak last, a touch of theatre that he hoped meant the massive crowd would not disperse early. He was right. Two hundred and fifty thousand Americans were in the Mall when King spoke on the afternoon of 28 August 1963, sweltering in their Sunday best as he set out his dignified encapsulation of all the movement's hopes. In 'I Have a Dream', he imagined a day in which his own four children would not be judged by the colour of their skin but the content of their character, at long last liberated from the prison of the body.

The problem for Rustin was that at this moment in time, homosexuality was not understood either as part of the inheritance of the body or as a valid choice for what you might want to do it with it. Instead, it was regarded as a component of character, which is to say a personal weakness rather than a source of solidarity and common struggle. Years later, he observed that though the civil rights movement was rife with affairs and promiscuity ('the crap that was going on in those motels . . . was totally acceptable'), it was only homosexuality that was regarded as a moral failing.

To be both black and queer was, he thought, to spend time on two crosses, existing in a punishing blind spot that even Reich had refused to address. Like his friend James Baldwin – who was kept off-stage at the March despite being the movement's most eloquent commentator, and who was likewise subject to rampant homophobia from those who shared his skin colour and rampant racism from those who shared his sexuality – Rustin was an outsider in every camp. He was still furious about it, right to the end of his life. A few months before he died, in the summer of 1987, he told an interviewer:

There is no question in my mind that there was considerable prejudice amongst a number of people that I worked with. But of course they would never admit that they were prejudiced. They would say that they were afraid that it might hurt the movement. The fact of the matter is, it was already known, it was nothing to hide. You can't hurt the movement unless you have something to reveal . . . They also said any more talk would hurt me. They would look at me soulfully and say, surely you don't want to go through any more humiliation? Well, I wasn't humiliated.

One of the most admirable things about Rustin is that he refused to serve as his own jailer, declining to live inside the closet even if he was ostracised or punished. His story viscerally demonstrates that prison is not simply an institution, but the concrete embodiment of a set of attitudes that control behaviour on the outside, too. Like Malcolm X, Rustin refused to obey, which gave him a kind of freedom, even when he was behind bars.

But to acknowledge that the prison extends far into society is not to diminish the power of the institution itself. By the time Rustin made this statement, the carceral landscape in America had become far more oppressive than when either he or Reich were serving time in Lewisburg. The Bureau of Prisons officially dropped the policy of reform in 1975 and in 1984 the Sentencing Reform Act abolished parole in federal prisons. The consequence was rapid overcrowding, since far more people stayed in the system for longer. At around the same time, the War on Drugs, rollbacks on welfare, higher sentences for minor crimes, minimum sentencing and a three-strike policy in many states created a substantial increase in the number of people sent to prison, despite a declining crime rate. Many of these changes disproportionately affected black people, creating a prison population that replicated the hateful old pattern of slavery.

By 2016, 2.3 million people were held in prisons in America, 20 per cent of the world's incarcerated population. A quarter of them had not been convicted or sentenced, mostly because they could not afford bail, and well over half had not committed violent crimes. Furthermore, the racial composition of the prison population did not reflect that of the nation as a whole. Based on calculations made by the Prison Policy Initiative using data from the 2010 census, African-Americans made up 13 per cent of the US population but 40 per cent of the prison population, while Hispanics made up 16 per cent of the population but 19 per cent of the incarcerated population.

2.3 million imprisoned bodies. Where do you put them all? The new generation of model institutions were not furnished with libraries and baseball diamonds. Instead, they prioritised surveillance, punishment and sensory deprivation. So-called problematic or difficult inmates could be held in solitary confinement, known euphemistically as 'indefinite administrative segregation', for years, even decades at a time. These supermax prisons and special management units were not built to reform souls or start new lives. They were in the business of generating unreformable bodies, which served no purpose other than to justify the escalating arduousness of the conditions in which they were kept.

As the abolitionist and civil rights activist Angela Davis observes in *Are Prisons Obsolete?*, no one likes to imagine the reality of prison, or how it might feel to be confined inside one. It's a source of terror, and so we prefer to 'think about imprisonment as a fate reserved for others, a fate reserved for the "evildoers".' But if the stories of Reich and Malcolm X, Jacobson and Rustin tell us anything at all, it's that any human body can be criminalised by the state, not because of a crime that's been committed, but because that particular body has been designated criminal in its own right. Davis again: 'Are we willing to relegate ever larger numbers of people to an isolated existence marked by authoritarian regimes, violence, disease, and technologies of seclusion that produce severe mental instability?' The transformations that Reich envisaged did not involve the tearing down of prisons, but it's hard to know how a shared freedom can be achieved while they exist in their present form, silos for bodies that were never dangerous in the first place.

# 7

# Block/Swarm

IN THE SUMMER OF 1988, when I was eleven, I went on my first protest march, with my mother and her friends. Pride is very corporate now, but back then there were no floats sponsored by banks or airlines or the police. We swept past the Houses of Parliament, a sea of bodies surging across Westminster Bridge chanting, 'Two, four, six, eight, is your MP really straight?' A Thatcher drag queen climbed up a lamppost in Parliament Square, handbag dangling from her elbow, conducting a vigorous round of 'Maggie Maggie Maggie, Out Out Out'. Section 28 of the Local Government Act had just passed into law, we were seven years into the Aids crisis, and thirty thousand people were on the march that year.

Did I write about it in the obligatory Monday morning school essay on 'My Weekend'? Probably not. Section 28 was designed above all to limit the visibility of gay families, and it applied especially to schools. It came into existence as the result of a moral panic about a children's book by the Danish writer Susanne Bösche. Using staged black-and-white photographs, *Jenny Lives with Eric and Martin* illustrated an ordinary weekend in the life of a gay couple with a small daughter. Shortly after it was published in English, it was swept up in a sustained tabloid attack on the so-called 'Loony Left' (Labour-run councils and their diversity initiatives, which included such madcap ideas as rape crisis centres and refuges for Asian women). Multiple newspapers reported that it was being handed out in junior schools as part of a campaign to indoctrinate children into perverted lifestyles. *The Sun* ran the story on the front page, under the headline 'Vile Book In School: Pupils See Pictures Of Gay Lovers'. In fact, a single copy had been purchased by the Inner London Education Authority, as a resource for teachers, not students. The panic and misinformation were not so dissimilar to reporting around trans children now.

Like every other pupil in Britain at the time, I never saw *Jenny Lives with Eric and Martin*, despite living in a bona fide lesbian household. Looking at the British Library copy now (it did own two, but one has been stolen or mislaid), it's not hard to see what so unsettled conservatives. Eric and Martin are two handsome, tousle-haired young hippies, often bare-chested or in leather jackets. They spend a lot of time lounging around in bed. On one page, Martin is dozing under his duvet. Eric lolls beside him, apparently naked, while Jenny snuggles in his lap with her doll. It's all very European, attesting to a casual bodily ease that if not actively erotic remains anathema to certain kinds of English sensibility. On subsequent pages, the family fix a bike puncture, argue about who will cook the supper and do their laundry. Racy stuff.

While walking home from the laundrette, towing Jenny in a cart, Eric and Martin are harangued by a female neighbour. 'You gays! Why don't you stay at home so the rest of us don't have to see you? Ugh!' she hisses. Jenny is terrified. Back home, she asks Eric why the woman was so angry and he explains that some people don't understand two men loving each other. Get some chalk, he tells her, and draws an explanatory cartoon on the paving stones in the back yard. A stick woman shouts at two stick men holding hands but this time she's corrected by her stick husband, who tells her about his own gay relationship and explains kindly, 'It can never be wrong to live with someone you are fond of.'

Hard to disagree with that unassuming 'fond' but by 1987, 74 per cent of British people thought homosexuality was mostly or always wrong; an increase of 13 per cent over five years that was largely the product of negative reporting around Aids. *Jenny* was raised in the House of Commons by several MPs, including the Education Secretary Kenneth Baker, who decried a permissive society and promised to clamp down on sexual deviance of all kinds, from homosexuality to abortion. At the Conservative Party Conference in October 1987, the Prime Minister herself attacked what she euphemistically described as 'positive images' in her keynote speech, adding: 'Children who need to be taught to respect traditional moral values are being taught that they have an inalienable right to be gay. All of those children need a sound start in life.'

Section 28 was proposed as an amendment to the Local Government Act less than two months later. It forbade local authorities from promoting or publishing material about homosexuality, and from promoting the teaching in state schools of 'the acceptability of homosexuality as a pretended family relationship'. It became law on 24 May 1988, and wasn't repealed until 2003. Like Paragraph 175 of the Prussian Penal Code or Executive Order 10450 in Eisenhower's America, it had tangible, material consequences (including the cutting off of funding to gay youth groups and helplines, more crucial than ever in the years of Aids) and it generated a hateful atmosphere.

By insisting that there could be no positive discussion of homosexuality in schools, it ensured the opposite. Homophobia spilled up unchecked. *Poof, lezzer, I hope you die of Aids*: the torrent of playground language to which any gay or gender non-conforming kid was subjected. I can still feel my school years in my body, every muscle clamped and clenched, defended against discovery of the so-called family situation, let alone my own sense of being at odds with my gender; not a girl at all, but something in between and as yet unnamed. Looking back, this unhappy legacy might have been why Reich's notion of body armour hit me so hard.

But the feeling of all those marching bodies on Westminster Bridge stayed with me too. One of the odd things about Section 28 was that in denying queer visibility it also served as a lightning rod for queer activism. It was my gateway into understanding that essential Reichian dynamic: that the political world can make bodies into prisons, but that bodies can also reshape the political world. Twice in 1988, lesbian campaigners breached the newly reinforced barrier against visibility, literally thrusting their way onto the news. On 2 February, four women snuck into the House of Lords the day the chamber voted on the bill. Seconds after the verdict was announced, two of them abseiled down from the public gallery on a washing line bought from a local market and smuggled in beneath a donkey jacket, a dyke staple of the time.

On 23 May, the evening before the bill passed into law, another quartet of women broke into the BBC News studios during the live transmission of the *Six O'Clock News*. One handcuffed herself to the camera, which wobbled ominously. You could hear thumps and muffled cries of 'Stop the Clause!' as Sue Lawley continued to read from her teleprompt. Eventually she interrupted herself to apologise for the noise, 'but I'm afraid we rather have been invaded.' In the background, the other newscaster, Nicholas Witchell, audibly rugby tackled one of the women and tried to drag her away, tricky since she was handcuffed to the desk. We watched it recapped all night in joyous disbelief. The *Daily Mirror*'s headline the next day was 'BEEB MAN SITS ON LESBIAN'.

That abseil line must have imprinted itself more deeply than I'd realised. By the time I was eighteen, I was immersed in the environmental direct action movement. For the most part, non-violent direct action meant physically occupying contested space. We lay in front of cars outside arms fairs (the first time I did this, tight-chested with adrenaline, I was picked up and slung bodily into railings by two policemen). We climbed on the roofs of oil companies and set up camps in the path of road building projects. As Rustin observed, the power of this kind of civil disobedience is directly indexed to the body's physical vulnerability. It was apparent that the more dangerous or precarious a position the protester took, the more powerful its effect, both in terms of the publicity it generated and the cost of their removal.

I became so involved in road protest that I dropped out of university altogether. My new home was an arboreal camp of treehouses in a beech wood due to be demolished for a bypass, from which I had to abseil thirty feet to get my breakfast cup of tea. The line was black and green, like a cartoon snake. 'It is not in the role of an artist to worry about life – to feel responsible for creating a better world', Agnes Martin once said. 'This is a very serious distraction.' All very well to say, but I did feel responsible for what was happening to the planet and it was intoxicating to believe that by putting my body where it wasn't supposed to be I might help to create a better world – or at least preserve the tarnished one that was already there, to roll back the oncoming apocalypse of climate change.

It astounds me now, the lengths to which people went to try and protect the earth, in a period just before internet usage became pervasive, when climate science was far less well known or believed. Road protests ran all through the 1990s, camps springing up in imperilled woods all over the UK. Solsbury Hill, Fairmile, Twyford Down, Newbury. The community was tight-knit and tribal, experimenting in low-impact, close to the earth living, cooking on fires and living under canvas. During the three months it took to evict the camps strung along the nine-mile Newbury Bypass site, protestors locked themselves to oil drums filled with concrete, set on rickety platforms in the canopies of trees. At Fairmile in Devon, another ancient woodland, they dug a labyrinth of narrow tunnels forty feet into the earth, punctuated by sealed doors, and it took a team of potholers armed with radar a week to ferret them all out. The undersheriff complained that the tunnellers had used rotten wood to shore the passageways, but precarity was the point. At a camp in Stringer's Common, a Site of Special Scientific Interest on the outskirts of Guildford, I once spent a day digging in one of those unshored tunnels, worming my way underground in a space barely bigger than my body, ten feet of sandy soil directly above my back, an experience too terrifying to repeat.

This kind of activism was made more complicated by the passage of yet another formidable law. As with Section 28, the 1994 Criminal Justice and Public Order Act had its origins in a tabloid panic, this time concerning the biggest illegal rave in UK history. In May 1992, local police prevented a group of New Age travellers from holding the annual Avon Free Festival, part of a long-running campaign to curtail nomadic, wandering lifestyles of all kinds. After being shunted from county to county, the ragged convoy of travellers and hippies in painted ambulances and buses was funnelled onto Castlemorton Common in Worcestershire, where, thanks to extensive media coverage, it was rapidly joined by dozens of sound systems, followed by around thirty thousand ravers in bucket hats and Umbro hoodies, who spent the sunny bank holiday weekend dancing in Dionysian abandon, off their faces on ecstasy and speed in the sublime landscape of the Malvern Hills.

Because Castlemorton was common land, the police lacked

the power as well as numbers to move people on. Local residents, understandably horrified by the invasion, not to mention ninety-six hours of non-stop techno, muttered to TV cameras about calling in the army. The tabloids revelled in describing the dirt, drugs and noise. Ecstasy, one correspondent explained, made people instantly defecate where they stood. 'Hippy tribes put village under siege', the *Telegraph* reported, while according to James Dalrymple in the *Times* ravers had killed and eaten a horse (his piece also referred queasily to the leaders of the rave as a 'black American man and a beautiful mixed-caste girl', adding a spot of racial othering to what was already a febrile mix of tabloid tropes, though one of the things that distinguished Castlemorton from the commercial festivals that followed was that there was no central organisation at all).

It's an odd feeling, looking through those papers now. Convoys of New Age travellers had been a staple on West Country roads since the 1960s. I spent my twenties living like that and now I can't remember the last time I saw a traveller vehicle rattling down a motorway, a welded-on chimney poking from its roof. Castlemorton was the last hurrah, the jubilant tail-end of a way of life that venerated both meanings of the word *free*: freedom of movement and doing things without a profit motive or charge. Its inadvertent marriage of subcultures was swiftly exploited by a Tory party limping in the polls and anxious to regain authority.

The 1994 Criminal Justice Bill, written in the wake of Castlemorton, gave the police fresh powers to prevent unauthorised camping and trespass, and created the new offence of aggravated trespass, which would soon be used widely in the policing of road protesters, hunt saboteurs and strikers. The section concerning raves became infamous for its attempt to criminalise the music itself, defined as 'the emission of a succession of repetitive beats'. It might have sounded ridiculous but it licensed the police to disperse open-air gatherings and meant organisers risked fines and prison sentences for putting on parties. There were plenty of commercial dance events in the years ahead, but no more free raves at the old Ovaltine Dairy or in the Black Mountains, to the sound of Spiral Tribe, Circus Warp and Circus Normal. No more temporary autonomous zones at Canary Wharf or in the Roundhouse, the beats going on for a full week, running off a power socket that belonged to British Rail. No more enraptured bodies sweating in an abandoned warehouse or underneath the stars, without the need to purchase a ticket or build the kind of barricaded fence you get at Glastonbury.

I don't mean to sound nostalgic. I was never a raver but I was immersed in protest culture and though I've long since relinquished the army boots and rainbow sweaters that were as much a uniform as the grey skirts and maroon blazers I wore to school, I remain susceptible to the abundant seductions of that time. The smell of wood smoke brings it all back: the storybook pleasures of living under canvas and up trees, the yips that sounded as we walked back into camp, the spells for hexing capitalism, the witchy mood that permeated everything. I know those things were only part of the story, the penny whistles and pantomime cows always teetering on the verge of an Ali G parody. Nor have I forgotten the widespread reliance on giros and Special Brew. No, what I really miss is hope. The larger truth of road protests is that they existed at a time when it still seemed possible that climate change could be averted, and my grief at the willed foreclosure of that future has only grown larger and more painful with the years.

After the Criminal Justice Bill passed into law, things became more violent. Protest marches and street parties were nearly always accompanied by the sight of riot buses gathering on a side street. Watch out, someone would say, it's kicking off. The police would come out, a black phalanx inching shoulder to shoulder in riot masks and shields. The boys in black from Class War would pull bandanas over their faces and jog to the front, to start lobbing bricks. My friend Simon had his leg broken by security guards at Newbury, who held him down and smashed it with a fire extinguisher. People were paranoid about police spies, who, it turned out years later, really were everywhere, concealed by false identities: dating your friends, making suggestions in meetings, lobbing bottles, even assisting in writing the McLibel leaflet, a critique of McDonald's that initiated one of the most famous British court cases of the 1990s.

I found an article recently in which locals bemoaned the filth of the protestors at Stringer's Common, saying our presence there scared away the birds and small mammals we claimed to care so much about. Two decades on, the Prime Minister Boris Johnson described the Extinction Rebellion protestors gathered in Trafalgar Square in 2019 as uncooperative crusties with nose rings in 'hemp-smelling bivouacs'. We were dirty, it's true. We washed in buckets if we washed at all, but as each new story of poisoned rivers and oceans full of plastic has come to light, it's become evident that lives which looked immaculate on the surface were actually causing degradation and despoilment on a massive scale. New clothes, new cars, washing machines, factory farms, all of it at an incalculable cost somewhere down the supply chain.

I find it hard to watch footage of protests from the 1990s, especially of the evictions at Newbury, because it feels as if I'm looking directly into a moment when the future could still have gone a different way, a microcosmic, speeded-up version of what is happening now to the planet as a whole. A woman lies in front of bulldozers, and then she is dragged away through the churned-up mud. The woods are intact and full of people, and then the trees are cut down; all bar the giant Middle Oak, which stands alone on a roundabout on the A30, looking as pointless and isolated as an animal in a zoo.

*

Witnessing a protest, especially if it's unreliably reported or violently suppressed, has the capacity to strip away naivety, to expose invisible power structures or to fling into doubt previously unquestioned assumptions and beliefs. One of the reasons I was so struck by Reich's writing back in the 1990s was that he too experienced this kind of awakening. In 1927, when he was thirty, he witnessed an uprising in Vienna that turned into a massacre. It seemed like a hinge in his strange life, a moment of revelation that still shone, despite everything that came after.

The inter-war years in Austria were a time of demonstrations and counter-demonstrations, of angry bodies assembling in the streets. During the 1920s, the controlling power nationally was the conservative, monarchist Christian Social Party, but Red Vienna itself was a bastion of socialism, a model of the welfare state that would be rolled out across Europe after the ruination of the Second World War. By 1927, the political situation had grown so fraught that nearly every Sunday in nearly every town and village you could find a uniformed militia marching, the socialist Schutzbund with red carnations in their caps and the right-wing Heimwehr in olive-green bonnets with outsized black grouse feathers sticking absurdly from the peak.

It was one of these rallies that catalysed the July Revolt. On 30 January 1927 the Schutzbund gathered in Schattendorf, a small town forty miles south of Vienna. After their march, they were walking back to the station when they passed an inn popular with the Frontkämpfer, a far-right, anti-Semitic paramilitary organisation associated with the Austrian government. The innkeeper's sons stood at the windows and fired rifles at the backs of the passing marchers, killing a veteran, Matthias Csmarits, who had lost an eye in the First World War, and his eight-year-old nephew, Josef Grossing.

Csmarits' funeral was attended by thousands of uniformed Schutzbund, and there was a fifteen-minute general strike in honour of the deaths. On 5 July, the three Frontkämpfer responsible were tried for the crime of public violence. They confessed to the shooting but claimed self-defence and nine days later were acquitted by the jury. 'A JUST VERDICT', the right-wing *Die Reichspost* proclaimed, but it was received with outrage, especially in Vienna. Nonetheless, the Social Democrats who controlled the city decided not to officially contest the verdict, in part because they didn't want to undermine the new institution of the jury trial.

Most people didn't hear the news until early the next morning, as they were walking to work. It surged through the city with the first papers, rushing through factory floors and depots. At 8am, the workers decided spontaneously to hold a peaceful demo. They switched off the electricity and stopped all public transport. As the city ground to a halt, tens of thousands of people gathered to express their frustration and disquiet. According to G. E. R. Gedye, a British journalist stationed in the city, at this stage the crowd were peaceful and good-humoured, laughing and joking as they jostled through the streets.

At ten in the morning, police on horseback tried to break up the gathering, firing at the crowd with revolvers, riding into them and refusing to let them pass. The bottleneck created chaos. The marchers armed themselves with sticks and cobblestones, planks and iron bars salvaged from a construction site, breaking into the police station and freeing anyone who'd been arrested (this scene is very like the Stonewall Riots, when the outnumbered police barricaded themselves in the Stonewall Inn, while the queers outside smashed their way in, armed likewise with cobblestones and street detritus). After setting the station on fire, the protestors were driven by the police to the square in front of the Justizpalast, which a small number stormed and set ablaze. By now a crowd of two hundred thousand had gathered, and they refused or were unable to let the fire engines pass.

Around the same time that Gedye heard the first isolated revolver shot, a patient arrived at Reich's office in a state of agitation. He said that the city workers were on strike, that the police were armed and that people were being killed. Reich cancelled the session and together they went outside to see what was happening in the streets. Everywhere, people were walking in silence, heading towards the University. To Reich's great surprise, he passed columns of Schutzbund marching in the opposite direction. Later, he learned that they had been sent back to barracks and ordered not to involve themselves in the dispute by the Social Democrats, though they were a trained force of fifty thousand that existed to protect the working people of Vienna.

On his way across town he passed the police headquarters, where he saw rifles being handed from a truck. He first heard the whip-crack of rifle fire as he crossed Rathaus Park, on the other side of Parliament from the burning Justizpalast. The crowd was screaming now, and running in and out of side streets, melting away and then re-forming, a terrified mass of bodies pursued by galloping horses. Most of the police had never been taught to use a gun, and held their rifles against their bellies, firing indiscriminately from left to right. They shot men, women and children, many of them onlookers who, like Reich, had only come to see the blaze. They shot at ambulances, fire engines, Red Cross workers, even at each other.

Tides of people ran in panic through the streets, chased by mounted police, sabres raised above their heads. Smoke rose from the Justizpalast. The sky turned red and the air smelt of burning paper. The lash of rifles, followed by boos and screams.

A man opened his coat in defiance and was shot in the chest. A woman kneeling over the wounded was shot in the back of the head. Later, it transpired that the chief of police had issued rifles to six hundred officers along with dumdum bullets, a type of ammunition that expands on impact, inflicting terrible wounds from the expanding lead, especially when fired at close range.

Reich ran home to get his wife Annie, and together they went back to the university. A phalanx of policemen was across the street. As the Reichs watched, they inched towards the crowd, 'slowly, very slowly', like children playing Grandmother's Footsteps. When they were fifty steps away they began to shoot. Dozens of people were lying on the ground. Reich grabbed Annie and hid behind a tree, unable to believe what he was seeing. One or two policemen deliberately aimed over people's heads but most of them were simply gunning people down. 'It was not a riot per se, with two antagonistic factions,' he wrote in his memoir, *People in Trouble*, 'but simply tens of thousands of people, and groups of policemen shooting into the defenceless crowd.'

As it grew dark he wandered the desolate streets, encountering weeping and traumatised strangers, many hunting for missing friends or family members. Eighty-nine people were dead, and a thousand more were in hospital, where doctors attempted to stitch up catastrophic wounds, some inflicted from less than a metre away. Shaken and exhausted, he and Annie decided to call in on a friend whose family were associated with the Social Democrat leadership. He wanted to discuss what he'd seen and to plan an urgent response, but instead he walked in on the preparations for a disconcertingly formal dinner. There were flowers and candles on the table. 'The gory events', he remembered later, 'appeared not to have penetrated this room.'

The guests arrived, and though they discussed the bloodshed Reich was sure none of them had seen it for themselves. They spoke in the same way that they customarily spoke of Goethe: cultured, reserved, intelligent, polite. He was beset with a sense of furious unreality and fantasised about tipping up the shining table and knocking the plates to the floor. Outside, protests were still flaring in suburbs and outposts of the city, but the next morning the strike was broken up by the right-wing Heimwehr. In the months that followed the Heimwehr received funds from Italian fascists and local industrialists keen to restore the nation to its lost imperialist glories. Within a few years, most would change their allegiance to the Nazis. As Reich's friends sat over their supper, the far-right had begun its Austrian ascent.

★

The things Reich saw in the streets of Vienna stayed with him. He was haunted by the spectacle of the brutalised crowd and the robotic policemen: a vision, though he didn't know it yet, of what would soon befall Europe. Why hadn't the people defended themselves, even though they far outnumbered their attackers? If the civil order was founded on and maintained by this kind of violence, how could a psychoanalyst be aiding their patients by insisting they accommodate themselves to it? And, most urgently of all, what force made the police shoot their undefended fellow citizens; like rabbits, Reich said. 'Somewhere', he wrote furiously in *People in Trouble*, 'a great deception was hidden.'

Freud too was troubled. He hadn't been in Vienna during the riots, and when Reich visited him at Villa Schuler a few weeks later it became apparent that he didn't regard the massacre as an injustice, but as something deplorable, the fault of the workers and not the police. All that spring, he'd been working on an essay about religion, and his disquiet about the events of 15 July trickled into it. In 'The Future of An Illusion', which he finished in September and published in November, he turned from a direct investigation of the psyche to the question of civilisation itself, an arena that had fascinated him since boyhood. 'Every individual', he wrote, thinking perhaps of the weeping, baying crowds outside the Palace of Justice, 'is virtually an enemy of civilisation, though civilisation is supposed to be an object of universal human interest.' He argued that disciplined leaders were vital in order to persuade the irrational, violent masses towards the instinctual sacrifice that civilisation required. While it wasn't an argument for fascism, it certainly didn't support the kind of egalitarian revolution Reich both longed for and believed was in sight.

Two years later, Freud refined this argument in *Civilisation and its Discontents*, the book that crystallised his battle with Reich. In it, he explains that the curtailment of individual rights is the necessary price to be paid for a world that is anything other than a stinking battlefield, a world in which the strongest don't trample, torture and murder the weak. *Homo homini lupus*, he concluded, adding grimly: 'civilisation overcomes the dangerous aggressivity of the individual by weakening him, disarming him and setting up an internal authority to watch over him, like a garrison in a conquered town.'

It wasn't that Reich didn't think the price worth paying; it's that he suspected that the garrison was the problem. What troubled him most about 15 July wasn't the crowds who marched for justice, but the behaviour of the police. They acted as if they were following orders in their sleep, incapable of shame or independent action, 'a stupid, idiotic automaton lacking reason and judgement . . . *Machine men!*' He recognised it from his own behaviour as an officer on the Italian front. What he'd witnessed on the streets of Vienna was not, he was certain, the natural or inevitable order of being. It was the product of patriarchal capitalism, which established a rigid, immobilising, sexually-repressed, authoritarian model of relationships from the moment a child was born, and it had culminated in a massacre.

This, I think, is the true crux of Reich's breach with Freud. They weren't arguing over psychoanalytic technique so much as two contrasting views of human nature, two visions of what freedom entails. The events in Vienna convinced Freud that humans needed civilisation – armed police, oppressive laws and all – to protect them from their anarchic, reckless selves, and that the compromise demanded in terms of individual freedom was worth it for the enlargement of communal security. Reich, on the other hand, could not believe humans were naturally hateful and cruel. He thought these behaviours were a consequence of the unequal and deforming systems in which they were forced to live. Freedom came from tearing the garrison down, not building it up.

I don't know how profitable it is to speculate about the essentials of human nature, but I am certain that civilisation has not yet provided equal levels of security for all bodies, and nor has it limited their freedoms to the same degree. Freud's pessimism can seem the more realistic position, but let's not forget that the price he was willing to pay for stability included appeasement of the Nazis, while Reich's belief in a better world allowed him to see that fascism must be resisted, a conviction that set into motion all the catastrophes of his later life.

But Reich and Freud were not the only people to have their ideas shaken by the events of 15 July. The question of the disenfranchised masses was one of the most prominent and widely discussed issues of the interwar period, and the riot became a central exhibit in a passionate debate about crowds, rationality and power. It preoccupied politicians and inspired novels and works of theory. Some people, like Reich, saw a warning in the behaviour of the police, while others regarded the burning of the Justizpalast as an indictment of lawless, nannyish Red Vienna, a sign that the masses were dangerously out of control.

For the twenty-two-year-old chemistry student who joined the crowd on his bicycle, 15 July was a crucial day: a prefiguration in perfect miniature of all that lay ahead, not to mention the beginning of a career as a writer that would culminate in the Nobel Prize. 'Fifty-three years have passed,' Elias Canetti wrote in his memoir, *The Torch in my Ear*, 'and the agitation of that day is still in my bones. It was the closest thing to a revolution that I have physically experienced.' Standing by the burning Justizpalast, he was especially struck by a man who stood plaintively on the sidelines, crying, 'The files are burning! All the files!' People matter more than paper, Canetti snapped, and the incident seeded his grotesque 1935 novel *Auto-da-fé*, in which a scholar, Peter Kien, secedes from humanity and its demands so totally that in the end he barricades himself in his beloved library and sets it on fire.

Like Reich, Canetti felt his physical experience that day made a nonsense of all the theories he'd read about crowd behaviour. It was all very well for Freud and Gustave Le Bon to write about the violence and irrationality of the crowd as a threat to civilisation, but his experience of dissolution was ecstatic, almost sublime. Even as people had fallen and died around him, he had felt himself subsumed and swept along, no longer an individual but part of a wild organism with its own dignity and desires. His account of the day is not journalistic, like Gedye, but metaphysical, conveying the temporospatial disruptions that accompany a radical shift in consciousness from *I* to *we*.

Everything yielded and invisible holes opened everywhere. However, the overall structure did not disappear; even if you suddenly found yourself alone somewhere, you could feel things tugging and tearing at you. The reason was that you *heard* something everywhere: there was something rhythmic in the air, an evil music. You could call it music; you felt elevated by it. I did not feel as if I were moving on my own legs. I felt as if I were in a resonant wind.

The experience of feeling the crowd as a kind of living being, one that had been mistrusted and maligned throughout history, pricked away at him, driving his vast and unclassifiable work of non-fiction, *Crowds and Power* – a book that Sontag, who loved Canetti, described as expounding a 'poetics of political nightmare'. There wasn't one crowd, Canetti argued, but many, among them the mob with pitchforks and the scapegoated or victimised herd. A crowd could be electric or ecstatic or zombie-like. It could be cowed or riotous, sprawling or disciplined. It could have a carnival atmosphere or it could bring terror. One of the most important aspects of Canetti's argument was that the crowd was complex and deserving of scrutiny. He refused the pervasive belief that it was automatically primitive and irrational, the opposite to the enfranchised and articulate individual. Crowds might not communicate in language, but that didn't mean they weren't expressing subtle hopes or fears.

I've been in a lot of different crowds but I've only once been in what might be called a mob. It was at a protest at Newbury in 1997, on the first anniversary of the final camp's eviction. The gathering was tightly organised by the police, and took place inside a cordon. It was very misty, and it was only once we got close to the fence that the construction site became visible. It was a shocking transformation, a whole landscape simply lifted up and taken away. There was a vast pit gouged into the earth, and at the edge of it was Middle Oak, a pathetic remnant of what had once been a whole forest.

I think it was seeing the tree that set people off. Someone cut a hole in the fence and then we were all through, followed by mounted police and security guards in hi-vis vests. There were maybe a thousand people there, scrambling on diggers and shinning up cranes. I was in a pair of tiger trousers with a tail (forgive us the tastes of our youth), and I clambered on a bulldozer and watched as people smashed windows and set Portakabins on fire. The fog never lifted, and the mood was a strange, muted mixture of wildness and despair.

What did we look like from the outside? What would Freud have thought? It's sometimes hard to remember that the bodies in a crowd are individuals, each with their own complex history and motivation for being there. When the Austrian novelist Heimito von Doderer used the 15 July riot in the final chapter of his panorama of bourgeois Vienna, *The Demons*, the crowd served as a pointillist backdrop to the stories of the individual characters whose heroism was tied up with their refusal of a communal identity. He used it as a way of bringing together his cast, neatly tying off all their narrative lines – marriage! inheritance! – against a background of terrible disorder. To the narrator, watching the events through binoculars, the crowd seemed like a mass of seething kaleidoscopic dots, punctuated by the dark bundles of corpses in the sunlight.

Doderer was temporarily a member of the Nazi Party, though he'd left by the time he wrote *The Demons*, and his sense of the crowd as something inchoate chimed with the way fascists regarded the masses as raw material, in need of sifting and moulding (Goebbels characterised the relationship as that of a painter to his paints). As Stefan Jonsson observes in his illuminating account of the masses in the interwar period, *Crowds and Democracy*, part of the fascist route to power is to cleave human bodies into two types of mass, the 'block' and the 'swarm': one hyper-disciplined, orderly and in service to the state; the other chaotic and transgressive, requiring inoculation, purging or extermination lest it contaminate the larger body politic.

> The block was an armoured mass, drilled and disciplined, violently cut to shape in order to fit the representative units of the soldier, the army, the race, the nation . . . On the other hand, there was the swarm, a mass not yet dammed up and disciplined and whose presence threatened to dissolve the hierarchic units of the fascist order. This was the Jewish mass and the Gypsy mass or the mass of hysteric females and irremediable communists, all of them associated with miscegenation, transgression, femininity, and egalitarianism.

This division of ordinary people into two distinct groups is what Reich glimpsed on 15 July. The transformation happened right before his eyes. The rhetoric of the swarm soon served to bolster the identity of the Nazis, facilitating their route to power. Characterising undesirable bodies as insects, vermin, degenerate trash is a mode of thinking that led directly to the Holocaust, and it also informs more recent genocidal acts. Take Rwanda, where the cry 'exterminate the cockroaches', *inyenzi*, broadcast on private RTLM radio in the spring of 1994, was the signal to begin the murder of over one million Tutsis, killed by their Hutu neighbours with machetes, guns and nail-studded clubs. Many of the killings were carried out by militias, organised blocks, among them the Interahamwe ('Those Who Attack Together') and the Impuzamugambi ('Those Who Have the Same Goal').

But the language of the swarm is not just confined to twentieth-century atrocities. In the past decade, it has once again infiltrated mainstream politics. During a discussion about the situation on the Calais border in the summer of 2015, the then-Prime Minister David Cameron spoke of 'a swarm of people coming across the Mediterranean, seeking a better life, wanting to come to Britain because Britain has got jobs.' The concept of the swarm is prevalent in the rhetoric of the Brexiteers and axiomatic of the thinking that has driven the hostile environment, government policy since 2012, which has seen thousands of refugees and asylum seekers deported, refused visas or held in indefinite detention in for-profit immigration removal centres like Yarl's Wood and Morton Hall.

In America, Trump too regularly uses terms like 'animals' to describe immigrants. He claims migrants 'pour into and infest' America, that it is a 'monstrosity', and has said of the Mexican border: 'You look at what is marching up, that's an invasion.' Against this so-called invasion he has deployed the paramilitary force of ICE to separate the children of the migrants from their desperate parents and to pen them in cages, likewise run for profit, where they sleep on concrete in filthy over-crowded rooms, where the lights are never turned off, where there is no medicine or soap or toothbrushes, no bedding and not enough food to eat. Five hundred bodies in a windowless warehouse, two thousand eight hundred children in a tent city in the Texan desert.

Invasion, killer, animal, insect, predator. The same old fantasies perpetuate themselves, the trigger terms about dirt and pollution, unbridled sexuality and unstoppable disease. *They* are coming: mysterious, invasive, contaminating, taking what is yours, infecting you with what is not (of course Trump would dub Covid-19 'the Chinese virus'). Freedom of movement is reconceptualised as burglary, yes, but also as an assault on purity: the terror of miscegenation, of different kinds of bodies mixing too freely. In this atmosphere of hostility, it's easy to believe that Freud was right, that civilisation is buckling once again under the deliberate stirring of aggression, the delicious libidinal thrill of hate.

★

What drives the block? What motivates them? On 11 August 2017, around five hundred white supremacists, Klansmen, Neo-Nazis and militias began to gather in Charlottesville, Virginia for the Unite the Right rally the following day, nominally organised as a protest against the removal of Confederate statues in southern cities by Black Lives Matter activists. That night, they marched across the University of Virginia campus with tiki torches, chanting 'Jews will not replace us' and 'Blood and soil'. They attacked a tiny group of counter-protestors, who had locked arms around a statue of Thomas Jefferson, and knocked down a journalist asking questions about the event.

The next morning protestors and counter-protestors, who now outnumbered them two to one, gathered in Lee Park, the site of a statue of the Confederate commander and slave-owner Robert E. Lee. The rally was mostly male: white men in button-down shirts and MAGA hats, white men carrying swastikas and wearing wraparound shades and helmets. Since Virginia is an open carry state, many of them carried weapons, most visibly the groups of militiamen in combat gear and backpacks, who stood menacingly on street corners and outside synagogues, clutching semi-automatic rifles.

Violence quickly broke out in the park, with counter-protestors punched, choked and attacked with pepper spray (some maintained a non-violent response, while others fought back). At eleven o'clock, an hour before the rally was due to start, the city declared a state of emergency, and an hour later police began clearing the park. During this chaotic process, which forced the two sides into close proximity, a twenty-year-old counter-protestor was dragged into a parking garage and beaten with poles and metal pipes by members of the Fraternal Order of the Alt-Knights, the Traditionalist Workers Party and the League of the South.

At 13:45, a white supremacist drove his car into a crowd of counter-protestors, smashing into people and then reversing at speed to hit more. In the news footage, you can see bodies flung entirely into the air, accompanied by a litter of stray shoes. He killed a young woman, Heather Heyer, and injured nineteen people. Later that day, the President condemned what he described as the 'egregious display of hatred, bigotry and violence on many sides, on many sides.' In his refusal to single out white supremacists, the President was 'the opposite of cuck' (alt-right slang for cuckold, meaning emasculated liberal), the editor of the Nazi website *Daily Stormer* approvingly concluded.

Like millions of people, I watched these events unfold in real-time on Twitter. The same photographs of the torchlight procession kept resurfacing: a snake of light, the fanatical young faces shining in the dark, arms raised in Nazi salutes. The block was back, fetishistic in its hatreds, incandescent at the notion that its privileges might be rescinded, that feminists should revoke access to sex, that people of colour might have the jobs or houses or cars to which they were surely entitled by birth. Most of the marchers were younger than I am: white boys with tidy haircuts and polo-shirts, their faces exultant, surfing the thrill that comes from making yourself the source of terror, converting your body into an ugly threat.

In the unsettled weeks that followed, an image kept resurfacing in my mind, of three Klansmen riding in a black car. *City Limits*, 1969, by the abstract expressionist painter Philip Guston. It looked like a joke, like a Krazy Kat version of the aftermath of a massacre. The car was ridiculous, clonking along on fat tractor tyres that didn't even pretend to be the same shape or size. The three pointy-headed figures were packed in like clowns, dressed in patched and tattered white hoods with worrying red flecks. One of them was puffing on a stogie, held in a fat gloved hand. They all looked straight ahead, their eyeholes a slick, unreflecting black. Apart from these small regions of black paint, the entire canvas was flooded, really drenched with turbulent strikes and swipes of filthy pink and oozing red. The phrase 'rivers of blood' came to mind.

In other paintings from the same series, the hoods drove around deserted towns in their cartoon jalopies, clutching their cigars, little flatulent speech bubbles of smoke floating overhead. Two stood neck-deep in a pool of black water, their hands bright red. Sometimes they were accompanied by weapons: lumpy bricks like baked potatoes, homemade crosses and guns, lengths of wood with nails sticking out, like those deployed in the Rwandan genocide. In 1970's *Bad Habits*, a Klansman scratched his back with a whip, his hood delicately spattered with carmine flecks. There were never any people around. Piles of discarded shoes kept cropping up (it might have been these shoes that subliminally called Guston to mind when I saw the photographs from Charlottesville), often with the lower legs still attached. Green trousers, meaty pink ankles, the post-match litter of some unspeakable event.

The lavish, juddery colours weren't new for Guston, but the figures were. They'd emerged from out of a crisis, one of those breaches in time, like the riots in Charlottesville and Vienna, that leave people stunned, certain the deck's been reshuffled in a malign, occluded way. On 4 April 1968, Martin Luther King was shot on the balcony of the Lorraine Motel in Memphis. All spring there were riots. In August, Guston was watching the anti-Vietnam protests at the Democratic Convention in Chicago on TV: ten thousand protestors, mostly peaceful, mostly young, getting beaten down with billy clubs by twenty-three thousand police and National Guardsmen.

That summer, while Agnes Martin was camping in the wilderness, he was in Woodstock, glued to the news. What he saw made him question the value of his exquisite abstract paintings. 'What kind of man am I,' he asked, 'sitting at home, reading magazines, going into a frustrated fury about everything – and then going into my studio to *adjust* a *red* to a *blue*?' Forget purity and its alchemical allure for the hyper-rich (around the same time he said that whenever he saw an abstract painting he smelled mink coats). Like Reich, he'd seen something he couldn't ignore, a vision of brutality he felt compelled to understand. He wanted to find out what it was like to be a body that fights not for freedom, but to take it away.

People laughed when they saw the Klan paintings, but Guston wasn't making light of the threat they represented. He knew the Klan of old. They'd haunted his childhood in Los Angeles, a mysterious, evil force. He'd been born in Montreal in 1913, the seventh and youngest child of immigrant Jews. The family's move to L.A. in 1919 coincided with the resurgence of the Klan, a white supremacist group that had been active during the Civil War and then died out. Like a zombie army, they were reanimated in 1915, inspired by D. W. Griffith's glamorising silent epic *Birth of a Nation*, which presented the Klan as American heroes. By the mid-1920s, there were around 4.5 million Klan members in the USA. They believed in an 'alliance of degeneracy' between Jews and African-Americans (degeneracy, another term that will not die), and they were figures of terror for Guston's family.

One of the most frightening things about this second incarnation of the Klan was that they normalised hatred and violence, making them palatable, domestic, even cosy. Alongside the beatings and burning crosses, the murders and lynchings, the tarring and feathering of prostitutes, vagrants and doctors who carried out abortions, this army of middle American vigilantes organised picnics and sponsored baseball teams. At the same time that they were attacking women like Louise Little, Malcom

X's pregnant mother, or lynching her husband and placing his body on the streetcar tracks, they were also running charity drives and performing in bands at state fairs.

Guston's first personal run-in with the Klan was in their guise as strike-breakers (union organisers and communists were among their most frequent non-racial targets). As a boy from a poor, working-class family, he took a series of menial jobs to support himself while he became an artist, including delivery truck driver and machinist. There were no unions, and workers were often expected to put in fifteen-hour days. When he was seventeen, Guston joined a strike and witnessed the force with which the Klan broke it up. That same year, 1930, he made a drawing called *Conspirators*, in preparation for a painting that has since been lost. It depicted a gathering of Klansmen, huddled together against a city wall, their gowned backs turned from the viewer. On the other side of the wall was the evidence of their hellish work: a crucifixion (the figure has a human body but a weird, wormy stump of a head) and a lynched black man hanging from a leafless tree. In the foreground of this new Golgotha, a solitary Klansman bows his head, penitential or in deep thought, fingering with his gloved white hands a thick dark rope.

By the time he was eighteen, Guston was deeply involved with radical politics. A year younger than Bayard Rustin, and on the opposite coast, he participated in many of the same struggles. In 1931, both joined communist groups that were protesting the racist imprisonment of the Scottsboro boys, nine African-American teenagers who'd been wrongfully accused of raping two white women. Guston was commissioned to produce murals inspired by the Scottsboro case for the Hollywood branch of the John Reed Club, a communist-affiliate organisation. He made a series of portable frescoes on cement, all depicting violence against African-Americans. On 12 February 1933, the infamous Captain William F. Hynes of the LAPD Red Squad – a police intelligence unit established to break up strikes and spy on unionists and left-wing radicals – came in and smashed the murals with lead pipes. To Guston's lasting disquiet, one of the Red Squad took a rifle and shot every single black body in his paintings through the eyes and genitals. That same year he had a painting show at the Stanley Rose Gallery, an artistically-minded Hollywood bookstore. It depicted Klan activity, and a group of Klansmen swung by and slashed two of the pictures.

In the 1930s, Guston had believed art was a force that could change the world as directly as marching or protesting. By 1968, when he was watching National Guardsmen beating anti-Vietnam protestors on live TV, he'd long since relinquished that particular dream, but that didn't mean the artist was entitled to turn his back. You have to bear witness, he kept saying, but he meant more than simply documenting events as they unfolded. Unlike Rustin, who sought to uncover the good in everyone, even racist prison guards, what Guston wanted to do was find out what it felt like to live alongside your own brutality, peering out at the world through slits in cloth.

He understood instinctively that one of the sources of the Klan's power was their anonymity. Their robes and hoods defend them against recognition, but concealing individuality also has a second, more significant role. Uniformed, disciplined, identical, any single Klansman automatically stands for the whole, just as a soldier, a stormtrooper or a National Guardsman is the metonymic embodiment of the entire force. This is the uncanny multiplicatory nature of the block, which is composed not of individual people but of identical, perpetually replaceable units. It's no coincidence that Guston's *hoods*, as he called them, look like cartoon ghosts or Hallowe'en costumes. To don the robes is to undergo a temporary death as an individual, to abnegate the identity of a creature with a face, which can empathise and be appealed to, in favour of a tool in an inhumane army, the 'stupid idiotic automaton' that Reich had witnessed in Vienna, endlessly capable of regeneration and replacement.

The white robes are also sexless, while the hoods have no mouths, which is to say no appetite. Everything about them is designed to attest to purity, to differentiate the Klansmen from the animal bodies of the swarm. It's funny how often this dynamic recurs, in racism, misogyny, anti-Semitism, homophobia, hatred of the poor and the disabled. The enemy body is always portrayed as being fashioned from grosser material, obscenely sexual or avaricious, greedy, primitive, uncontrolled, infectious, spilling over, barely human, a kind of disgusting fleshy jelly. It makes me wonder if what drives prejudice is at root horror of the body itself. After all, as Sade observed, the body can be a terrifying place: open and insatiable, helpless and dependent. Hatred is a way of displacing this annihilating fear onto other bodies, asserting a magnificent autonomy, a freedom from the sullying, hopelessly interdependent life of flesh.

One of the things that Guston was doing in his Klan paintings was refusing this aspect of the block's power, as ready a source of terror as the weapons they used. He didn't humanise them in the sense of making them likeable, so much as strip them of their projective power, the sinister glamour of their masks. His hoods are tattered and paunchy, manifestly not in control of their own base appetites. They puff away, they're surrounded by butts and stubs, ashes and empty bottles. They look, in fact, a lot like the hard-drinking, chain-smoking Guston himself. As he explained in 1974, the paintings were self-portraits.

> I perceive myself as being behind the hood . . . My attempt
> was really not to illustrate, to do pictures of the KKK, as I
> had done earlier. The idea of evil fascinates me, rather like
> Isaac Babel who had joined the Cossacks, lived with them,
> and written stories about them. I almost tried to imagine
> that I was living with the Klan. What would it be like to
> be evil? To plan, to plot.

This is such an unusual, risky thing to do. Was he disguising himself as his potential assailants in order to understand them, or was he trying to gauge his own potential for violence? 'In masking himself as his would-be persecutor,' the critic Aaron Rosen observes, 'the victim gains a unique understanding of the aggressor, but at the cost of humanizing – perhaps even being seduced by – this role.' It's a dangerous game to play, using art as a court in which you take the role of victim and perpetrator, judge and jury.

As Guston says, there was a precedent for this work. The Russian writer Isaac Babel travelled with the anti-Semitic

Cossacks as a correspondent during the Soviet–Polish War, disguising his identity as a Jew. He rode with them on their sorties, drank with them after battles, slept among them in a smelly litter of sabres and saddles. He documented everything he saw, the shtetls torched, the villagers raped, filling his 1926 short-story collection *Red Cavalry* with a jumbled baggage of violence, boredom and courage. In 1930, Guston had dedicated his painting *Conspirators* to 'I.B.' He admired Babel's ironic restraint, the grim detachment with which he set down horrors.

The Cossacks sound like something from ancient history, but for Guston they were almost as immediate a source of malevolence as the Klan. His parents had emigrated to Canada to escape pogroms in the Ukraine. They left their home in Odessa, where Babel too was born, in 1905, during an upsurge of attacks by Cossacks and a Tsarist militia called the Black Hundreds, who targeted, tortured and killed Jews. (Reich too was from this milieu. When he fled his farm during the Russian invasion, ten years later and four hundred miles away, he looked back and saw the hill behind him 'black with Cossacks'.)

As a boy, Philip grew up on stories about hiding from Cossacks in the basement. With the Klan series, he gave himself licence to imagine his own way into the bleak rooms of his family's past. *Cellar*, 1970: four pairs of hob-nailed shoes attached to legs, some sticking ridiculously into the air, some bent at an unpleasantly floppy angle, surrounded by a mess of trashcan lids and chairs. He said he was painting people in the act of diving into the cellar, but from where I'm sitting it looks like they got caught. As a Jewish artist working in the aftermath of the

Holocaust, Guston knew there was no end to the capacity for human harm; that, as Freud had said, man is wolf to man. In a letter written just after the 1973 coup in Chile, he wrote: 'Our whole lives (since I can remember) are made up of the most extreme cruelties of holocausts. We are the witness of this hell. When I think of the victims, it is unbearable. To paint, to write, to teach, in the most dedicated sincere way, is the most intimate affirmation of creative life we possess in these despairing years.'

This is where Guston's feeling of identification with the Klansmen becomes more complicated. It turns out that he too was wearing a mask; he too had committed a violent act. In 1935, he'd changed his name from Phillip Goldstein to Philip Guston. He repainted the signature on some of his early works and kept the switch secret until the final year of his life. He asked his biographer Dore Ashton not to mention it, a request to which she acquiesced, and it wasn't made public until 1980, in a catalogue essay for his retrospective at the San Francisco Museum of Modern Art. By the 1960s, the decision had begun to eat away at him. Had he been trying to conceal his Jewishness, even to Aryanise himself? And if he hadn't, did it look like he had?

His daughter Musa wasn't told her father's real name until she was in college. As she explains in her sorrowing memoir, *Night Studio*, she knew nothing about her father's family. She never met her aunts and uncles. There were no photographs, no albums. What she did know is that 'my father had felt tremendous regret about having changed his name, that in his eyes it had become a shameful, cowardly act. And I knew that after the Second World War and the revelations of the Holocaust, when it became crucial for him to reclaim his Jewish identity, it was too late to change it back. His reputation was already established with the new name.'

A name change is at the very least a breach in continuous identity, severing the self into past and future elements, if not a kind of murder, the former existence decisively erased (Guston kept all the documents concerned hidden in a locked safety deposit box). It represents an aspirational attitude to the life that lies ahead, and also begs the question of what or who is being discarded. Guston said the main motivating force was his love for the painter and poet Musa McKim, who he married two years after he changed his name. He thought her parents wouldn't accept him as Phillip Goldstein, though he also said he didn't attempt to hide his identity as a non-observant Jew.

No longer being Phillip Goldstein also reshaped his relationship to his father, removing the permanent marker of patrilineal identity. There were reasons why this might have been appealing, and reasons too why it might have come to feel like a betrayal. Guston's father Leib, known as Louis or Wolf, had never been happy in America. In Odessa he had been a blacksmith and in Montreal a machinist on the railway, but in L.A. he was reduced to working as a rag and bone man, spending every day gathering up the city's trash and selling it from a horse-drawn wagon. He hung himself in 1923 or 1924, slinging a rope over the rafters of an outbuilding alongside the family home, where he was found by Phillip, his youngest son. 'Can you imagine', Guston sometimes asked his friends, 'how it feels to find your father like that?'

It was after Leib's death that Guston began to draw seriously. From the beginning he saw it as a way of transporting himself, reinventing and erasing all at once. On Sundays, his older brothers and sisters would come with their crowds of children to his mother's apartment. He'd beg her to lie about his whereabouts, instructing her to say he was out with friends. Hidden in the closet with its single light bulb, he'd listen to them talk and feel safe and remote, reading and drawing 'in this private box', yet another version of Reich's magic accumulator. Even as an adult he longed 'to be hidden and feel strange', a function that a false name can't help but serve.

Who knows whether Leib's death was in its specifics a tragedy or a relief? In discussing the personal aspect of Guston's paintings, I'm not saying that it trumps or overwrites the abundant political meanings of his work. What it does mean is that the objects in his canvases cannot be considered neutral. Rope. Light bulb. Klansman. Cossack. Everything is imbued with meaning, at once acutely personal and a consequence of the tumbling dominoes of global events. The rope the Klansman fingers in *Conspirators* might not be the same one that Phillip Goldstein found his father hanging from, but it is unmistakably the rope that ties us into history, that lashes us to time. What Guston's paintings tell us is that evil is not confined to specific bodies in specific eras. It bleeds out, seeping and staining through the years. History always comes home to roost. There is no possibility of a life uncompromised by the violence of the past.

In the reddish light cast by the tiki torches of Charlottesville, these meanings seemed painfully clear. Guston was trying to investigate the drives that underpin white supremacy, in himself as well as in the outside world. It's hard to imagine more significant work for an artist. But when he first showed the Klan paintings at the Marlborough Gallery in New York in November 1970, critics and colleagues alike reacted with fury at his defection from abstract painting ('embarrassing', Lee Krasner said). Several of his friends dropped him and he received almost uniformly brutal reviews. The harshest, by Hilton Kramer in the *New York Times*, accused him of being 'a mandarin pretending to be a stumblebum', feigning primitivism to catch a vogueish wave in politically engaged painting that had anyway already ebbed.

'It was as though I had left the church', Guston remembered. 'I was excommunicated for a while.' No one could understand why he'd abandoned his sublime, shuddering regions of pure colour for such ham-fisted, lurid work. Writing decades later in the *New Yorker*, Peter Schjeldahl recalled that he'd felt personally betrayed by the transition from refinement to abjection, a deliberate nose-dive into the trash heap. And what was the point anyway? It was 1970. The Klan weren't even a threat any more, Robert Hughes complained in *Time*.

Imagine being that cosseted, that certain. Two weeks before the Klan show opened, the civil rights activist Angela Davis was arrested by the FBI, and less than a month later, James Baldwin wrote his famous open letter to her in prison. In it, he said that racism would never end until white Americans stopped taking refuge in their whiteness. He described whiteness as putting a 'sinister . . . distance' between the experience of white people and the experience of others. It's this 'sinister distance' that allows some humans to consider others as a swarm, as trash, and it's this 'sinister distance' that drives the block in their noxious work. It will not be dismantled, not until each one of us looks at what our silence is facilitating, peering, as Guston did, into the blind spot in which atrocity keeps on and on occurring.

# 8

# 22nd Century

THE CLOSEST THING TO Reich's orgone box that I have found is a room on Lafayette Street in New York City. When I felt most locked up inside my body, almost the only thing that made me feel free was going to Joe's Pub to see Justin Vivian Bond, a transgender singer and performance artist who had the gift of duende, the knack for going so far beyond the edge of safety that everyone in the room felt shaken loose, transported to somewhere strange and new.

I'd first come across Viv a decade earlier, as the mistress of ceremonies in *Shortbus*, a 2006 film with a distinctly Reichian sensibility. The central character, Sofia, is a sex therapist who can't have an orgasm. Her quest for release takes her to a sex salon in Brooklyn populated by a diverse cast of queers and freaks. Despite the copious sex, which includes the national anthem being sung into somebody's asshole, it's appealingly sceptical about free love, not so much a manifesto of polyamory as a melancholy account of the difficulties of being a sexual body in the world. Many of the characters, particularly the dominatrix Severin, use sex as a way of hiding from real feeling.

The act itself isn't necessarily a cure for loneliness or a way of creating connection. Instead, it's the ability to open to other people that's presented, Reich-style, as the source of liberation: emotional vulnerability as the gateway to joy. All the sex is real and unsimulated, including Sofia's long-awaited orgasm, adding to the tender, shaky, naked mood.

Bond was ravishing in that film, a vision beyond age or gender, in a flapper's sequinned dress and elbow-length gloves, projecting a smoky, after-hours world-weariness that was immensely seductive. The first time I ever encountered the concept of being non-binary was when I was talking about it a few years later, on a sofa in New Hampshire with my friend Joseph, who had a cameo in the orgy scene. I said something about Bond, and he gently corrected my description, informing me that the pronoun wasn't *he* but *v*.

At the time, my own gender was like a noose around my neck. I was non-binary, even if I didn't yet know the word. I'd always felt like a boy inside, a femme gay boy, and the dissonance between how I experienced myself and how I was assumed to be was so painful that often I didn't want to leave my room and enter the world at all. Ten years ago, trans issues were nothing like as visible or widely discussed as they are now, and what discussion there was focused on the transition from male to female, female to male. It was a step forward, but it didn't address the problem of what to do if neither gender fitted you. What I wanted as a trans person was to escape the binary altogether, which seems so natural if it includes you and so unnatural and violently enforced if it does not. I wanted Hirschfeld's forty-three million genders, resplendent and unpoliced, a pool you could dive into and swim away.

You can hate what happens to bodies categorised as female while also remaining sceptical about the notion of two rigidly opposed genders, coloured pink and blue. Even Andrea Dworkin understood that. Though we think of her now as reifying gender, what she actually wanted to do was to dissolve the binary altogether, whatever the transphobes who've claimed her might say. 'We want to destroy sexism, that is polar role definitions of male and female, man and woman', she wrote in *Intercourse*. 'Androgyny as a concept has no notion of sexual repression built into it . . . It may be the one road to freedom open to women, men, and that emerging majority, the rest of us.'

Bond was the most visible non-binary person at the time, a pioneer who as well as creating the pronoun *v* had invented the gender-inclusive honorific *Mx*, now so prevalent that my English bank offers it as an option. The experience of encountering someone who insisted on claiming their own gender was so exciting it made me feel dizzy. My feelings of confinement would start to lift each time I walked across the East Village to Joe's Pub, climbing the big steps on Lafayette with my heart running a little fast. I always sat at a table in the front, usually with a friend or two, drank a glass of bourbon and waited for the things that weighed on me to be transformed. I was never sure if it would happen, but it always did, and afterwards I was at a loss to say exactly what had taken place, only that I felt some constriction or binding had been removed and that my body was streaming with life.

There was a cover Bond used to do at the time of two linked songs from near the end of Kate Bush's 2005 album *Aerial*. The first was a dreamy account of a naked moonlit swim on a deserted beach, a testament to voluptuous bodily pleasure. Then the sun came up and the mood changed with it, becoming witchy and feral. Bond stood poised on the edge of chaos, controlling dark knots of energy that swirled through the room. It was physical, the sense of space expanding. It always reminded me of Lorca, who in his famous lecture on duende said of the flamenco singer Pastora Pavon: 'she managed to tear through the scaffolding of the song, but allow through a furious burning *duende*.' A few paragraphs on, he added: 'when this escape is perfected, everyone feels the effects.'

I loved hearing those songs, but they were only a prelude to the psychic turmoil of the closing number, '22nd Century', which Viv always introduced the same way. 'This is a song by a Bahamian voodoo priest by the name of Exuma, but I do feel that it speaks to my experience and the experience of my people.' Then v would snap the word *HA*, and launch into a death rattle of images, swaying like a cobra. Back in 1970, Exuma had looked into a dark glass, seeing a strange ashy version of the decades ahead. He predicted a world where everything was in apocalyptic disarray. It came very fast, the words tumbling over each other, a vision of turbulence and instability that hung menacingly in the air. A plague in the 1990s that made me think of Aids, and now of course of Covid-19. Men becoming women, women becoming men. Animal liberation, liberation of women, the end of disease, no babies being born, man as his own god, no oxygen in the air. It was coming and it was coming now, radiant and terrifying. Viv's head was flung back, hair sleeked into a chignon, arms aloft, clawing the future into being.

★

The Obeah man Exuma might have written '22nd Century', but the most famous rendition belongs to Nina Simone, though it nearly dropped out of history altogether. She recorded it in February 1971 as part of the session for *Here Comes the Sun*, but it wasn't included on the album or written in the session log. It didn't resurface again until 1998, when a researcher who was putting together a compilation album stumbled across it in the RCA vaults, where I imagine it had been pulsing ominously in the cloistered dark.

Simone could find deep registers of emotion in even the flimsiest of lyrics, and she could also channel those emotions towards political ends. The most powerful numbers in her repertoire were the ones that allowed her to express mixed feelings, to carry rage, hatred, bitterness alongside yearning, joy coupled with despair. She once said she had a narrow vocal range, but she knew how to make her voice change shape, roiling from gravel to honey and back again. Like 'Pirate Jenny' and 'Mississippi Goddam', '22nd Century' is one of the gravel songs, in which her ongoing vision of liberation is yoked to a nine-minute fantasy of retribution and punishment, judgement day come at last. Exuma's apocalypse song allows her to slice back and forth, a prophetess of a post-human future in which all the tortuous old bodily categories have been dissolved.

Guitar, shaker, something wooden, clicking out a clave.

Then steel drums rolling repeated notes. She comes in at her leisure, almost remote against the pulsing calypso rhythm, unfolding a harrowing vision of unbreathable air, deformed and damaged people. Everything is changing, changing, changing. Gender has become unstable, right wing slips into left, the people with the power no longer have control, time itself upends. Her voice is menacing, absolutely authoritative and yet she also wrings something joyful from the litany of disasters ahead. The drums bubble as she bends a wordless *aaaaaa*, keening slowly, keening fast. Dogs and death, the end of marriage, the end of god. She shouts it out like a preacher, hexing the powers that be. 'Don't try to sway me over to your way. Your day, your day will go away.' Near the end she shifts into a rapid-fire scat, language itself breaking down into syllable and sound. It's frightening in the way that freedom is frightening: a world in which all the things that occasion subjugation can no longer be said to exist.

Simone's version of '22nd Century' is an artefact of the same political moment as Philip Guston's Klan paintings, emerging in response to the shattering events of the late 1960s, when it seemed as if the civil rights movement had been destroyed by the assassination or imprisonment of many of its leaders. The Nina singing was a woman in frank despair. Her marriage to Andy Stroud, the ex-cop who managed her career, had just broken up. She'd recently left what she'd taken to calling the United Snakes of America and gone into exile, but like her friend James Baldwin she'd fled pursued by ghosts. As she recounted in her memoir, *I Put a Spell on You*, they were all dragging along behind her: her father, her sister, the movement, Martin Luther King Jr., Malcolm X, her marriage and all her hopes, every one of them a corpse.

She'd come late to the civil rights movement, but once she decided to involve herself she'd gone all in, total commitment. Like Andrea Dworkin, like Malcolm X, it had taken her a while to process the stunning realisation that the injustices she'd experienced and witnessed were not reality per se, the natural and permanent order of events, but instead a deliberate system built on exclusion and supremacy: a situation that could be resisted, perhaps even remade. What she remembered from her childhood in Tryon, North Carolina was silence. No one spoke about the racism that everyone could see, and she understood even then that the silence was a product of violence, the consequence of an unspoken and omnipresent physical threat. 'I had not made a connection between the fights I had and any wider struggle for justice because of how I was raised', she explained. 'The Waymon way was to turn away from prejudice and to live your life as best you could, as if acknowledging the existence of racism was in itself a kind of defeat.'

Her name wasn't Nina back then. She was born Eunice Waymon in 1933, a month after Susan Sontag, the sixth of eight children. When she was three, her capable, beloved father nearly died from an intestinal obstruction. She was appointed his nurse through the long and painful convalescence, making him liquid meals from eggs and sugar and washing the ugly wound perhaps ten times a day while her mother kept the family afloat working as a housekeeper for white people. Mary Kate Waymon was a Methodist preacher, a cold, purposeful woman; in Simone's own word a 'fanatic' who disparaged all

worldly things, regarding even popular songs as sinful and polluting. The whole family was musical, but Eunice was
unprecedented in her talent, and from the moment she first
picked out 'God Be With You 'Til We Meet Again' in the key
of F, her legs too short to reach the pedals, it was decreed that
she would become the first black American concert pianist, a
phrasing she stuck to throughout her life, though she must have
known by adulthood that at least three women had preceded
her to the title, Hazel Harrison, Natalie Hinderas and Philippa
Schuyler.

A kind of severing went on in her childhood, a descending
line that cut her off from everyone around her. Her parents
couldn't afford piano lessons, but one of the women for whom
her mother cleaned offered to pay for a year of tuition. For 75
cents a lesson, the piano teacher, who she called Miz Mazzy,
introduced her to Bach and gave her so much of the affection
and attention she lacked at home that Eunice came to regard
her as 'my white momma'. After the year was up, Miz Mazzy
badgered the citizens of Tryon into setting up a town fund to
pay for her continuing musical education in return for regular
concerts (according to Simone's biographer Nadine Cohodas,
the fund only had two donors, both wealthy white women).

Eunice became public property, the black prodigy, the
chosen one permitted to pass through doors that were otherwise securely locked. It was the beginning of her long isolation
– the loneliness of practising six, seven, eight speechless, unac-
companied hours a day multiplied by the loneliness of being
invited to cross tracks that were mortally dangerous to everyone
who shared the colour of her skin. Not that she was allowed to

forget, in those Jim Crow years, the reality of segregation. She might be the town project, but she still had to take her grilled-cheese sandwich outside the pharmacy while the white children ate inside, a humiliation that stayed with her no matter how rich she got.

This isn't to say that she made no attempts at resistance. In 1944, she gave a recital at the Tryon library. It was an all-white affair but she insisted her parents attend. Sitting at the piano, she saw them being moved from the front row to make room for a white couple. She announced to the audience at large that she would not play unless her parents were sat where she could see them. They were allowed to return to their seats, though Eunice also heard snickers, hardly the last time she'd be laughed at on stage. She was eleven years old.

She was brought up to believe in the American dream: that effort and talent will lead unequivocally to success, never mind what kind of body you inhabit. This powerful illusion held until April 1951, when she was rejected by the Curtis Institute of Music, the Philadelphia conservatory that had been her consuming goal since childhood. At first she believed she simply wasn't good enough, but people kept telling her the decision had been racist. The realisation that the door was not open after all was what forced Eunice Waymon to create her second self, the doppelganger who became a world-famous star.

The stopping-up of her talent meant she needed an outlet as well as a source of funds. In the summer of 1954 she began to play in a bar in Atlantic City under a new name, Nina Simone, chosen because she didn't want her mother to know she was performing what Mary Kate had always called *real*, as opposed to holy music. She brought concert hall airs to the Irish drunks, wearing a chiffon evening dress and demanding total silence as she played. She hadn't intended to sing, but the owner of the Midtown Bar & Grill on Pacific Avenue insisted on the very first evening: sing or go.

Music was a lodging place where she could temporarily house her feelings, pouring her anger, sorrow and self-hatred into songs she knew were too small, too superficial for her prodigious gifts. She put everything she'd learned into it, making a single tune float into hours, taking it to places no other person had the dexterity or intelligence to imagine, let alone to reach. Performing was from the very first a ghetto and a trap, a manifestation of her disgrace and a reminder of the unjust outside world, but it was also a place in which she could enact her own original vision, as a concert hall could never have been. Refused the category she wanted, she refused category altogether, sailing from blues to jazz to gospel to soul, often in the space of a single song, while the piano underneath yearned its way always back to Bach.

Soon she was playing clubs in New York and putting out records; soon she was driving around Greenwich Village in a steel-grey Mercedes with red leather seats, top down, a queen in a red hat. By the late 1950s, fame and money had arrived, neither quite the blessing that it seemed. She wanted to be listened to, insisting on it even in those early years, but she didn't always want to be looked at. '*I can't be white* and I'm the kind of colored girl who looks like everything white people despise or have been taught to despise', she wrote in an undated note to herself. 'If I were a boy, it wouldn't matter so much, but I'm a girl and in front of the public all the time wide open for them to jeer and approve of or disapprove of.'

It wasn't until after she'd been married twice and had a daughter of her own that she really began to focus on the civil rights movement, to realise that the miseries she was confiding to her diary were in themselves political. She knew about Rosa Parks and the Montgomery bus boycott, she was friends with the writers James Baldwin and Langston Hughes, but it took the playwright Lorraine Hansbury to make her see that her own experiences were connected to the ongoing legacy of slavery, to wake her up to the realities of race and class. Hansbury was a dynamic, brilliant young lesbian, who at the age of twenty-seven had written *A Raisin in the Sun*, the first play by an African-American woman to be staged on Broadway. 'We never talked about men or clothes or other such inconsequential things when we got together,' Simone said of their electrifying friendship. 'It was always Marx, Lenin, revolution – real girls' talk.'

1963, the year of the March on Washington, was the turning point in her political awakening, the moment she finally shed her reluctance to be involved. On 12 April, Good Friday, Martin Luther King Jr. was arrested and jailed in Birmingham for taking part in a non-violent demonstration against segregation. Protestors were attacked with Alsatians and cudgels and drenched with fire hoses as they walked from the 16th Street Baptist Church (the city's first black church and the organisational headquarters of the movement) to City Hall, where they hoped to encourage the mayor to discuss segregation. While King and fifty other Birmingham citizens were in jail, Nina was playing a show in Chicago at the time, a frivolity that Lorraine was quick to ring and point out.

Two months later, on 12 June, the civil rights activist Medgar Evers was shot to death, two hours after President Kennedy had announced his Civil Rights Bill. Evers was the field secretary of the Mississippi branch of the NAACP, the National Association for the Advancement of Colored People, and had helped to organise mass protests to desegregate its beaches, buses and parks, all of which had been met with violent resistance by white residents, parading with swastikas and armed with just the sort of homemade weapons wielded by Guston's Klansmen. Evers was a close friend of James Baldwin, who had written the play *Blues for Mister Charlie* about their nocturnal journey together to discover the white murderer of a black man.

Evers was shot in the driveway of his own home by a member of the White Citizens' Council, while carrying an armful of T-shirts to give out to demonstrators the next day. Each was stamped with the legend: JIM CROW MUST GO. The hospital in which he died was segregated too, and at first he was refused entry, though he was plainly bleeding to death. Years before, when he was a boy, a friend of his father's had been killed for talking to a white woman. His bloody clothing lay on a fence for months afterwards, and Evers said that for the rest of his life he could still see it in his mind's eye, a visceral symbol of what racism really was.

Like that death, Evers's assassination ignited something in Simone, but there was worse to come. She couldn't go to the March on Washington on 28 August because she was rehearsing for a tour. She watched it live on television from the big house she'd bought in Mount Vernon, a suburb of New York City. Eighteen days later, she was sitting alone in her den above the garage, still rehearsing songs, when she heard on the radio that four members of the Klan had planted sticks of dynamite in the 16th Street Baptist Church in Birmingham during Sunday school, killing four little girls. Later that day, there were two more murders in the city. A white policeman shot a sixteen-year-old black boy who was throwing stones at a car full of white men waving Confederate flags and hurling bottles, and then two white men on a motor scooter plastered with more Confederate stickers pulled a thirteen-year-old black boy off the handlebars of his brother's bicycle and shot him too. The Confederate flag, the same symbol waved at Charlottesville, had recently been resurrected as a symbol of opposition to civil rights, if not active nostalgia for the era of slavery.

Addie May Collins, Cynthia Wesley, Carole Robertson, Carol Denise McNair, Johnny Robinson and Virgil Ware, all of them dead, all of them children. This was what Lorraine had been trying to tell her. 'I suddenly realized', she wrote in *I Put a Spell on You*, 'what it was to be black in America in 1963.' She went down to the garage in a trance, out of her mind with rage. When her husband Andy walked in he saw at once that she was trying to make a zip gun, a homemade firearm. 'Nina, you don't know anything about killing,' he said. 'The only thing you've got is music.' An hour later she emerged again with the sheet music to 'Mississippi Goddam'. When she sang it, she felt as if she'd flung 'ten bullets' back at the Birmingham killers.

As she became more involved with the movement, her

performances changed. She wasn't a popular entertainer any more. She was a freedom fighter, using music as a 'political weapon' for rallying her people, providing sustenance and education. The movement thrilled her. There was so much hope, so much to discuss. Was non-violence really the best technique? Was separatism necessary? What kind of future society should be created? Her own inclinations were closer to the militant Black Power teachings of Stokely Carmichael and Huey Newton than the turn-the-other-cheek Christianity espoused by Bayard Rustin and the NAACP. When she met Martin Luther King, she burst out, 'I'm not non-violent,' before he even had the chance to say hello ('That's OK, sister,' he replied).

For the first time since she'd been rejected by Curtis, her life felt meaningful. As an activist, she had a sense of dignity and purpose that had been lacking right through her adult years. Singing freedom songs, she told an interviewer, 'helps to change the world . . . To move the audience, to make them conscious of what has been done to my people around the world.' When the organiser Vernon Jordan asked her in 1964 why she wasn't more involved, she had snapped, 'Motherfucker, I *am* civil rights.' A song is not a gun, just as a painting is not a protest march, but that doesn't mean it has no effect on the outside world. In a radio interview in 1969, Simone explained that she didn't think artists had to take a political stand, but that it was their duty to reflect the reality they live in. Striking a Reichian note, she described American society as a cancer that had to be exposed before it could be cured. 'I am not the doctor to cure it however, sugar,' she said. 'All I can do is expose the sickness, that's my job.'

Over the years, she thought a lot about what music could do, trying to understand the strange transaction that took place when she sat down at the keys and opened her mouth. Some of her tracks were plainly cathartic, like her cover of 'Pirate Jenny', a song from Brecht's *Threepenny Opera*, which had been playing everywhere in Berlin the year that Reich arrived in the city. Simone pours everything she knows about invisibility and hard labour into the role of the servant girl Jenny, intoning the sinister line 'I'm counting their heads as I'm making the beds' as the prelude to a retributive murder spree.

The lyrics of 'Mississippi Goddam' also struck a vengeful note. Sometimes she sang 'we're all going to die', a protest against the cautious pace of the Lyndon B. Johnson administration, crawling towards incremental shifts in the law while the bodies kept mounting up. *Too slow*, Nina and her band bellowed in the chorus. Other times, she changed the pronoun, flipping the line from prophecy to threat. 'Oh but this whole country is full of lies/You're all going to die and die like flies', she sang at Carnegie Hall on 17 May 1964, to an audience that grows audibly more unnerved by the verse. She told the filmmaker Peter Rodis that when she performed it: 'I just want them to be in pieces. I want to go in that den of those elegant people with their old ideas, smugness, and just drive them insane.' In response, boxes of broken records were sent to her label and the song was banned on the radio in several Southern states.

But fantasies of retribution were not the entirety of Simone's activism (and nor do threats delivered from a stage exist in the same order of reality as centuries of actual and ongoing atrocity). She might have been, as she put it herself, a woman on fire, but the Old Testament tone was always mixed with something tender, a yearning for contact. As a child back in North Carolina, she'd played the piano at revival meetings for hours on end, the congregation testifying and speaking in tongues, 'just running back and forth . . . and the preacher gathering up all that spiritual energy and throwing it back out on the people. Women would have to go to hospital sometimes, they got so transported.' It was this experience that she began to feel in her concerts in the 1960s, an uncanny energy that moved between her and the audience, as if every last body in the crowd was a source of power and she had found the communal switch.

Sex, she wrote in her diary, was the 'source of power' for her performances, the way she transformed the concert hall into an orgone box. I don't know if she ever read Lorca on duende, but when she tried to explain what she meant, the best comparison she could think of was to a bullfight. She'd been to one in Barcelona, on a sweltering afternoon, and when the bull was finally killed she'd vomited with shock. A real bloodletting, she called it, the same phrase they used in Tryon when someone became enraptured, beside themselves, foaming at the mouth. It was 'the same sense of being transformed, of celebrating something deep, something very deep. That's what I learned about performing, that it was real, and I had the ability to make people *feel* on a deep level . . . And when you've caught it, when you've got the audience hooked, you always know because it's like you've got electricity hanging in the air . . . I was the toreador mesmerizing this bull and I could turn around and walk away, turning my back on this huge animal . . . And, like they did with the toreadors, people came to see me because they knew I was playing close to the edge and one day I might fail.'

It's funny, she sounds like Susan Sontag in that statement, when she was talking in the wake of her first brush with cancer about death as a bull, a black bull that she wanted to run ahead of. The difference is that Simone wasn't just doing it for herself. I never saw her play, but I've felt that electricity sometimes at shows. Canetti said that there were many kinds of crowds, and once or twice I've been in one that felt like a huge animal. It's an experience that comes close to the ecstasy of sex, the joy of shedding your own burdened, individual body and merging with a wild, surging collective instead. For Simone, it was a transaction that went both ways, which was why she screamed at audiences for chatting or getting up when she was playing. She needed their focus, their attention, as the raw material from which she could enact her transformations; the fuel for a long journey out.

As to where she was headed, I think what she was doing in the 1960s was carrying her audience down into their own most painful feelings, a high-risk, cathartic passage through fury, mourning, horror, hurt, despair and out again to joy, just as Vivian Bond did in Joe's Pub on Lafayette Street five decades later. It wasn't so much that she sang about freedom as that she enacted it by way of her own supple transformations, her ability to slip fluidly, spontaneously from mood to mood, to interpolate, to interrupt, to feint, to float away, to cut to the heart. Reich developed a kind of touch to break down his patients' armour, the traumatic history that exists in every human body, and I think Simone did the same thing with song.

'Everybody is half dead,' she told an interviewer in 1969, setting out once again what sounds very much like a Reichian philosophy. 'Everybody avoids everybody. All over the place, in most situations, most all of the time. I know. I'm one of those everybodies, and to me it is *terrible*. And so all I'm trying to do all the time is just open people up so they can feel themselves and let themselves be open to somebody else. That is all. That's it.'

These days we tend to be sceptical of the political effects of opening up. It sounds like too much like careless hippie platitudes. But in his despairing 1972 account of the civil rights movement, *No Name in the Street*, Simone's friend James Baldwin took the same idea about emotional closeness even further. He was always among the most consistently insightful of Reich's readers. Like Foucault, he'd raised a sceptical eyebrow at the notion of orgasms ending violence, and yet in this devastated book he drew on Reich to argue that curtailments or repressions of the private life had the gravest of consequences in the public world, identifying it as the root cause of racism itself.

I have always been struck, in America, by an emotional poverty so bottomless, and a terror of human life, of human touch, so deep that virtually no American appears able to achieve any viable, organic connection between his public stance and his private life. This failure of the private life has always had the most devastating effect on American public conduct, and on black-white relations. If Americans were not so terrified of their private selves, they would never have become so dependent on what they call the 'Negro problem.' This problem, which they invented in order to safeguard their purity, has made of them criminals and monsters, and it is destroying them.

On Simone's thirty-second birthday, 21 February 1965, Malcolm X was assassinated during a lecture at the Audubon Ballroom by three members of the separatist Nation of Islam, the organisation he'd left the previous year, in part because he wanted to collaborate with other civil rights groups. To her abiding regret, Nina had never met him, but she knew his pregnant wife, Betty Shabazz, who soon afterwards moved next door to her in Mount Vernon along with her six daughters; two of whom, the twins Malikah and Malaak, were born after their father's murder.

A month after Malcolm's death, Simone cancelled a string of lucrative dates in New York and flew to Alabama with her band for the concert at the culmination of the third Selma to Montgomery march for voting rights (in Alabama at the time, black citizens could register to vote on two days of the year. Each registration took an hour). That night Nina played on a stage made, in lieu of any other materials, from empty coffins donated by a local black mortuary. Whatever it took, up there in her plaid skirt, giving love and fury back to an exhausted and footsore crowd of twenty-five thousand, pressed together in the drenching rain.

The talk in those days was of revolution: not if but when.

Like Reich in the aftermath of the Vienna riots, Nina couldn't understand why everybody didn't rise up and fight. She no longer believed that there was any possibility of freedom being handed over peacefully by people who bombed churches, murdered activists and openly mourned slavery. If you wanted it, you'd have to take it. As she pointed out, the Ku Klux Klan weren't non-violent, and nor were the police.

The movement didn't just give her a purpose. It was also a way to channel her own complicated private feelings into something larger. She could alchemise her depression, her abiding sense of ugliness, both legacies of racism, and convert them into anthems of joy and pride like 'Ain't Got No/I Got Life' or 'Young, Gifted and Black', which was written for Lorraine. But the constant touring took a toll, and the bad feelings kept seeping back. Many nights she couldn't sleep at all, the lyrics she'd just sung tracking endlessly through her head. It was all very well acting as a conduit for the energies of thousands of people, but what did you do when they went home and you were left in a dressing room alone, staring at your own spectral face in the full-length mirror? Drink helped, or seemed to, as did pills: 'sleeping pills to sleep + yellow pills to go on stage'.

Sex was a better medicine, the only thing, she once wrote, that let her be a warm and open human being. In her diary she acknowledged her desire for both sexes, charting too the descent of her relationship with Andy. He was cold, he worked her like a dog, he made her beg for affection and sometimes he hit her. She found his violence shattering and unendurable, just as Dworkin would when her husband began to beat her in

Amsterdam a year or two later. 'They don't know that I'm dead and my ghost is holding on', Nina wrote in an undated note in her journal. Reality winked in and out. While she was on tour with Bill Cosby in 1968, Andy found her in the dressing room, putting brown make-up in her hair. She was hallucinating and when she looked up at him, for a minute she could see clean through his skin. Years later, she was diagnosed bipolar and put on medication, but in the 1960s the only thing she had was work, never mind that the world was degrading around her as she sang.

Malcolm X's autobiography was published in November 1965, nine months after his death. She loved it, but the part about his education in a progressive prison was bitter, considering prison was already being deployed as a tactic to destroy the movement. Rustin and his contemporaries had used arrest as a technique of non-violent resistance, the cry of *fill the jails* presenting the state with non-compliant bodies as a physical problem to solve. But in the late 1960s, the state reconfigured imprisonment as a weapon, instituting drastically longer sentences, often on false charges. The threat of prison had a chilling effect on people's willingness to engage in activism and marked the beginning of today's era of mass incarceration and long-term solitary confinement, both of which disproportionately affect people of colour.

Many of the civil rights organisers who weren't in jail were subject to an FBI programme of surveillance, infiltration and discreditation known as Cointelpro, which was explicitly designed to undermine and sabotage the movement. In what was by no means their most malevolent act, the FBI bugged

Martin Luther King's hotel rooms for two years, creating an audio record of the affairs he'd been so frantic to conceal that he'd stopped working with Rustin rather than risk them being leaked to the press. In an anonymous letter sent on 21 November 1964, the Bureau warned that the audio tape would be released to the media if King didn't commit suicide before the Nobel Peace Prize was awarded to him three weeks later. *Filthy, evil, animal* were among the words used to address him.

By the late 1960s, Simone felt as if all her former comrades were either dead, 'exiled, jailed or underground'. Langston Hughes was dead. Lorraine Hansberry was dead of pancreatic cancer at the age of thirty-four (her friend Baldwin suspected, à la Reich, 'that what she saw contributed to the strain that killed her, for the effort to which Lorraine was dedicated is more than enough to kill a man'). Malcolm X was dead at the age of thirty-nine. Huey Newton was in prison. Stokely Carmichael was under surveillance and hobbled by a travel ban.

The last blow was the worst. Nina was preparing for a show on Long Island when she saw people huddled around a television. 4 April 1968. Martin Luther King Jr. had been shot, the newscaster informed her, and there were riots in one hundred and twenty-five cities, among them Washington, Detroit, New York, Chicago. Like Malcolm, he was thirty-nine. Three days later, with America still in flames, Nina played at the Westbury Music Fair. She sang 'Mississippi Goddam', and she also sang a song her bass player had written for King, which, she told the audience, they had only learned that day. She repeatedly broke off to address the audience, sometimes openly sobbing. 'Do you realise how many we have lost?' she asked them. She listed the dead, many among them her own close friends. 'We can't afford any more losses. They're shooting us down one by one.' This is was what was roiling inside her when she recorded '22nd Century' three years later: frank despair.

★

Say you wanted a better world. Say you fought for it, and say that it unravelled, that people were irrevocably damaged, that there were deaths. Say that the dream was freedom. Say that you dreamt of a world in which people were not hobbled or hated or killed because of the kind of body they inhabited. Say that you thought the body could be a source of power or delight. Say that you imagined a future that did not involve harm. Say that you failed. Say that you failed to bring that future into being.

From feminism to gay liberation to the civil rights movement, the struggles of the last century were at heart about the right to be free of oppression based on the kind of body you inhabited: able to live where you pleased, work where you pleased, eat where you pleased, walk where you pleased without the risk of violence or death; able to have an abortion, kiss in public, engage in consensual sex without the threat of a prison sentence. The victories that did arise were hard-won, but they weren't permanently secured, and already they are vanishing away.

Perhaps Freud was right. Perhaps there is something atavistic in humans, an irrepressible will to violence, an instinctive desire to generate notions of *us* and *them*, to enforce borders between good and bad bodies, and to obsess over purity, degeneration, miscegenation and pollution. And yet the dream of the free body doesn't go away. It buzzes in the air. It smells of honey. While I was writing these pages I went to dinner with a friend who works as a teacher in Hong Kong. He described the protests that took place at the end of 2019 and he said that some of his students were facing prison sentences just for carrying a mask, for walking down the wrong street. Many things had been banned, including the word *protest*, so when they communicated with each other the students used the word *dreaming* instead. I know that *dreaming* is dangerous, one of them told my friend, but *dreaming* gives me hope.

What does freedom mean to you, the film-maker Peter Rodis once asked Simone. In the footage, she's sitting on the floor in her house in Mount Vernon, leaning up against the couch, wearing a brown batik print dress and big hoops in her ears. Her hair is short and her face amazingly expressive. It's 1969, so she is thirty-six years old and at a very low ebb, in that painful space between King's death and her escape from the United Snakes of America, though she looks full of life. 'What's free to me?' she asks, fiddling with her dress. 'Same thing it is to you. You tell me.' The interviewer laughs and says no, and then she laughs too. She puts her hands around her knees and shakes her head slowly. 'It's just a feeling. It's just a feeling . . . I've had a couple of times on stage where I really felt *free*, and that's something else.'

She pulls herself more upright, swivels round to face the camera. 'That's really something else.' Her hands are up now, palms out, tracking the space in front of her. 'Like, like.' Then she gets it. 'I'll tell you what freedom is to me. No fear! I mean really, no fear.' She looks almost shocked by what she's saying, puts her hand to her head. 'If I could have that half of my life,' she shakes her head again, 'no fear.' In a softer voice: 'Lots of children have no fear. That's the closest way, that's the only way I can describe it. That's not all of it, but it is *something* to really, really feel.' The interviewer starts to stutter a new question but she is completely caught up in examining what she's just articulated. She looks down, still shaking her head, laughing a little. As he continues to speak she abruptly leans forward and reaches out her hand. 'Like a new way of seeing! A new way of seeing something.'

Like Reich, the tragedy of Simone's later life is not that she struggled with alcohol or mental illness. It's not that she had periods of poverty, lived in unhappy exile, was sometimes violent or gave performances that descended into chaos. It's that the freedom she fought for did not come to pass in her lifetime, not as she had hoped. When she was asked about the civil rights movement in the 1990s, while she was living in France, she said bitterly: 'There is no civil rights movement. Everybody's gone.' And yet even at the very end of her life she was singing the old songs. São Paulo, Brazil, 13 April 2000. Monumental now, hair braided into a topknot, she sits at the piano and sings 'The King of Love is Dead', power still flooding through her ravaged, unmistakable voice. Right at the end, she breaks off to speak directly to the crowd. 'This is 2000 now,' she tells them. 'No more time for wasting time about this racial problem.' She repeats it three times, like a spell. 'No more time, no more time. No more time.'

Reich's dream, Dworkin's dream, Nina's dream: none of

these better worlds have yet transpired. There is no republic of unencumbered bodies, free to migrate between states, unharried by any hierarchy of form. It's impossible to know if it will ever be achieved, but if I'm certain about anything at all, it's that freedom is a shared endeavour, a collaboration built by many hands over many centuries of time, a labour which every single living person can choose to hinder or advance. It is possible to remake the world. What you cannot do is assume that any change is permanent. Everything can be undone, and every victory must be refought.

I still don't believe in orgone boxes but I do think Reich found his way to two durable truths. I think the weight of history abides in our private bodies. Each of us carries a legacy of personal and inherited trauma, operating within an unequal grid of rules and laws that depends upon the kind of body we were born into. At the same time, we are porous and capable of mysterious effects on each other's lives. If, as Angela Carter said of Sade, 'my freedom makes you more unfree, if it does not acknowledge your freedom', then surely the opposite is also true. This is what differentiates the marchers in Charlottesville from those in Washington in 1963 or from the Black Lives Matter protesters gathered in cities across the world in the spring of 2020. Contrary to what the white supremacists might think, claiming the right to deny other people their liberty is not a freedom movement, and nor is refusing to wear a mask designed to protect other people's health.

When I listen, as I often do, to '22nd Century', I feel fear move through my body like a contaminating fog. If I look into the future, I too see ashes. I'm afraid every day of what lies ahead, especially the cruelties that will inevitably occur as resources diminish. There is so little time left. Already, the soil is poisoned, the glaciers melting, the oceans full of plastic; already a new plague has exposed the drastic inequalities in how our lives are valued and protected. Every day as I've sat down to write there have been more stories about bodily harm on account of bodily difference. Precarious bodies, bodies as a brutalised, limitless resource. I'm devastated by what is happening, and by how difficult it, it being capitalism, is to change. It's not the world I want, in which difference is cherished: not a planet like a prison, but a planet like a forest.

Violence is a fact, and yet whenever I've sat in Joe's Pub watching Viv or listened to Nina Simone sing, I've felt the room expand around me. This is what one body can do for another: manifest a freedom that is shared, that slips under the skin. Freedom doesn't mean being unburdened by the past. It means continuing into the future, *dreaming* all the time. A free body need not be whole or undamaged or unaugmented. It is always changing, changing, changing, a fluid form after all. Imagine, for a minute, what it would be like to inhabit a body without fear, without the need for fear. Just imagine what we could do. Just imagine the world that we could build.

# Notes

## CHAPTER 1: THE LIBERATION MACHINE

5   '*the acceptability of homosexuality . . .*': Local Government Act 1988.

6   '*He listened, observed, then touched . . .*': Peter Reich, *A Book of Dreams* (John Blake, 2015 [1974]), p. xi.

9   '*vibrating soundless hum . . .*': William Burroughs, *Naked Lunch* (John Calder, 1964 [1959]), p. 207.

9   '*the message of orgasm . . .*': William Burroughs, *The Ticket That Exploded* (John Calder, 1968), p. 76.

12   '*that most optimistic of sexual liberationists . . .*': Andrea Dworkin, *Intercourse: Twentieth Anniversary Edition* (Basic Books, 2007 [1987]), p. 179.

12   '*I just know that something good is going to happen*': Kate Bush, 'Cloudbusting', *Hounds of Love* (1985).

13   '*My body is talking louder . . .*': Katie Roiphe, *The Violet Hour: Great Writers at the End* (The Dial Press, 2016), p. 44.

13   '*the people I had been raised among . . .*': James Baldwin, 'The New Lost Generation', in *Collected Essays* (Library of America, 1998), p. 663.

## CHAPTER 2: UNWELL

26   '*His body was a graveyard of buried emotions . . .*': Edward St Aubyn, *At Last* (Picador, 2011), pp. 171–2.

28 'open, lost, hungry . . .': Myron Sharaf, *Fury on Earth: A Biography of Wilhelm Reich* (Da Capo Press, 1994), p. 51.

29 'an adventurer': Sigmund Freud, ed. Jeffrey Moussaieff Masson, *The Complete Letters of Sigmund Freud to Wilhelm Fliess, 1887–1904* (Harvard University Press, 1985), p. 398.

30 'I have become convinced that sexuality . . .': Wilhelm Reich, *The Function of the Orgasm* (Panther, 1968), p. 44.

31 'He looked straight at you . . .': Wilhelm Reich, *Reich Speaks of Freud* (Pelican Books, 1975 [1967]), p. 47.

31 'still at an uncodified, experimental stage . . .': Christopher Turner, *Adventures in the Orgasmatron* (Fourth Estate, 2012), p. 22.

36 'My body froze . . .': *Norton Grim and Me*, dir. Tony Gammidge (2019).

36 'almost wholly inadequate . . .': Susan Sontag, *As Consciousness Is Harnessed to Flesh: Journals & Notebooks 1964–1980* (Farrar, Straus and Giroux, 2012), pp. 233–4.

37 'rigidity and antisexuality . . .': Jonathan Cott, *Susan Sontag: The Complete Rolling Stone Interview* (Yale University Press, 2013), p. 41.

38 'I was my mother's iron lung . . .': Susan Sontag, *As Consciousness Is Harnessed to Flesh*, p. 220.

38 'My earliest childhood decision . . .': David Rieff, *Swimming in a Sea of Death* (Granta, 2008), p. 23.

38 'The lesson was: stay away from bodies . . .': Susan Sontag, *As Consciousness Is Harnessed to Flesh*, p. 217.

39 'leaky': David Rieff, *Swimming in a Sea of Death*, p. 29.

39 'bordered on the unbearable': ibid., p. 34.

39 'One pushes and pulls and pokes . . .': ibid., p. 35.

39 'I feel like the Vietnam War . . .': ibid., p. 35.

40 'Cancer = death': ibid., p. 29.

41 'it is my impression . . .': Denis Donoghue, *New York Times*, 16 July 1978.

41 'gloomy . . .': Susan Sontag, *Illness as Metaphor & AIDS and its Metaphors* (Penguin Modern Classics, 1991), pp. 97–8.

41 'opaque': David Rieff, *Swimming in a Sea of Death*, p. 33.

41 'I felt my tumour . . .': Susan Sontag, *As Consciousness Is Harnessed to Flesh*, p. 223.

NOTES

'*I feel my body has let me down . . .*': David Rieff, *Swimming in a Sea of Death*, p. 36.

43 '*Let the bitch die*': Lorena Munoz-Alonso, 'Adele Mailer, Visual Artist Once Stabbed by Husband Norman Mailer, Dies at 90', *Artnet*, 26 November 2015.

43 '*a murderous nest of feeling*': Susan Sontag, *Illness as Metaphor*, p. 23.

44 '*I'm allergic to the couch*': *Safe*, dir. Todd Haynes (1995).

45 '*I . . . love . . . you?*': ibid.

45 '*I've been under a lot of stress*': ibid.

46 '*There's nothing wrong with you, Carol*': ibid.

48 '*Her book literally states . . .*': Tod Haynes, *Bomb 52*, Summer 1995.

48 '*Ultimately, what was it in people . . .*': Julia Leyda, ed., *Todd Haynes: Interviews* (University Press of Mississippi, 2014), p. 91.

49 '*A demonic pregnancy*': Susan Sontag, *Illness as Metaphor*, p. 14.

50 '*A healthy person is one who can say . . .*': Kathy Acker, 'The Gift of Disease', *Guardian*, 18 January 1997.

50 '*a piece of life history . . .*': Wilhelm Reich, trans. Vincent R. Carfango, *Character Analysis* (Farrar, Straus and Giroux, 1990 [1933]) p. 154.

51 '*a girlish mother . . .*': Chris Kraus, *After Kathy Acker* (Allen Lane, 2017), p. 44.

52 '*On a very deep level, she couldn't stand me*': Nina Burleigh, 'Kathy Acker', *Chicago Tribune*, 28 August 1988.

54 '*My search for a way to defeat . . .*': Kathy Acker, 'The Gift of Disease', *Guardian*, 18 January 1997.

55 '*It's fantastic knowing . . .*': 'Susan Sontag Found Crisis of Cancer Added Fierce Intensity to Life', *New York Times*, 30 January 1978.

58 '*What does make sense . . .*': Jonathan Cott, *Susan Sontag: The Complete Rolling Stone Interview*, p. 8.

58 '*Each woman responds to the crisis . . .*': Audre Lorde, *The Cancer Journals* (Aunt Lute Books, 1997 [1980]), p. 7.

60 '*She remained unsheltered . . .*': Avital Ronell, in Amy Scholder, Carla Harryman and Avital Ronnell, eds., *Lust for Life: On the Writings of Kathy Acker* (Verso, 2006) p. 15.

60 '*her reasoning here wasn't flawless*': Chris Kraus, *After Kathy Acker*, p. 267.

61   '*The first thing that I did . . .*': Kathy Acker, 'The Gift of Disease', *Guardian*, 18 January 1997.

63   '*strange, chemical immortality*': David Rieff, *Swimming in A Sea of Death*, p. 16.


CHAPTER 3: SEX ACTS

70   '*gold and inferno-red*': Christopher Isherwood, *Goodbye to Berlin* (Hogarth Press, 1954 [1939]), p. 296.

70   '*Sodom and Gomorrah at a Prussian tempo . . .*': Norman Page, *Auden and Isherwood: The Berlin Years* (Macmillan Press, 1998), p. 86.

70   '*you had this feeling that sexually. . .*': Michael Peppiatt, *Francis Bacon: Anatomy of an Enigma* (Constable, 2008 [1996]), p. 35.

71   '*the buggers daydream*': Norman Page, *Auden and Isherwood: The Berlin Years*, p. 14.

71   '*To Christopher, Berlin meant Boys*': Christopher Isherwood, *Christopher and His Kind: 1929–1939* (Magnum, 1977 [1976]), p. 10.

72   '*natural*': ibid., p. 16.

72   '*an intimate physical shame*': ibid., p. 13.

73   '*This is what freedom is . . .*': ibid., p. 24.

73   '*was the coming of warmth and colour . . .*': ibid., p. 39.

73   '*a Black Forest of furniture*': ibid., p. 22.

74   '*I suppose you wouldn't care to have lunch here?*': ibid., p. 18.

74   '*freakish fellow-tribesmen . . .*': ibid., p. 20.

75   '*he encouraged his friends . . .*': ibid., p. 32.

76   '*that which nearly strangled my heart*': Heike Bauer, *The Hirschfeld Archives: Violence, Death, and Modern Queer Culture* (Temple University Press, 2017), p. 40.

78   '*I have always expressed the view . . .*': Charlotte Wolff, *Magnus Hirschfeld: A Portrait of a Pioneer in Sexology* (Quartet Books, 1986) p. 256.

79   '*The number of actual and imaginable . . .*': Elena Mancini, *Magnus Hirschfeld and the Quest for Sexual Freedom* (Palgrave Macmillan, 2010), p. 62.

80   'all *love should be a private matter . . .*': Charlotte Wolff, *Magnus Hirschfeld*, p. 91.

81   *'haunting grocery stores . . .'*: Peter C. Engelman, ed., 'Sanger's Hunger Games: A Post-War German Odyssey', *The Margaret Sanger Papers Project Newsletter*, No. 61, Fall 2012.

81   *'beautiful dwelling'*: ibid.

82   'I *had ceased to be* . . .': Wilhelm Reich, trans. Mary Boyd Higgins, *Passion of Youth: An Autobiography, 1897–1912* (Farrar, Straus and Giroux, 1988), p. 43.

82   *'forced marriage'*: ibid., p. 175.

83   *'That thick?'*: Christopher Turner, *Adventures in the Orgasmatron*, p. 94.

83   *'It is not just to fuck* . . .': Wilhelm Reich, *Reich Speaks of Freud*, p. 37.

84   *'The repercussions, the shock waves* . . .': Benjamin Moser, *Sontag: Her Life* (Allen Lane, 2019), p. 175.

87   *'Freud had to give up* . . .': Wilhelm Reich, *Reich Speaks of Freud*, p. 33.

89   *'a gatekeeper's house* . . .': Elizabeth Ann Danto, *Freud's Free Clinics* (Columbia University Press, 2005), p. 95.

89   *'From now onward* . . .': Wilhelm Reich, *Reich Speaks of Freud*, p. 51.

91   *'What was new* . . .': Wilhelm Reich, trans. Philip Schmitz, *People in Trouble* (Farrar, Straus and Giroux, 1976 [1953]), p. 108.

91   *'the great freedom movement'*: ibid., p. 118.

92   *'individuals living under the same working conditions* . . .': ibid., p. 148.

94   *'and especially towards homosexuals* . . .': Norman Haire, ed., *World League for Sexual Reform: Proceedings of the Third Congress* (Kegan Paul, Trench, Trubner & Co., 1930), p. 591.

94   *'shrouded in darkness* . . .': Wilhelm Reich, *People in Trouble*, p. 17.

96   *'most of those that now dominate* . . .': Patrick Wintour, 'Genetics outweighs teaching, Gove adviser tells his boss', *Guardian*, 11 October 2013.

96   *'the best stock'*: Alison Bashford and Lesley Hall, eds., *The Oxford Handbook of Eugenics* (Oxford University Press, 2010), p. 5.

98   *'They demanded whether or not tuberculosis* . . .': Wilhelm Reich, *People in Trouble*, p. 109.

98   *'social struggle to eliminate* . . .': ibid., p. 111.

99  'There is no difference . . .': Charlotte Wolff, *Magnus Hirschfeld*, pp. 404–405.

99  'If you believe you are a citizen of the world . . .': Theresa May, Conservative Party Conference, 5 October 2016.

99  'mentally . . . stupid': Ralf Dose, *Magnus Hirschfeld: The Origins of the Gay Liberation Movement* (Monthly Review Press, 2014), p. 77.

99  'on the contrary . . .': Elena Mancini, *Magnus Hirschfeld and the Quest for Sexual Freedom*, p. 69.

100  'asymmetry of face and head . . .': Charlotte Wolff, *Magnus Hirschfeld*, p. 252.

101  'it would stamp out homosexuality . . .': Christopher Isherwood, *Christopher and His Kind*, p. 21.

101  'Hitler's weather': ibid., p. 96.

103  'as soon as Heinz has been . . .': ibid., p. 152.

104  'Heinz is my one support . . .': ibid., p. 109.

104  'I'd say it was the sort of letter . . .': ibid., p. 124.

105  'importation, production, or sale . . .': Atina Grossman, *Reforming Sex: The German Movement for Birth Control and Abortion Reform, 1920–1950* (Oxford University Press, 1995), p. 151.

105  'if the perpetrator through such deeds . . .': ibid., p. 152.

106  'unworthy': ibid., p. 152.

107  'Poison Shop': ibid., p. 146.

## CHAPTER 4: IN HARM'S WAY

111  'An object had been used to mutilate her . . .': *Daily Iowan*, Vol. 106, No. 203, 14 May 1974.

113  'The authoritarian state has a representative . . .': Kate Millett, *Sexual Politics* (Columbia University Press, 2016 [1970]), p. 158.

113  'for lack of more inspired terminology . . .': Barbara Hardy, 'De Beauvoir, Lessing – Now Kate Millett', *New York Times*, 6 September 1970.

113  'Anyone who would try to break . . .': Angela Neustatter, *Hyenas in Petticoats: A Look at Twenty Years of Feminism* (Penguin, 1989), p. 24.

115  'and by real I mean I wanted . . .': Stephanie Rosenthal, ed., *Traces: Ana Mendieta* (Hayward Publishing, 2013), p. 90.

117 'I think all my work has been like that . . .': ibid., p. 90.

117 'A young woman was killed . . .': Howard Oransky, ed., *Covered in Time and History: The Films of Ana Mendieta* (University of California Press, 2015), p. 82.

120 'You become unable to use language . . .': Andrea Dworkin, *Letters From a War Zone* (E.P. Dutton, 1989), pp. 331–2.

120 'protect': ibid., p. 330.

122 'just some bleeding thing cut up on the floor': Andrea Dworkin, ed. Johanna Fateman and Amy Scholder, *Last Days at Hot Slit* (Semiotext(e), 2018), p. 296.

122 'turns anybody who is subjected to it . . .': Simone Weil and Rachel Bespaloff, *War and the Iliad* (New York Review of Books, 2007), pp. 3–5.

123 'obstacles that litter the path . . .': Jacqueline Rose, 'Feminism and the Abomination of Violence', *Cultural Critique*, Vol. 94 (Fall 2016), pp. 4–25.

124 'more terrifying than rape . . .': Andrea Dworkin, *Last Days at Hot Slit*, pp. 314–15.

124 'women who had been sleeping . . .': ibid., p. 20.

126 'sexual terrorist': Andrea Dworkin, *Pornography: Men Possessing Women* (The Women's Press, 1981), p. 100.

126 'In him, one finds rapist and writer . . .': ibid., p. 70.

127 'far, far under the surface': Andrea Dworkin, *Last Days at Hot Slit*, p. 314.

128 'sexual extravaganzas': Andrea Dworkin, *Pornography*, p. 76.

128 'only doing what all men do': Marquis de Sade, trans. Richard Seaver, *Letters From Prison* (The Harvill Press, 2000), p. 180.

128 'a spanking to a whore': Andrea Dworkin, *Pornography*, p. 82.

128 'a sore behind': ibid., p. 82.

128 'a rather disagreeable hour or two': ibid., p. 84.

129 'a woman so badly wounded . . .': Geoffrey Gorer, *The Life and Ideas of the Marquis de Sade* (Peter Owen, 1963), p. 28.

129 'the sort of girls . . .': Neil Schaeffer, *The Marquis de Sade: A Life* (Harvard University Press, 1999), p. 185.

129 'advocacy and celebration of rape and battery . . .': Andrea Dworkin, *Pornography*, p. 99.

129 '*by its bedrock conviction . . .*': ibid., p. xxxvii.

130 '*de Sade and sexuality . . .*': Edmund Gordon, *The Invention of Angela Carter: A Biography* (Chatto & Windus, 2016), p. 219.

130 '*as long as a year to complete it*': ibid., p. 220.

132 '*Throughout the literature on him . . .*': Andrea Dworkin, *Pornography*, pp. 88–9.

133 '*leeches always lying in wait . . .*': Marquis de Sade, trans. Will McMorran and Thomas Wynn, *The 120 Days of Sodom* (Penguin Classics, 2016 [1785]), p. 3.

133 '*One of Sade's cruellest lessons . . .*': Angela Carter, *The Sadeian Woman: An Exercise in Cultural History* (Virago, 1992 [1979]), p. 89.

136 '*I think that he really didn't understand . . .*': Jonathan Cott, *Susan Sontag: The Complete Rolling Stone Interview*, p. 41.

136 '*From now on, sexuality is indeed distorted . . .*': Wilhelm Reich, *The Mass Psychology of Fascism* (Noonday Press, 1970), cited in Juliet Mitchell, *Psychoanalysis and Feminism* (Allen Lane, 1974), p. 212.

137 '*only (!) the sound . . .*': Wilhelm Reich, *Passion of Youth*, p. 31.

137 '*deep groan*': ibid.

137 '*ghastly scenes . . .*': ibid., p. 35.

139 '*the only male one to abhor rape really*': Andrea Dworkin, *Intercourse*, p. 179.

140 '*the darkness of the pre-verbal realm*': Edward St Aubyn, *At Last*, p. 171.

140 '*the ur-figure of so-called anti-sex feminism . . .*': Johanna Fateman, 'The Power of Andrea Dworkin's Rage', *New York Review of Books*, 15 February 2019.

141 '*Angela's socialist consciousness . . .*': Edmund Gordon, *The Invention of Angela Carter*, p. 218.

141 '*I think some of the Sisters . . .*': ibid., p. 217.

143 '*I had played a game . . .*': Angela Carter, 'The Bloody Chamber', in *Burning Your Boats: Collected Short Stories* (Chatto and Windus, 1995 [1979]), p. 137.

143 '*The blade did not descend . . .*': ibid., p. 142.

146 '*I don't think that you can separate . . .*': Ana Mendieta, in Linda Montano, ed., *Performance Artists Talking in the Eighties* (University of California Press, 2001), p. 396.

146 *'announcing that women . . .'*: A.I.R., 'Short History', www.artgallery. org/shorthistory.

147 *'My wife is an artist . . .'*: Robert Katz, *Naked by the Window: The Fatal Marriage of Carl Andre and Ana Mendieta* (Atlantic Monthly Press, 1990), pp. 11–12.

148 *'You see, I am a very successful artist . . .'*: ibid., p. 4.

149 *'Do you know the art . . .'*: ibid., p. 340.

149 *'in which she depicted . . .'*: ibid., p. 330.

150 *'Why does everybody think . . .'*: Chris Kraus, *I Love Dick* (Semiotext(e), 2015), p. 211.

150 *'Submission can be refused and I refuse it'*: Andrea Dworkin, *Intercourse*, p. xxxii.

151 *'Do it with a size 5 feet . . .'*: Stephanie Rosenthal, *Traces: Ana Mendieta* (Hayward Publishing, 2013), pp. 200–201.

## CHAPTER 5: A RADIANT NET

156 *'Now I'm very clear that the object is freedom'*: Agnes Martin, 'The Untroubled Mind', in Arne Glimcher, *Agnes Martin: Paintings, Writings, Remembrances* (Phaidon, 2012), p. 216.

159 *'the darkness wiped me out . . .'*: Sylvia Plath, *The Bell Jar* (Harper Collins, 2006 [1971]), p. 214.

160 *'a tiny orgone box of a room . . .'*: Terry Castle, 'Travels with My Mom', *London Review of Books*, 16 August 2007.

160 *'full-scale interplanetary battle'*: Christopher Turner, *Adventures in the Orgasmatron*, p. 374.

161 *'I am doing my best . . .'*: Reich to Eisenhower, 23 February 1957, Aurora Karrer Reich Collection, National Library of Medicine.

162 *'Freud wanted nothing of politics . . .'*: Wilhelm Reich, *Reich Speaks of Freud*, p. 54.

163 *'what my father finds offensive . . .'*: Christopher Turner, *Adventures in the Orgasmatron*, p. 142.

163 *'a horrible triage centre . . .'*: Elizabeth Ann Danto, *Freud's Free Clinics*, p. 259.

164 *'I lost literally all . . .'*: Wilhelm Reich, *People in Trouble*, p. 232.

166 'as a theory of the psychological . . .': Susan Sontag, *Illness as Metaphor*, p. 69.

166 'at the bottom of an ocean of orgone energy': Wilhelm Reich, *American Odyssey: Letters and Journals, 1940–1947* (Farrar, Straus & Giroux, 1999), p. 34.

168 'those straight genital Reichians . . .': William Burroughs, *Letters, 1945–59* (Penguin Modern Classics, 2009), p. 19.

169 'I tell you Jack . . .': ibid., p. 51.

169 'very organic, like a fur-lined bathtub': William Burroughs, 'My Life in Orgone Boxes', in *The Adding Machine: Selected Essays* (Arcade, 1993), p. 166.

169 'It seemed to me that people . . .': James Baldwin, *Collected Essays* (Library of America, 1998), p. 662.

170 'I still dream of Orgonon': Kate Bush, 'Cloudbusting', *Hounds of Love* (1985).

170 'the new cult of sex and anarchy': Mildred Edie Brady, 'The New Cult of Sex and Anarchy', *Harper's Magazine*, April 1947.

172 'when faced with the relatively minor . . .': James S. Turner, ed., *The Chemical Feast: Ralph Nader's Study Group Report on the Food and Drug Administration* (Penguin, 1976), p. 1.

172 'I request the right to be wrong': Wilhelm Reich, *American Odyssey*, p. 442.

172 'perpetually enjoined and restrained from': Wilhelm Reich et al. v. United States of America, US Court of Appeals for the First Circuit, 1957.

173 'the first human beings to engage . . .': Peter Reich, *A Book of Dreams*, p. 31.

174 'I'm not a woman . . .': Jill Johnston, 'Surrender & Solitude', *The Village Voice*, 13 September 1973.

174 'I'm not a woman, I'm a doorknob': ibid.

175 'deep voice . . .': David K. Johnson, *The Lavender Scare: The Cold War Persecution of Gays and Lesbians in the Federal Government* (University of Chicago Press, 2014), p. 130.

176 'was terrified . . .': Henry Martin, *Agnes Martin: Pioneer, Painter, Icon* (Schaffner Press, 2018), p. 94.

176 *'sociopathic personality disturbance'*: Jack Drescher, 'Out of DSM: Depathologizing Homosexuality', *Behavioural Science*, Vol. 5, Issue 4, Dec. 2015, pp. 565–75.

177 *'You feel as if you've climbed . . .'*: Nancy Princenthal, *Agnes Martin*, p. 68.

177 *'the Slip, like Taos . . .'*: ibid., p. 73.

179 *'the guys there were so beautiful . . .'*: Lucian Truscott, 'Gay Power Comes to Sheridan Square', *The Village Voice*, 3 July 1969.

179 *'defend the fairies'*: ibid.

180 *'the satisfaction of appetite happens to be impossible'*: Agnes Martin, 'The Untroubled Mind', in Arne Glimcher, *Agnes Martin*, p. 216.

182 *'Everything falls in a tremendous shower . . .'*: Virginia Woolf, *The Waves* (Vintage Books, 2004 [1931]), p. 137.

182 *'conceptual traffic jam . . .'*: Peter Schjeldahl, 'Life's Work', *New Yorker*, 7 June 2004.

183 *'My paintings are about merging, about formlessness . . .'*: Ann Wilson, 'Linear Webs', *Art & Artists*, Vol. 1, No. 7 (October 1966), p. 47.

183 *'Solitude and independence for a free mind'*: Agnes Martin, 'The Untroubled Mind', in Arne Glimcher, *Agnes Martin*, p. 220.

184 *'Fifteen minutes of physical abrasion'*: Jenny Attiyeh, 'Agnes Martin: An Artist on Her Own', *Horsefly*, Spring 2001.

184 *'I can't deal with distraction . . .'*: Arne Glimcher, *Agnes Martin*, p. 77.

185 *'you make me feel mighty real'*: Sylvester, 'You Make Me Feel (Mighty Real)', *Step II* (1978).

186 *'My mother didn't like children . . .'*: Benita Eisler, 'Life Lines', *New Yorker*, 25 January 1993.

186 *'Nature is like parting a curtain . . .'*: Frances Morris and Tiffany Bell, eds., *Agnes Martin* (Tate Publishing, 2015), p. 232.

187 *'Reality may be denied . . .'*: Edith Jacobson, 'The Self and the Object World: Vicissitudes of Their Infantile Cathexes and Their Influence on Ideation and Affective Development', *The Psychoanalytic Study of the Child*, Vol. 9, Issue 1, 1954, p. 115.

187 *'A great day in Puerto Rico yesterday . . .'*: @realdonaldtrump, Twitter, 4 October 2017.

187 *'Wow, so many Fake News . . .'*: @realdonaldtrump, Twitter, 4 October 2017.

188 '*Wilhelm Reich was living in a dream world*': Box 2, Folder 12, Aurora Karrer Reich Collection, National Library of Medicine.

188 '*In 1956 WR believed himself a spaceman*': ibid.

188 '*WR had massive delusions of grandeur . . .*': ibid.

188 '*You, are you not deeply ashamed of your own rotten nature . . .*': ibid.

188 '*Watch out . . .*': ibid.

189 '*The pile was crumpled and broken . . .*' Peter Reich, *A Book of Dreams*, p. 66.

190 '*Willie violent and threatening . . .*': Box 2, Folder 12, Aurora Karrer Reich Collection, National Library of Medicine.

190 '*What gets passed off as the effects of Oranur . . .*': ibid.

190 '*I do not plan to sit calmly . . .*': ibid.

191 '*Absolutely NOT true*': Christopher Turner, *Adventures in the Orgasmatron*, p. 340.

192 '*the continued pressure forced him . . .*': ibid.

193 '*Not because biologically . . .*': Andrea Dworkin, *Last Days at Hot Slit*, p. 133.

## CHAPTER 6: CELLS

197 '*I still dream of Orgonon, I wake up crying*': Kate Bush, 'Cloudbusting', *Hounds of Love* (1985).

199 '*60-year-old divorced . . .*': Myron Sharaf, *Fury on Earth: A Biography of Wilhelm Reich* (Da Capo Press, 1994)), p. 470.

201 '*a runway for hugging*': Peter Reich, *A Book of Dreams*, p. 80.

201 '*Oh my God, oh my God!*': ibid., p. 81.

201 '*His heart had stopped . . .*': ibid., p. 82.

201 '*Come back, come back*': ibid., p. 85.

205 '*unceasing vigilance*': Sarah Handley-Cousins, 'The Auburn System: Prison and Punishment in the 19th Century United States', digpodcast.org, 11 March 2018.

206 '*in prison, all work . . .*': Karen M. Morin, 'Security Here is Not Safe: Violence, Punishment, and Space in the Contemporary US Penitentiary', *Environment and Planning D: Society and Space*, Vol. 31, Issue 3, 1 January 2013.

207 'His welcome to white America': Bayard Rustin, ed. Devon W. Carbado and Donald Weise, *Time on Two Crosses: The Collected Writings of Bayard Rustin* (Cleis Press, 2015), p. 173.

208 'Our anchor giving way': Malcolm X with the assistance of Alex Haley, *The Autobiography of Malcolm X* (Penguin, 2007 [1965]), p. 99.

208 'A white man in charge . . .': ibid., p. 101.

209 'like a pink poodle': ibid., p. 112.

209 'groovy, frantic': ibid., p. 140.

210 'I never will forget how shocked . . .': ibid., p. 266.

211 'Months passed . . .': ibid., p. 267.

212 'Any person who claims . . .': ibid., p. 245.

213 'Who will still be there . . .': Edith Jacobson, 'Notes From Prison', translated for the author by Rebecca May Johnson, in Ulrike May, Elke Muhleitner and Otto F. Kernberg, *Edith Jacobson: Sie selbst und die Welt ihre Objekte* (Psychosozial-Verlag, 2005), p. 181.

214 'had put the analytic movement in danger': Per Anthi and Svein Haugsgjerd, 'A note of the history of the Norwegian Psychoanalytic Society from 1933 to 1945', *The International Journal of Psychoanalysis*, Vol. 94, 2013, p. 718.

215 'a rare opportunity to observe . . .': Edith Jacobson, 'Observations on the Psychological Effect of Imprisonment on Female Political Prisoners', in K. R. Eissler, ed., *Searchlights on Delinquency: New Psychoanalytic Studies* (Imago, 1949), p. 343.

216 'sudden violent attack . . .': ibid., p. 344.

217 'estranged body parts': Edith Jacobson, 'Depersonalization', *Journal of the American Psychoanalytic Association*, Vol. 7, Issue 4, 1 October 1959, p. 587.

218 'the contradictory educational system of cleanliness and order': Edith Jacobson, 'Observations on the Psychological Effect of Imprisonment on Female Political Prisoners', p. 353.

219 'hard labour, hard fare, and a hard bed': The Prisons Act 1865.

219 'in a strong grown man . . .': Oscar Wilde, Letter to the editor, *Daily Chronicle*, 28 May 1897.

220 'I have the most urgent need of fresh air': Marquis de Sade, *Letters from Prison*, p. 120.

220 *'the panic of complete helplessness drives us to fantastic extremes'*: Nancy Princenthal, *Agnes Martin: Her Life and Art*, p. 161.

222 *'truly constructive development'*: Edith Jacobson, 'Observations on the Psychological Effect of Imprisonment on Female Political Prisoners', p. 359.

222 *'exceptional'*: ibid.

222 *'social and cultural development . . .'*: ibid., p. 367.

223 *'War is wrong . . .'*: Bayard Rustin, ed. Michael G. Long, *I Must Resist: Bayard Rustin's Life in Letters* (City Lights, 2012), pp. 11–12.

223 *'There is little doubt that Rustin . . .'*: ibid., p. 10.

224 *'plausible, smooth and ingratiating . . .'*: ibid., p. 19.

224 *'the lovely natural scenes . . .'*: ibid., p. 19.

225 *'I shall not help them rob me . . .'*: ibid., pp. 29-30.

225 *'a constitutional homo . . .'*: ibid., p. 44.

226 *'he never knew there was a closet to go into'*: Rachelle Horowitz, *We Were There: The March on Washington – An Oral History*, 2013.

226 *'For these are our only weapons'*: Bayard Rustin, *I Must Resist*, p. 63.

226 *'We are willing to pay a price for freedom'*: ibid., p. 72.

226 *'I am needed on the outside'*: ibid., p. 83.

227 *'Unjust social laws and patterns . . .'*: Jervis Anderson, *Bayard Rustin: Troubles I've Seen* (Harper Collins, 1997), p. 115.

229 *'Hell no . . .'*: Bayard Rustin, *Time on Two Crosses*, p. 36.

229 *'these men and thousands like them . . .'*: ibid., p. 40.

230 *'If the law of cause and effect . . .'*: ibid., p. 57.

232 *'torn . . . distressed . . . uneasy'*: Bayard Rustin, *Time on Two Crosses*, p. 285.

232 *'the greatest demonstration for freedom . . .'*: Martin Luther King, 'I Have a Dream', March on Washington, 28 August 1963.

233 *'The conviction was sex perversion'*: Strom Thurmond, *We Were There: The March on Washington – An Oral History*, 2013.

234 *'the crap that was going on in those motels . . .'*: Bayard Rustin, *Time on Two Crosses*, p. 302.

234 *'There is no question in my mind . . .'*: ibid., p. 299.

236 *'think about imprisonment as a fate . . .'*: Angela Davis, *Are Prisons Obsolete?* (Seven Stories Press, 2003), p. 15.

236 *'Are we willing to relegate . . .'*: ibid., p. 16.

## CHAPTER 7: BLOCK/SWARM

243 '*You gays! Why don't you . . .*': Susanne Bösche, *Jenny Lives with Eric and Martin* (Gay Men's Press, 1983), p. 38.

243 '*It can never be wrong . . .*': ibid., p. 44.

243 '*positive images*': Margaret Thatcher, Speech to Conservative Central Council, Margaret Thatcher Foundation, 21 March 1987.

243 '*Children who need to be taught . . .*': Margaret Thatcher, Conservative Party Conference, 9 October 1987.

244 '*the acceptability of homosexuality . . .*': Local Government Act 1988.

245 '*but I'm afraid we rather have been invaded*': 'Lesbian protest at the BBC', *BBC News*, 23 May 2018.

245 '*BEEB MAN SITS ON LESBIAN*': *Daily Mirror*, 24 May 1988.

246 '*It is not in the role of an artist . . .*': Agnes Martin, 'Beauty is the Mystery of Life', in Frances Morris and Tiffany Bell, eds. *Agnes Martin*, p. 156.

248 '*black American man and a beautiful mixed-caste girl*': James Dalrymple, *The Times*, 31 May 1992.

249 '*the emission of a succession of repetitive beats*': Criminal Justice and Public Order Act 1994.

250 '*hemp-smelling bivouacs*': Hayley Dixon and Izzy Lyons, 'Boris Johnson calls Extinction Rebellion activists "crusties" who live in "hemp-smelling bivouacs" ', *Telegraph*, 7 October 2019.

255 '*slowly, very slowly*': Wilhelm Reich, *People in Trouble*, p. 26.

255 '*It was not a riot per se . . .*': ibid., p. 25.

257 '*The gory events . . .*': ibid., p. 32.

257 '*Somewhere a great deception was hidden*': ibid., p. 28.

257 '*Every individual is virtually an enemy . . .*': Sigmund Freud, trans. James Strachey, 'The Future of an Illusion', in *The Standard Edition of the Complete Psychological Works of Sigmund Freud*, Volume XXI (Hogarth Press, 1973), p. 6.

257 '*civilisation overcomes the dangerous aggressivity . . .*': Sigmund Freud, trans. James Strachey, 'Civilisation and its Discontents', in ibid., pp. 123–4.

258 '*a stupid, idiotic automaton . . .*': Wilhelm Reich, *People in Trouble*, p. 27.

259 *'Fifty-three years have passed . . .'*: Elias Canetti, trans. Joachim Neugroschel, *The Torch in My Ear* (Pan Books, 1990 [1980]), p. 245.

260 *'The files are burning! All the files!'*: ibid., p. 245.

260 *'Everything yielded and invisible holes . . .'*: ibid., p. 248.

261 *'poetics of political nightmare'*: Susan Sontag, 'Elias Canetti', *Granta 5: The Modern Common Wind*, 1 March 1982.

263 *'The block was an armoured mass . . .'* Stefan Jonsson, *Crowds and Democracy: The Idea and Image of the Masses from Revolution to Fascism* (Columbia University Press, 2013), p. 46.

264 *'a swarm of people coming across . . .'*: Jessica Elgot and Matthew Taylor, 'Calais crisis: Cameron condemned for "dehumanising" description of migrants', *Guardian*, 30 July 2015.

264 *'animals'*: Dara Lind, 'Trump's Animals remark and the ensuing controversy, explained', *Vox*, 21 May 2018.

264 *'pour into and infest'*: Ben Zimmer, 'What Trump Talks About When He Talks About Infestation', *Politico*, 29 July 2019.

264 *'monstrosity'*: 'Trump calls immigration crisis "a monstrosity"', *CNN*, 19 June 2018.

264 *'You look at what is marching up, that's an invasion'*: Peter Baker and Michael D. Shear, 'El Paso Shooting Suspect's Manifesto Echoes Trump's Language', *New York Times*, 4 August 2019.

266 *'egregious display of hatred . . .'*: Ben Jacobs and Warren Murray, 'Donald Trump under fire after failing to denounce Virginia white supremacists', *Guardian*, 13 August 2017.

266 *'the opposite of cuck'*: Maya Oppenheim, 'Neo-Nazis and White Supremacists applaud Donald Trump's response to deadly violence in Virginia', *Independent*, 13 August 2017.

268 *'What kind of man am I . . .'*: Robert Slifkin, *Out of Time: Philip Guston and the Refiguration of Postwar American Art* (University of California Press, 2013), p. 65.

273 *'I perceive myself as being behind the hood . . .'*: Philip Guston, ed. Clark Coolidge, *Philip Guston: Collected Writings, Lectures, and Conversations* (University of California Press, 2011), p. 282.

273 *'In masking himself as his would-be persecutor . . .'*: Aaron Rose,

*Imagining Jewish Art: Encounters with the Masters in Chagall, Guston, and Kitaj* (Legenda, 2009), p. 71.

274 '*black with Cossacks*': Wilhelm Reich, *Passion of Youth*, p. 57.

275 '*Our whole lives (since I can remember) . . .*': Dore Ashton, *A Critical Study of Philip Guston* (University of California Press, 1992), p.177

275 '*my father had felt tremendous regret . . .*': Musa Mayer, *Night Studio: A Memoir of Philip Guston* (Thames and Hudson, 1988), p. 229.

276 '*Can you imagine how it feels to find your father like that?*': ibid., p. 12.

277 '*in this private box . . . to be hidden and feel strange*': ibid., p. 24.

278 '*embarrassing*': David Kaufmann, *Telling Stories: Philip Guston's Later Work* (University of California Press, 2010), p. 19.

278 '*a mandarin pretending to be a stumblebum*': Hilton Kramer, 'A Mandarin Pretending to be a Stumblebum', *New York Times*, 25 October 1970.

278 '*It was as though I had left the church . . .*': Robert Slifkin, *Out of Time*, p. 108.

279 '*sinister . . . distance*': James Baldwin, 'Open Letter to Angela Davis', in Angela Davis, *If They Come in the Morning: Voices of Resistance* (Orbach and Chambers, 1971), p. 22.

## CHAPTER 8: 22ND CENTURY

285 '*We want to destroy sexism . . .*': Andrea Dworkin, *Last Days at Hot Slit*, p. 60.

286 '*she managed to tear through . . .*': Federico Garcia Lorca, *In Search of Duende*, trans. A. S. Kline, www.poetryintranslation.com.

286 '*This is a song by a Bahamian . . .*': Justin Vivian Bond, Joe's Pub, 20 September 2013.

288 '*Don't try to sway me over to your way. Your day, your day will go away*': Exuma, '22nd Century', *Do Wah Nanny* (1971).

289 '*I had not made a connection . . .*': Nina Simone, with Stephen Cleary, *I Put a Spell on You* (Da Capo Press, 1991), p. 86.

289 '*fanatic*': ibid., p. 16.

290 '*my white momma*': ibid., p. 24.

292 '*I can't be white . . .*': Alan Light, *What Happened, Miss Simone?* (Canongate, 2016), p. 128.

293 *'We never talked about men . . .'*: Nina Simone, *I Put a Spell on You*, p. 87.

295 *'I suddenly realized what it was to be black in America in 1963'*: ibid., p. 89.

295 *'Nina, you don't know anything about killing . . .'*: ibid., p. 89.

295 *'ten bullets'*: Cohodas, *Princess Noire: The Tumultuous Reign of Nina Simone* (Pantheon Books, 2010), p. 145.

296 *'political weapon'*: Nina Simone, BBC Hardtalk, 25 March 1999.

296 *'I'm not non-violent'*: Joe Hagan, 'I Wish I Knew How It Would Feel To Be Free: The Secret Diary of Nina Simone', *The Believer*, August 2010.

296 *'That's OK, sister'*: ibid.

296 *'helps to change the world . . .'*: Nina Simone, BBC Hardtalk, 25 March 1999.

296 *'Motherfucker, I am civil rights'*: Alan Light, *What Happened, Miss Simone?*, p. 102.

296 *'I am not the doctor to cure it however, sugar . . .'*: ibid., p. 158.

297 *'I'm counting their heads as I'm making the beds'*: Bertolt Brecht, trans. Marc Blitzstein, 'Pirate Jenny', *The Threepenny Opera* (1928).

297 *'Oh but this whole country is full of lies / You're all going to die and die like flies'*: Nina Simone, 'Mississippi Goddam', *Nina Simone in Concert* (1964).

297 *'I just want them to be in pieces . . .'*: Alan Light, *What Happened, Miss Simone?*, p. 148.

298 *'just running back and forth . . .'*: Nina Simone, *I Put a Spell on You*, p. 18.

298 *'source of power'*: Joe Hagan, 'I Wish I Knew How It Would Feel To Be Free: The Secret Diary of Nina Simone', *The Believer*, August 2010.

298 *'the same sense of being transformed . . .'*: Nina Simone, *I Put a Spell on You*, p. 92.

300 *'Everybody is half dead . . .'*: *Nina Simone: Historical Perspective*, dir. Peter Rodis (1970).

300 *'I have always been struck . . .'*: James Baldwin, *No Name in the Street* (Vintage, 2007 [1972]), pp. 53–4.

# NOTES

302 *'sleeping pills to sleep + yellow pills to go on stage'*: Joe Hagan, 'I Wish I Knew How It Would Feel To Be Free: The Secret Diary of Nina Simone', *The Believer*, August 2010.

303 *'They don't know that I'm dead and my ghost is holding on'*: *What Happened, Miss Simone?*, dir. Liz Garbus (2015).

304 *'exiled, jailed or underground'*: Nina Simone, *I Put a Spell on You*, p. 115.

304 *'that what she saw contributed to the . . .'*: James Baldwin, 'Sweet Lorraine', *Esquire*, 1 November 1969.

304 *'Do you realise how . . .'*: Nina Simone, Westbury Music Fair, 7 April 1968.

306 *'What's free to me? Same thing it is to you. You tell me . . .'*: *Nina Simone: Historical Perspective*, dir. Peter Rodis (1970).

307 *'there is no civil rights movement. Everybody's gone'*: ibid.

307 *'This is 2000 now . . .'*: Nina Simone, São Paulo, 13 April 2000.

# Bibliography

Acker, Kathy, *Blood and Guts in High School, Plus Two* (Pan Books, 1984)

— *Don Quixote* (Paladin, 1986)

— *Eurydice in the Underworld* (Arcadia Books, 1997)

— *Bodies of Work: Essays* (Serpent's Tail, 1997)

— *The Last Interview and Other Conversations* (Melville House, 2008)

Anderson, Jervis, *Bayard Rustin: Troubles I've Seen: A Biography* (Harper Collins, 1997)

Annan, Gabriele, 'Glee', *London Review of Books*, Vol. 17, No. 17, 7 September 1995

Anthi, Per and Svein Haugsgjerd, 'A Note on the History of the Norwegian Psychoanalytic Society from 1933 to 1945', *The International Journal of Psychoanalysis*, 94:4, pp. 715–24, 2013

Antonic, Thomas, 'Genius and Genitality: William S. Burroughs Reading Wilhelm Reich', *Humanities*, Vol. 8, Issue 2, June 2019

Arenas, Reinaldo, *Before Night Falls* (Serpent's Tail, 2001)

Ashton, Dore, *A Critical Study of Philip Guston* (University of California Press, 1992)

Baldwin, James, 'The New Lost Generation', *Esquire*, July 1961

— *Blues for Mister Charlie* (Dell, 1964)

— 'Sweet Lorraine', *Esquire*, November 1969

— *No Name in the Street* (Vintage, 2007 [1972])

— *Collected Essays* (Library of America, 1998)

— *I Am Not Your Negro*, compiled and edited by Raoul Peck (Penguin, 2017)

Barthes, Roland, *Sade, Fourier, Loyola* (Jonathan Cape, 1977)

Bashford, Alison and Lesley Hall, *The Oxford Handbook of Eugenics* (Oxford University Press, 2010)

Bauer, Heike, *The Hirschfeld Archives: Violence, Death, and Modern Queer Culture* (Temple University Press, 2017)

Beachy, Robert, *Gay Berlin: Birthplace of a Modern Identity* (Vintage, 2015)

Blocker, Jane, *Where is Ana Mendieta?* (Duke University Press, 2002)

Bond, Justin Vivian, *Tango: My Life in High Heels* (The Feminist Press, 2011)

Bösche, Susanne, *Jenny Lives with Eric and Martin* (Gay Men's Press, 1983)

Bry, Gerhard, *Resistance: Recollections from the Nazi Years* (Leo Baeck Institute Archives, LBI Berlin Collection)

Burroughs, William, *Naked Lunch* (John Calder, 1964 [1959])

— *The Ticket That Exploded* (John Calder, 1968)

— 'My Life in Orgone Boxes', in *The Adding Machine: Selected Essays* (Arcade, 1993)

— *Letters, 1945–59* (Penguin Modern Classics, 2009)

Butler, Judith, *Precarious Life: The Powers of Mourning and Violence* (Verso, 2004)

Canetti, Elias, trans. Carol Stewart, *Crowds and Power* (Phoenix Press, 20 [1962])

— trans. Joachim Neugroschel, *The Torch in My Ear* (Pan Books, 1990 [1980])

Carter, Angela, *The Sadeian Woman: An Exercise in Cultural History* (Virago, 1979)

— *The Bloody Chamber* (Gollancz, 1979)

— *Burning Your Boats: The Collected Short Stories* (Chatto & Windus, 1995)

Carter, David, *Stonewall: The Riots that Sparked the Gay Revolution* (St Martin's Griffin, 2004)

Castle, Terry, 'Travels with My Mom', *London Review of Books*, Vol. 29, No. 6, 16 August 2007

Cocks, Geoffrey, *Psychotherapy in the Third Reich* (Oxford University Press, 1985)

Cohodas, Nadine, *Princess Noire: The Tumultuous Reign of Nina Simone* (Pantheon Books, 2010)

Colley, Zoe A., *Ain't Scared of Your Jail: Arrest, Imprisonment, and the Civil Rights Movement* (University Press of Florida, 2013)

Conlin, Michelle and Kristina Cooke, '$11 toothpaste: Immigrants pay big for basics at private ICE lock-ups', *Reuters*, 18 January 2019

Cott, Jonathan, *Susan Sontag: The Complete Rolling Stone Interview* (Yale University Press, 2013)

Dabrowski, Magdalena, *The Drawings of Philip Guston* (Museum of Modern Art, 1988)

Danto, Elizabeth Ann, *Freud's Free Clinics: Psychoanalysis & Social Justice, 1918–1938* (Columbia University Press, 2005)

Davis, Angela, *Are Prisons Obsolete?* (Seven Stories Press, 2003)

— ed., *If They Come in the Morning: Voices of Resistance* (Orbach & Chambers, 1971)

Davis, Mike, 'Hell Factories in the Field: A Prison-Industrial Complex', *The Nation*, Vol. 260, No. 7, 20 February 1995

Diski, Jenny, 'Queening It', *London Review of Books*, Vol. 31, No. 12, 25 June 2009

District of Columbia Corrections Information Council, 'USP Lewisburg Special Management Unit', 6 April 2018

Dworkin, Andrea, *Woman Hating* (Plume, 1974)

— *Pornography: Men Possessing Women* (The Women's Press, 1981)

— *Intercourse: Twentieth Anniversary Edition* (Basic Books, 2007 [1987])

— *Letters From a War Zone* (E.P. Dutton, 1989)

— *Last Days at Hot Slit* (MIT Press/Semiotext(e), 2019)

Eisler, Benita, 'Life Lines', *New Yorker*, 25 January 1993

Elkind, David, 'Wilhelm Reich – The Psychoanalyst as Revolutionary', *New York Times*, 18 April 1971

Elliott, Richard, *Nina Simone* (Equinox, 2013)

Evans, Richard, 'Weimerama', *London Review of Books*, Vol. 12, No. 21, 8 November 1990

Faludi, Susan, 'Death of a Revolutionary', *New Yorker*, 8 April 2013

Feldstein, Ruth, *How It Feels to Be Free: Black Women Entertainers and the Civil Rights Movement* (Oxford University Press, 2017)

Firestone, Shulamith, *The Dialectic of Sex* (Verso, 2015 [1970])

Foucault, Michel, trans. Alan Sheridan, *Discipline and Punish: The Birth of the Prison* (Penguin, 1991 [1975])

— trans. Robert Hurley, *The Will to Knowledge, The History of Sexuality: Volume One* (Penguin, 1990 [1976])

— trans. Robert Hurley, *The Use of Pleasure, The History of Sexuality: Volume Two* (Penguin, 1992 [1984])

— trans. Robert Hurley, *The Care of Self, The History of Sexuality: Volume Three* (Penguin 1990 [1984])

Foucault, Michel, Nicole Morar and Daniel W. Smith, 'The Gay Science', in *Critical Inquiry*, Vol. 37, No. 3, Spring 2011

Freud, Sigmund, trans. David McLintock, *Civilisation and its Discontents* (Penguin, 2002 [1930])

— trans. James Strachey, *The Standard Edition of the Complete Psychological Works of Sigmund Freud*, Volume XXI (Hogarth Press, 1973)

— trans. James Strachey, *On Sexuality: Three Essays on the Theory of Sexuality and other works* (Pelican, 1977)

Gedye, G. E. R., *Fallen Bastions* (Victor Gollancz, 1939)

Glimcher, Arne, *Agnes Martin: Paintings, Writings, Reminiscences* (Phaidon Press, 2012)

Gomez, Lavinia, *An Introduction to Object Relations* (Free Association Books, 1997)

Gordon, Edmund, *The Invention of Angela Carter: A Biography* (Chatto & Windus, 2016)

Gorer, Geoffrey, *The Life and Ideas of the Marquis de Sade* (Peter Owen, 1963) [1934)]

Greenfield, Jerome, *Wilhelm Reich vs. the U.S.A.* (W.W. Norton, 1974)

Griffin, Susan, *Made From This Earth: Selections from her writings* (The Women's Press, 1982)

Grossman, Atina, *Reforming Sex: The German Movement for Birth Control and Abortion Reform, 1920–1950* (Oxford University Press, 1995)

Guston, Philip, ed. Clark Coolidge, *Philip Guston: Collected Writings, Lectures, and Conversations* (University of California Press, 2011)

Hagan, Joe, 'I Wish I Knew How It Would Feel To Be Free: The Secret Diary of Nina Simone', *The Believer*, August 2010

Haire, Norman, ed., *World League for Sexual Reform: Proceedings of the Third Congress* (Kegan Paul, Trench, Trubner & Co., 1930)

Hampton, Sylvia and David Nathan, *Nina Simone: Break Down and Let It All Out* (Sanctuary, 2004)

Harrington, Anne, *The Cure Within* (W.W. Norton, 2008)

Haynes, Todd, ed. Julia Leyda, *Todd Haynes: Interviews* (University Press of Mississippi, 2014)

Heyd, Milly, *Mutual Reflections: Jews and Blacks in Art* (Rutgers University Press, 1999)

Hopwood, Nick, Rebecca Fleming and Lauren Kassell, eds., *Reproduction: Antiquity to the Present Day* (Cambridge University Press, 2018)

Isherwood, Christopher, *Mr Norris Changes Trains* (Vintage, 2001 [1935])

— *Goodbye to Berlin* (Hogarth Press, 1954 [1939])

— *Christopher and His Kind* (Magnum, 1978)

Jacobson, Edith, 'Observations on the Psychological Effect of Imprisonment on Female Political Prisoners', in K. R. Eissler, ed., *Searchlights on Delinquency: New Psychoanalytic Studies* (Imago, 1949)

— 'The Self and the Object World: Vicissitudes of Their Infantile Cathexes and Their Influence on Ideation and Affective Development', *The Psychoanalytic Study of the Child*, Vol. 9, Issue 1, 1954

— 'Depersonalization', *Journal of the American Psychoanalytic Association*, Vol. 7, Issue 4, 1 October 1959

— *The Self and the Object World* (Hogarth Press, 1964)

— Interview with David Milrod (Archives & Special Collections, A.A. Brill Library, New York Psychoanalytic Society and Institute, 1971)

Jacoby, Russell, *The Repression of Psychoanalysis: Otto Fenichel and the Political Freudians* (Chicago University Press, 1983)

Jewles, Yvonne, ed., *Handbook of Prisons* (Routledge, 2007)

Johnson, David K., *The Lavender Scare: The Cold War Persecution of Gays and Lesbians in the Federal Government* (University of Chicago Press, 2006)

Jonsson, Stefan, *Crowds and Democracy: The Idea and Image of the Masses from Revolution to Fascism* (Columbia University Press, 2013)

Johnston, Norman, *Forms of Constraint: A History of Prison Architecture* (University of Illinois Press, 2000)

Kane, Sarah, *Collected Plays* (Methuen, 2001)

Katz, Robert, *Naked by the Window: The Fatal Marriage of Carl Andre and Ana Mendieta* (The Atlantic Monthly Press, 1990)

King, Richard, *The Lark Ascending: The Music of the British Landscape* (Faber, 2019)

Klein, Melanie, *The writings of Melanie Klein. Vol. 1, Love, guilt and reparation and other works 1921–1945* (Free Press, 1984 [1975])

— *Envy and Gratitude and Other Works, 1946–1963* (The Hogarth Press, 1975)

Kraus, Chris, *After Kathy Acker* (Allen Lane, 2017)

Lahr, John, 'Backlash Blues', *London Review of Books*, Vol. 38, No. 12, 16 June 2016

Landau, Ellen, 'Double Consciousness in Mexico: How Philip Guston and Reuben Kadish Painted a Morelian Mural', *American Art*, Vol. 21, No. 1 (Spring 2007)

Lever, Maurice, *The Marquis de Sade: A Biography* (Flamingo, 1995)

Lewy, Gunter, *Harmful and Undesirable: Book Censorship in Nazi Germany* (Oxford University Press, 2016)

Light, Alan, *What Happened, Miss Simone?* (Canongate, 2016)

Light, Alison, *Mrs Woolf and the Servants* (Penguin, 2008)

Long, Michael G., *I Must Resist: Bayard Rustin's Life in Letters* (City Lights Books, 2012)

Lorca, Federico Garcia, 'Theory and Play of the Duende', in *In Search of Duende* (New Directions, 1998)

Lorde, Audre, *The Cancer Journals* (Aunt Lute Books, 1997 [1980])

Lynn, Lukkas and Howard Oransky, *Covered in Time and History: The Films of Ana Mendieta* (Katherine E. Nash Gallery/ University of California Press, 2015)

Malcolm, Janet, *In the Freud Archives* (Granta, 2018 [1984])

Mancini, Elena, *Magnus Hirschfeld and the Quest for Sexual Freedom* (Palgrave Macmillan, 2010)

Mancini, Matthew J., 'Race, Economics, and the Abandonment

of Convict Leasing', *The Journal of Negro History*, Vol. 63, No. 4, October 1978

Martin, Henry, *Agnes Martin: Pioneer, Painter, Icon* (Schaffner Press, 2018)

May, Ulrike, Elke Muhleitner and Otto F. Kernberg, *Edith Jacobson: Sie selbst und die Welt ihre Objekte* (Psychosozial-Verlag, 2005)

Mayer, Musa, *Night Studio: A Memoir of Philip Guston by His Daughter* (Knopf, 1988)

Mendieta, Ana, *A Book of Works* (Grassfield Press, 1993)

Merz, Beatrice, ed., *Ana Mendieta. She Got Love* (Skira, 2013)

Millet, Kate, *Sexual Politics* (Virago, 1977)

Mitchell, Juliet, *Psychoanalysis and Feminism* (Allen Lane, 1974)

Montano, Linda, ed., *Performance Artists Talking in the Eighties* (University of California Press, 2001)

Moran, Joe, *On Roads: A Hidden History* (Profile, 2009)

Morin, Karen M., 'Security Here is Not Safe: Violence, Punishment, and Space in the Contemporary US Penitentiary', *Environment and Planning D: Society and Space*, Vol. 31, Issue 3, 1 January 2013

Morris, Frances and Tiffany Bell, eds., *Agnes Martin* (Tate, 2015)

Moser, Benjamin, *Sontag: Her Life* (Allen Lane, 2019)

Moure, Gloria, *Ana Mendieta* (Editiones Poligrafa, 1996)

Nelson, Maggie, *The Art of Cruelty: A Reckoning* (W.W. Norton, 2011)

Neustatter, Angela, *Hyenas in Petticoats: A Look at Twenty Years of Feminism* (Penguin, 1989)

Page, Norman, *Auden and Isherwood: The Berlin Years* (Macmillan, 1998)

Penman, Ian, 'Always Searching For a Key', *The Wire*, Issue 232, June 2003

Peters, Justin, 'How America's Model Prison Became the Most Horrific Facility in the Federal System', *Slate*, 20 November 2013

Phillips, Adam, *Becoming Freud: The Making of a Psychoanalyst* (Yale University Press, 2014)

Phillips, John, *How to Read Sade* (Granta, 2005)

Pick, Daniel, *Faces of Degeneration: A European Disorder, c. 1848–1918* (Cambridge University Press, 1989)

Pierpoint, Claudia Roth, 'A Raised Voice: How Nina Simone turned the movement into music', *New Yorker*, 11 and 18 August 2014

Princenthal, Nancy, *Agnes Martin: Her Life and Art* (Thames & Hudson, 2015)

Reich, Peter, *A Book of Dreams* (John Blake, 2015 [1974])

Reich, Wilhelm, ed. Mary Higgins and Chester M. Raphael, trans. Vincent R. Carfagno, *Character Analysis* (Farrar, Straus & Giroux, 1990 [1933])

— trans. Theodore P. Wolfe, *The Function of the Orgasm* (Panther, 1970 [1942])

— ed. Mary Higgins and Chester M. Raphael, trans. Vincent R. Carfagno, *The Mass Psychology of Fascism* (Souvenir Press, 1970 [1946])

— trans. Philip Schmitz, *People in Trouble* (Farrar, Straus & Giroux, 1976 [1953])

— ed. Mary Boyd Higgins, *Selected Writings: An Introduction to Orgonomy* (Farrar, Straus & Giroux, 1960)

— trans. Thérèse Pol, *Reich Speaks of Freud* (Penguin, 1967)

— ed. and trans. Mary Boyd Higgins, *Passion of Youth: An Autobiography, 1897–1922* (Farrar, Straus & Giroux, 1988)

— ed. Mary Boyd Higgins, *American Odyssey: Letters and Journals, 1940–47* (Farrar, Straus & Giroux, 1999)

— ed. Mary Boyd Higgins, *Where's the Truth: Letters and Journals, 1948–1957* (Farrar, Straus & Giroux, 2012)

Reiff, David, *Swimming in a Sea of Death* (Granta, 2008)

Richardson vs Thomas R. Kane et al, 'Complaint', United States District Court for the Middle District of Pennsylvania, 7 December 2011

Robins, Ahley H. and Sean L. Sellars, 'Oscar Wilde's Terminal Illness: Reappraisal After a Century', *The Lancet*, Vol. 356, Issue 9244, 25 November 2000

Roiphe, Katie, *The Violet Hour* (The Dial Press, 2016)

Rose, Jacqueline, 'Feminism and the Abomination of Violence', *Cultural Critique*, Vol. 94 (Fall 2016), pp. 4–25

Rosen, Aaron, *Imagining Jewish Art: Encounters with the Masters in Chagall, Guston, and Kitaj* (Legenda, 2009)

Rosenthal, Stephanie, ed., *Traces: Ana Mendieta* (Hayward Publishing, 2013)

Rothman, Joshua, 'When Bigotry Paraded Through the Streets', *The Atlantic*, 4 December 2016

Rowbotham, Sheila, *Edward Carpenter: A Life of Liberty and Love* (Verso, 2008)

Rustin, Bayard, *Time on Two Crosses: The Collected Writings of Bayard Rustin*, ed. Devon W. Carbado and Donald Weise (Cleis Press, 2015)

Sade, Marquis de, trans. Will McMorran and Thomas Wynn, *The 120 Days of Sodom* (Penguin Classics, 2016 [1785])

— trans. and ed. Richard Seaver, *Letters from Prison* (The Harvill Press, 2000)

— trans. John Philips, *Justine, or the Misfortunes of Virtue* (Oxford Modern Classics, 2012 [1781])

— trans. Austryn Wainhouse, *Juliette* (Grove Press, 1968 [1797])

Scarry, Elaine, *The Body in Pain* (Oxford University Press, 1985)

Schaeffer, Neil, *The Marquis de Sade: A Life* (Harvard University Press, 1999)

Schjeldahl, Peter, 'The Junkman's Son', *New Yorker*, 26 October 2003

— 'Life's Work', *New Yorker*, 7 June 2004

Schlosser, Eric, 'The Prison-Industrial Complex', *The Atlantic*, December 1998

Scholder, Amy, Carla Harryman and Avital Ronnell, *Lust for Life: On the Writings of Kathy Acker* (Verso, 2006)

Sedgwick, Eve Kofosky, 'Paranoid and Reparative Reading, Or, You're So Paranoid You Probably Think This Essay Is About You', *Touching Feeling* (Duke University Press, 2003)

Sharaf, Myron, *Fury on Earth: A Biography of Wilhelm Reich* (Da Capo Press, 1994)

Simone, Nina, with Stephen Cleary, *I Put a Spell on You* (Da Capo Press, 1991)

Slifkin, Robert, *Out of Time: Philip Guston and the Refiguration of Postwar American Art* (University of California Press, 2013)

Sontag, Susan, 'Elias Canetti', *Granta*, Vol. 5, 1 March 1982

— *Illness as Metaphor & AIDS and its Metaphors* (Penguin Modern Classics, 1991)

— *Regarding the Pain of Others* (Penguin, 2004)

— *As Consciousness is Harnessed to Flesh*, ed. David Rieff (Farrar, Straus & Giroux, 2012)

— *Essays of the 1960s and 70s*, ed. David Rieff (Library of America, 2013)

Srinivasan, Amia, 'Does Anyone Have the Right to Sex', *London Review of Books*, Vol. 40, No. 6, 22 March 2018

Stern, J. P., 'Canetti's Later Work', *London Review of Books*, Vol. 8, No. 12, 3 July 1986

Tamagne, Florence, *A History of Homosexuality in Europe: Berlin, London, Paris, 1919–1939*, Volume I (Algora, 2004)

Theweleit, Klaus, trans. Chris Turner, Erica Carter and Stephen Conway, *Male Fantasies, Vol. I: Women, Floods, Bodies, Histories* (Polity, 1987)

— trans. Chris Turner, Erica Carter and Stephen Conway, *Male Fantasies, Vol. II: Male Bodies: Psychoanalysing the White Terror* (Polity, 1989)

Thompson, Christie and Joseph Shapiro, '28 Days in Chains', The Marshall Project/NPR, 26 October 2016

Thompson, Heather Ann, *Blood in the Water: The Attica Prison Uprising of 1971 and Its Legacy* (Vintage, 2016)

Tomkins, Calvin, 'The Materialist', *New Yorker*, 5 December 2011

Totton, Nick, *The Water in the Glass: Body and Mind in Psychoanalysis* (Rebus Press, 1998)

Turner, Christopher, *Adventures in the Orgasmatron: The Invention of Sex* (Fourth Estate, 2012)

Turner, James S., ed., *The Chemical Feast: Ralph Nader's Study Group Report on the Food and Drug Administration* (Penguin, 1976 [1970])

Van Der Kolk, Bessel, *The Body Keeps the Score* (Penguin, 2014)

Viso, Olga, ed., *Ana Mendieta, Earth Body* (Hatje Cantz, 2004)

— ed., *Unseen Mendieta: The Unpublished Work of Ana Mendieta* (Prestel, 2008)

Walder, Joyce, 'A Death in Art', *New York Magazine*, 16 December 1985

Weil, Simone and Rachel Bespaloff, *War and the Iliad* (*New York Review of Books*, 2007)

Whitehurst, Andrew, 'Free Party Politics: Castle Morton', *DJ Mag*, 28 March 2014

Wilson, Colin, *The Quest for Wilhelm Reich* (Panther, 1982)

Winnicott, D. W., *Playing and Reality* (Routledge, 1971)

— *Babies and Their Mothers* (Free Association Books, 1988)

Wolff, Charlotte, *Magnus Hirschfeld: A Portrait of a Pioneer in Sexology* (Quartet Books, 1986)

Woodfox, Albert, *Solitary* (Text Publishing Company, 2019)

Woodman, Donald, *Agnes Martin and Me* (Lyon Art Books, 2016)

Wood, Sarah, *Civilisation & Its Malcontents* (Ma Bibliothèque, 2017)

Woollen, Peter, 'Death (and Life) of the Author', *London Review of Books*, Vol. 20, No. 3, 5 February 1998

de Zegher, M. Catherine, ed., *Inside the Visible: an elliptical traverse of 20th century art* (Les editions La Chambre, 1996)

# Acknowledgements

First up, this book wouldn't exist without my beloved agent Rebecca Carter. Thank you for your abundant faith and tireless labours. It's been a slog! Vast thanks too to my American agent PJ Mark, who always seems to grasp what it is and why it matters. The deepest gratitude to you both.

Major thanks to Christopher Turner, who wrote the definitive Reich biography, and has been so helpful and generous as I've worked on this book. No matter what obscure corner of Reichiana I turned up, Chris had already been there, which is what makes *Adventures in the Orgasmatron* so fascinating, both as a portrait of Reich and of his role in the culture at large.

To all at the family at Picador, present and departed: Paul Baggaley, Philip Gwyn Jones, George Morley, Jeremy Trevathan, Ravi Mirchandani, Gaby Quattromini, Paul Martinovic, Nicholas Blake, Stuart Wilson: thank you, thank you. Major gratitude to my editor, Kishani Widyaratna, who kept saying 'why' until I figured it out. This book is so much richer for your involvement, and I am very grateful.

And to everyone at Norton, especially my editor Jill Bialosky, Drew Weitman and Erin Sinesky Lovett.

Very special thanks to John Pittman, my travelling companion to Orgonon, a trip which is a whole other story, and to Sarah Schulman, for our conversations about Reich over eggs at Mogador.

I'm grateful too to the following early readers: Joseph Keckler, who accompanied me on research trips, discussed ideas and has cameos in half my books, including this one. Charlie Porter, boon BL companion, who said Freud needed to have a body. Jenny Lord, for everything, but especially the potato story. Matt Wolf, radical connector, brilliant writer of notes. Francesca Segal, who not only provided meticulous edits but posted them during a pandemic too. Lauren Kassell, who knows a lot more about sex than most people. Chantal Joffe, my electrifying friend, who also found page references in *The Bell Jar* while all Britain's libraries were closed. Jean Hannah Edelstein, especially for suggesting I elaborate on Guston's personal story. Lauren John Joseph, dear heart. Sarah Wood, always.

While I was working on *Everybody* I won a Windham Campbell prize. Hard to express the difference cold hard cash makes in a writer's life. Thank you to Michael Kelleher and Megan Eckerle, for all your support, and to Donald and Sandy too.

Ideas in this book have been evolving since the 1990s, and arise out of discussions over many years. My thanks, in no particular order, to Tony Gammidge, who introduced me to the work of both Ana Mendieta and Philip Guston, Lili Stevens, with whom I've been talking about bodies for decades now,

# ACKNOWLEDGEMENTS

Tom de Grunwald and Tamora James, treetop companions, Bob Dickinson, Sherri Wasserman, David Dernie, Rich Porter, Carl Williamson, Mary Manning, Carole Villiers, Nick Davies (always), Nick Blackburn, Alex Halberstadt, David Adjmi, Brian Dillon, Emily LaBarge, Jon Day, Ali Smith, Esme Joffe, Jack Partlett.

To my teachers, back in the herbal day: Peter Conway and Julian Barker.

Much gratitude to Rebecca May Johnson, who translated Edith Jacobson's prison diaries from the German for me.

For help with image permissions, thank you to Aileen Corkery and Emily Rothrum at Hauser and Wirth, Jackie Burns at the Getty Museum, and Amanda Wilkinson.

Thank you to the staff of the National Library of Medicine, where the Aurora Karrer Reich collection is housed, to Nellie Thomson at the Brill Library, and to Will McMorran, who discussed the Marquis de Sade with me in the slightly incongruous setting of the BL cafe.

To my family: Denise Laing, Kitty Laing, Peter Laing, Tricia Murphy, thank you all.

And to Ian Patterson, of course: librarian, poet, interlocutor, love.

# EVERYBODY

*Olivia Laing*

# EVERYBODY

## *Olivia Laing*

### DISCUSSION QUESTIONS

1. Were you familiar with renegade psychoanalyst Wilhelm Reich before reading this book? What did you think as you read about his work? What most interested or surprised you?

2. "Listening to their stories, [Reich] came to realise that the problems he was seeing, the psychic disarray, weren't just a consequence of childhood experience but of social factors like poverty, poor housing, domestic violence and unemployment. Each individual was plainly subject to larger forces, which could cause just as much trouble as Freud's central site of interest, the crucible of the family" (p. 7). Do you agree with this understanding of trauma? Do you feel like American society is structured in such a way as to mitigate or maximize these traumas? What else could be done?

3. Over the course of this book Olivia Laing explores many wrenching transgressions of the human body, including violence, imprisonment, terror, and degradation. Why do you think Laing chose the physical body as a lens through which to reexamine the great freedom movements of the twentieth century?

4. There are many artists, thinkers, and writers included here—did any of them particularly resonate with you? Did Laing's writing about their work challenge or expand your previous understanding of their work?

5. "It was beginning to seem as if the great liberation movements of the twentieth century were failing, the victories of feminism, gay liberation and the civil-rights movement overturned one by one, assuming they'd ever been secured at all" (p. 11). It is very easy to succumb to a feeling of despair at the current moment, but Laing resists hopelessness, advocating for the power of community in

resistance and the profound impact of art and writing as political weapons. How did reading this book influence your thinking about life in the current moment?

6. Do you consider yourself an activist? Why or why not? Did reading this book challenge or change your perspective on activism? What work is happening right now in your community?

7. "A free body need not be whole or undamaged or unaugmented. It is always changing, changing, changing, a fluid form after all. Imagine, for a minute, what it would be like to inhabit a body without fear, without the need for fear. Just imagine what we could do. Just imagine the world that we could build" (p. 309). How has your relationship to your own body changed or evolved over time? Has your feeling of safety, or lack thereof, within the wider world changed in similar ways?

8. Laing writes about the opposing experiences of cancer by Susan Sontag and Kathy Acker. In your own life or the lives of loved ones, have you experienced extreme illness? Did you feel a pressure or desire to find a broader "meaning" in the experience? Were there writers or particular works that you connected with during this time?

9. Laing explores so many fraught intersections of the physical body and cultural/societal outside forces. The varying responses to vaccination during the COVID-19 health crisis have proven to be yet another battleground for the fight for freedom—the freedom to make personal choices in opposition with the freedom to be safe within the wider community. What does freedom look like when we must take personal action to protect others? How has your thinking about your personal body and your obligations to the world around you been shaped by this global pandemic?

10. "There is no steel-lined box that can protect you from the grid of forces that limits in tangible, tormenting ways what each private body is allowed to be or do. There is no escape, no possible place to hide. Either you submit to the world or you change the world" (p. 193). Have you felt these limitations in your own life or seen them at work against the lives of those you love? Have you ever felt

yourself to be at the fraught, even dangerous, intersection of the personal and political? How did your gender, sexuality, race, or physical health influence that experience?

11. Have you ever been a part of a protest? What brought you out of your home and into the streets? What was the experience like?

12. Laing resists rigid answers or strict conclusions as she explores so many different perspectives and philosophies throughout this work. Why do you think this is? How does this approach reflect her subject? What conclusions do you draw from the book?

13. "Freedom doesn't mean being unburdened by the past. It means continuing into the future, *dreaming* all the time" (p. 309). What does "freedom" mean to you? What change do you think is needed? How can you help further that work?

Don't miss other titles by
"astute and consistently surprising culture critic" (NPR)

# OLIVIA LAING

OLIVIALAING.CO.UK

"Laing's arts writing is sharp-minded, and her manner is generous toward both subject and reader."

—John Glassie, *Washington Post*

A *New York Times* Notable Book, *The New Yorker*, *Washington Post*, NPR, *Guardian*, *Esquire*, and *Bustle* Best Book of the Year

"Love may not be original, but this funny, fervent novel is."

—*The New Yorker*

**W. W. NORTON & COMPANY**
*Independent Publishers Since 1923*